A Compa

A Company of Tanks

A British Company Commander's view
of tank warfare during the First World War

W. H. L. Watson

LEONAUR

A Company of Tanks
A British Company Commander's view
of tank warfare during the First World War
by W. H. L. Watson

First published under the title
A Company of Tanks

Leonaur is an imprint
of Oakpast Ltd

ISBN: 978-1-84677-980-0 (hardcover)
ISBN: 978-1-84677-979-4 (softcover)

http://www.leonaur.com

Publisher's Notes

In the interests of authenticity, the spellings, grammar and place names
used have been retained from the original editions.

The opinions of the authors represent a view of events in which he
was a participant related from his own perspective,
as such the text is relevant as an historical document.

The views expressed in this book are not necessarily
those of the publisher.

Contents

The words of an eye-witness, flowing naturally from first impressions, are frequently more expressive, and convey ideas more just than studied descriptions; though the language may often be such as it would scarcely be allowable in other persons to write.

Captain James Burney, 1806.

TO PATRICK AND DAVID

CHAPTER 1

On the 11th Corps Front
(OCTOBER TO DECEMBER 1916.)

The village of Locon lies five miles out from Bethune, on the Estaires road. Now it is broken by the war: in October 1916 it was as comfortable and quiet a village as any four miles behind the line. If you had entered it at dusk, when the flashes of the guns begin to show, and passed by the square and the church and that trap for despatch-riders where the *chemin-de-fer vicinal* crosses to the left of the road from the right, you would have come to a scrap of orchard on your left where the British cavalrymen are buried who fell in 1914.

Perhaps you would not have noticed the graves, because they were overgrown and the wood of the crosses was coloured green with lichen. Beyond the orchard was a farm with a garden in front, full of common flowers, and a flagged path to the door. Inside there is a cheerful little low room. A photograph of the Prince of Wales, a sacred picture, and an out-of-date calendar, presented by the '*Petit Parisien*,' decorate the walls. *Maman*, a dear gnarled old woman—old from the fields—stands with folded arms by the glittering stove which projects into the centre of the room. She never would sit down except to eat and sew, but would always stand by her stove.

Papa sits comfortably, with legs straight out, smoking a pipe of *caporal* and reading the *Télégramme*. Julienne, pretty like a sparrow, with quick brown eyes, jerky movements, and fuzzy hair, the flapper from the big grocer's at La Gorgue, for once is quiet and mends Hamond's socks. In a moment she will flirt like a kitten or quarrel with Louie, a spoilt and altogether unpleasant boy, who at last is going to school. The stalwart girl of seventeen, Adrienne, is sewing laundry marks on Louie's linen. It is warm and cosy.

The coffee is ready. The little bowls are set out on the table. The moment has come. From behind a curtain Hamond produces, with the solemnity of ritual, a battered water-bottle. He looks at Papa, who gravely nods, and a few drops from the water-bottle are poured into each steaming bowl of coffee. The fragrance is ineffable, for it is genuine old Jamaica. . . .

We talk of the son, a *cuirassier*, and when he will come on leave; of the Iron Corps who are down on the Somme; of how the men of the Nord cannot be matched by those of the Midi, who, it is rumoured, nearly lost the day at Verdun; of Mme. X. at Gonnehem, who pretends to be truly a *Parisienne*, but is only a carpenter's daughter out of Richebourg St Vaast; of the oddities and benevolence of *M. le Maire*. Adrienne discusses learnedly the merits of the divisions who have been billeted in the village. She knows their names and numbers from the time the Lahore Division came in 1914.[1]

We wonder what are these heavy armoured motorcars of a new type that have been a little successful on the Somme. And we have our family jokes. "*Peronne est prise*," we inform *Maman*, and make an April fool of her—while, if the line is disturbed and there is an outbreak of machine-gun fire or the guns are noisy, we mutter, "*Les Boches attaquent!*" and look for refuge under the table.

In April of last year, when the Boche attacked in very truth, *Maman* may have remembered our joke. Then they piled their mattresses, their saucepans, their linen, and some furniture on the big wagon, and set out for Hinges—Bethune was shelled and full of gas. I wonder if they took with them the photograph of the Prince of Wales? There was bitter fighting in Locon, and

---

1. Every intelligent person in every French village or town knew the numbers of all the divisions in the neighbourhood.

we must afterwards have shelled it, because it came to be in the German lines. . .

Hamond knew the Front from the marshes of Fleurbaix to the craters of Givenchy better than any man in France. He had been in one sector of it or another since the first November of the war. So, when one of the companies of the 11th Corps Cyclist Battalion, which I commanded, was ordered to reinforce a battalion of the 5th Division in the line at Givenchy and another of my companies to repair the old British line by Festubert, and to work on the "islands,"[2] I determined to move from my dismal headquarters in a damp farm near Gonnehem and billet myself at Locon. It was the more convenient, as Hamond, who commanded the Motor Machine-Gun Battery of the Corps, was carrying out indirect fire from positions near Givenchy.

We lived in comfort, thanks to *Maman* and Starman, Hamond's servant. I would come in at night, saying I was *fatigué de vivre*. Old Maman, understanding that I was too tired to live, would drag out with great trouble grandfather's armchair, place a pillow in it, and set it by the stove. And Julienne, a little subdued at my imminent decease, would forget to flirt.

We would start, after an early breakfast, in Hamond's motor-cycle and side-car, and drive through the straggling cottages of Hamel, where the *cuirassiers*, in October 1914, protected the left flank of the advancing 5th Division, through Gorre, with its enormous ramshackle *château*, and along the low and sordid banks of the La Bassée Canal. We would leave the motor-cycle just short of the houses near Pont Fixe, that battered but indomitable bridge, draped defiantly with screens of tattered sackcloth.

I would strike along the Festubert road, with the low ridge of Givenchy on my left, until I came to the cross-roads at Windy Corner.

A few yards away were the ruins of a house which Brigadier-General Count Gleichen,[3] then commanding the 15th Infantry

---

2. Detached posts, which could not be approached by day, in front of the main trench system.
3. Now Major-General Lord Edward Gleichen, K.C.V.O., C.B., C.M.G., D.S.O.

Brigade, had made his headquarters when first we came to Givenchy, and were certain to take La Bassée. That was in October 1914, and the line ran from the houses near Pont Fixe through the farm-buildings of Canteleux to the cottages of Violaines, whence you looked across open fields to the sugar factory, which so greatly troubled us, and the clustered red walls of La Bassée. The Cheshires held Violaines. They were driven out by a sudden attack in November. The line broke badly, and Divisional Headquarters at Beuvry Brewery packed up, but a Cyclist officer with a few men helped to rally the Cheshires until a battalion from the 3rd Division on the left arrived to fill the gap. We did not again hold Violaines and Canteleux until the Germans retired of their own free-will.

Now once again, exactly two years later, the 5th Division was in the line.

I would take to the trench at Windy Corner, and tramp along to call on the cheery young colonel of the battalion to which my men were attached. There is a little story about his headquarters. A smell developed, and they dug hard, thinking it came from a corpse. The sergeant-major discovered the cause. A fond relative had sent the mess-waiter a medicated belt to catch the little aliens in the course of their traditional daily migration. . . .

We would go round the line, which then was quiet, exploring the intricacies of Red Dragon Crater. Afterwards I would walk through the complicated defences of Givenchy to join Hamond at "Dirty Dick's," [4] by the shrine, for the ride back. . . .

The 5th Division was afraid of an attack on Givenchy at this time. It was a key position. If Givenchy went, the line south of the canal must crumble and the left flank of the Loos salient would be in the air. But the attack did not come until April 1918, and the story of how Givenchy held then, when the line to the north was flowing westwards, is history.

On the left of Givenchy the line ran in front of Festubert through stagnant fields, where the water in the summer is just below the surface. It is dreary country, full of ghosts and the

---

4. A famous dugout.

memories of fighting at night. It is all a sodden cemetery.

There my men were rebuilding the breastworks of the old British line, for in these marshes it was impossible to dig trenches, and working on the "islands."

Breastworks continued to the north. Our lines were overlooked from the Aubers Ridge. In winter they were flooded and men were drowned. Behind were dead level meadows, often covered with water, and dismal ruined villages. The country was filthy, monotonous, and stunted. In the summer it stank. In the winter it was mud. Luckily, for many months the line was quiet.

In November of this year the corps, to vary the picture, took over the Cuinchy sector on the right of Givenchy and immediately south of the La Bassée Canal. It was a unique and damnable sector, in which a company of my men were set to dig tunnels from the reserve to the support and front trenches.

It was unique by reason of the brick-stacks, and damnable by reason of the Minenwerfer and the Railway Triangle. Our line ran in and out of a dozen or so brick-stacks, enormous maroon cubes of solid brick that withstood both shell and mine. Some we held and some the enemy held. Inside them tiny staircases were made, and camouflaged snipers, impossible to detect, made life miserable. Occasionally we tried to take each other's brick-stacks, but these attempts were unsuccessful, and we settled down, each as uncomfortable as he well could be. And in this sector the enemy employed *minenwerfer* with the utmost enterprise. Our trenches were literally blown to pieces.

In the daytime we ran about like disturbed ants, ever listening for the little thud of the "minnie's" discharge and then looking upwards for the black speck by day or the glow of it by night. For "minnies" can be avoided by the alert and skilful. Finally, a triangle of railway embankments, fortified until they had become an impregnable field-work, held for the German the southern bank of the canal.

To the occasional tall visitor the main communication trench added irritation and certain injury to fear. Some ingenious fellow had laid an overhead rail some six feet above the trench boards. On this rail material was slung and conveyed forwards. It was an excellent substitute for a light railway, but it compelled a tall man to walk along the trench with his head on one side. This strained attitude did not conduce to stability on slippery trench boards. Again, the height of the rail above the floor of the trench varied. A moment's absent-mindedness and the damage was done.

My officers and men worked well. We were lucky, and our casualties were few, but it was a trying time. An occasional day in Bethune just made life bearable.

The one redeeming feature of the 11th Corps front was the excellent town of Bethune.

Of all the towns immediately behind the line, none could rival Bethune in the providing of such comforts, relaxations, and amenities as the heart of the soldier desired. The billets were notoriously comfortable. The restaurants were varied and good. The *pâtisserie* was famous before the war. The oyster-bar approached that of Lillers. I know of but one *coiffeur* better than "Eugene's." The shops provided for every reasonable want. The theatre was palatial. The canteen was surpassed only by Meaulte, of ill-fated memory. The inhabitants were civil, friendly, and, in comparison with their neighbours, not extortionate.

On the morning in October 1914, when the 5th Division— the first British troops Bethune had seen—passed through the town to take up the line Vermelles-Violaines, I breakfasted at the "Lion d'Or," round the corner from the square. I was received with grateful hospitality by *madame*. An extremely pretty girl of fourteen, with dark admiring eyes, waited on me. She was charmingly hindered by Annette, a child of three or four, who with due gravity managed to push some bread on to my table and thus break a plate.

When I returned in the summer of 1916, I expected that I would at least be recognised. I found the tavern crowded. Agnes, who had just recovered from an illness, served the mob of officers with unsmiling disdain. She was not even flurried by the entreaties of multitudinous *padres* who were doubtless celebrating some feast-day. And Annette, decorated with appalling ribbons, was actually carrying plates.

The alternative was the "Hôtel de France"—a solemn and pretentious hostelry, at which the staff and French officials congregated. When the enemy began to shell Bethune, the "Hôtel de France" was closed.

The "Lion d'Or" carried on until the house opposite was hit, and afterwards reopened spasmodically; but in 1916 and 1917 it was wiser to try the "Paon d'Or" in the outskirts of the town, near the canal. At that stuffy restaurant' it was possible to lunch peacefully while shells dropped at intervals in the square and centre of the town.

"Eugene: Coiffeur," was an institution. Eugene must have been dead or "serving," for *madame* presided. She was a thin and friendly lady, with tiny feet, and a belief that all her customers required verbal entertainment. It was touching to see *madame* seat herself briskly beside a morose colonel who knew no respectable word of French, and endeavour, by the loud reiteration of simple phrases, to assure him that he was welcome and the weather appalling.

I would linger over Bethune, because no town has been a greater friend to the soldier for a brief period out of the line. Now it is shattered, and the inhabitants are fled.

My headquarters at this time were in a farm near Gonnehem, six miles or so from Bethune. The farm was good of its kind, and in summer the casual visitor might even have called it smart, after Wiggans, my adjutant, had cleared away the midden-heap, drained the courtyard, and had whitewashed everything that would take the colour—all in the face of violent and reiterated protests from madame. The centre of the courtyard, encircled by a whitewashed rope, was particularly effective.

In winter no polite epithet could describe the place. The hamlet consisted of a few farms, each surrounded by innumerable little ditches, hidden by rank undergrowth and sheltered by large trees. At the best of times the ditches were full of soaking flax, which gave out a most pungent odour. After rain the ditches overflowed and flooded the roads and paths. The hedges and bushes sagged with water. The trees dripped monotonously. Some of us caught influenza colds: some endured forgotten rheumatism and lumbago.

We had but one pastime. Certain of our transport horses were not in use. These we were continually exchanging for riding horses more up to our weight with a friendly "Remounts" who lived in solitude nearby. In due course Wiggans became the proud owner of a dashing little black pony and I of a staff officer's discarded charger. In spite of the dreariness of our surroundings, we felt almost alive at the end of an afternoon's splash over waterlogged fields. Nobody could damp Wiggans' cheerfulness when he returned with a yet more fiery steed from his weekly deal, and the teaching of the elements of horsemanship to officers, who had never ridden, produced an occasional laugh. We may ourselves have given pleasure in turn to our friends, the yeomanry, who were billeted in Gonnehem itself.

To us in our damp and melancholy retreat came rumours of tanks. It was said that they were manned by "bantams." The supply officer related that on the first occasion on which tanks went into action the eardrums of the crews were split. Effective remedies had been provided. We learned from an officer, who had met the quartermaster of a battalion that had been on the Somme, the approximate shape and appearance of tanks. We pictured them and wondered what a cyclist battalion could do against them. Apparently the tanks had not been a great success on the Somme, but we imagined potentialities. They were coloured with the romance that had long ago departed from the war. An application was made for volunteers. We read it through with care.

I returned from leave. It was pouring with rain and there was nothing to do. The whole of my battalion was scattered in small parties over the Corps area. Most of my officers and men were under somebody else's command. I sent in an application for transfer to the heavy branch of the Machine-Gun Corps, the title of the Tank Corps in those days. I was passed as suitable by the Chief Engineer of the Corps, and waited.

It was on the 28th December 1916 that I was ordered by wire to proceed immediately to the headquarters of the tanks. Christmas festivities had cheered a depressed battalion, but there was at the time no likelihood of the mildest excitement. Hamond had disappeared suddenly—it was rumoured to England and tanks. I was left with a bare handful of men to command. It was still raining, and we were flooded. I was not sorry to go. . . .

We set out on a bright morning, in a smart gig that Wiggans had bought, with his latest acquisition in the shafts, bedecked with some second-hand harness we had found in Bethune, and clattered through Lillers to the Hôtel de la Gare.

Lillers was a pleasant town, famous principally for the lady in the swimming-bath and its oyster-bar. Every morning, in the large open-air swimming-bath of the town, a lady of considerable beauty was said to disport herself. The swimming-bath was consequently crowded. The oyster-bar provided a slight feminine interest as well as particularly fine *marennes verts*. Lillers was an army headquarters. Like all towns so fated it bristled with neat notices, clean soldiers with wonderful salutes, and many motorcars. It possessed an under-world of staff officers who hurried ceaselessly from office to office and found but little time to swim in the morning or consume oysters in the afternoon.

The Hôtel de la Gare was distinguished from lesser hotels by an infant prodigy and champagne cocktails. The infant prodigy was a dumpy child of uncertain age, who, with or without encouragement, would climb on to the piano-stool and pick out simple tunes with one finger. The champagne cocktails infected a doctor of my acquaintance with an unreasoning desire to change horses and gallop back to billets.

At last the train came in. My servant, my baggage, and myself were thrown on board, and alighted at the next station in accordance with the instructions of the R.T.O. . . .

A few months later the Cyclist Battalion went to Italy, under Major Percy Davies. It returned to France in time for the German offensive of April 1918, and gained everlasting honour by holding back the enemy, when the Portuguese withdrew, until our infantry arrived. For its skilful and dogged defence this battalion was mentioned by name in the despatches of the commander-in-chief.

CHAPTER 2

Fred Karno's Army
(JANUARY TO APRIL 1917.)

My servant, Spencer, and I arrived at St Pol, where officers going on leave used to grow impatient with the official method of travel, desert the slow uncomfortable train, and haunt the Rest House in the hope of obtaining a seat in a motorcar to Boulogne. I had expected that the R.T.O. would call me into his office, and in hushed tones direct me to the secret lair of the tanks. Everything possible, it was rumoured, had been done to preserve the tanks from prying eyes. I was undeceived at once. An official strode up and down the platform, shouting that all men for the tanks were to alight immediately. I found on inquiry that the train for the tank area would not depart for several hours, so, leaving my servant and my kit at the station, I walked into the town full of hope.

I lunched moderately at the hotel, but, though there was much talk of tanks there, I found no one with a car. I adjourned in due course to the military hairdresser, and at dusk was speeding out of St Pol in a luxurious Vauxhall. I was deposited at Wavrans with the Supply Officer, a melancholy and overworked young man, who advised me to use the telephone. Tank headquarters informed me that I was posted provisionally to D Battalion, and D Battalion promised to send a box-body. I collected my servant and baggage from the station at Wavrans, accepted the supply officer's hospitality, and questioned him about my new corps.

Tanks, he told me, were organised as a branch of the Machine-Gun Corps for purposes of camouflage, pay, and records. Six companies had been formed, of which four had come to France and two had remained in England. The four overseas companies had carried out the recent operations on the Somme (September–October 1916). The authorities had been so much impressed that it was decided to expand each of these companies into a battalion, by the embodiment of certain Motor Machine-Gun Batteries and of volunteers expected from other corps in response to the appeal that had been sent round all formations. Thus A, B, C, and D Battalions were forming in France, E, F, and sundry other battalions, in England. Each battalion, he believed, consisted of three companies. Each company possessed twelve or more tanks, and the Company Commander owned a car.

Primed with this information and some hot tea, I welcomed the arrival of the box-body. We drove at breakneck speed through the darkness and the rain to Blangy-sur-Ternoise. I entered a cheerful, brightly-lit mess. Seeing a venerable and imposing officer standing by the fire, I saluted him. He assured me that he was only the equipment officer. We sat down to a well-served dinner, I discovered an old 'Varsity friend in the doctor, and retired content to a comfortable bed after winning slightly at bridge.

In the morning I was sent in a car to Bermicourt, where I was interviewed by Colonel Elles.[1] As the result of the interview I was posted to D Battalion, and on the following evening took over the command of No. 2 Company from Haskett-Smith. . . .

The usual difficulties and delays had occurred in the assembling of the battalions. Rations were short. There was no equipment. The billets were bad. Necessaries such as camp kettles could not be obtained. That was now old if recent history. The battalions had first seen the light in October. By the beginning of January officers and men were equipped, fed, and under cover.

The men were of three classes. First came the "Old Tankers," those who had been trained with the original companies.

---

1. Now Major-General H. J. Elles, C.B., D.S.O.

They had been drawn for the most part from the A.S.C.: M.T. Some had been once or twice in action; some had not. They were excellent tank mechanists. Then came the motor machine gunners—smart fellows, without much experience of active operations. The vast majority of officers and men were volunteers from the infantry—disciplined fighting men.

On parade the company looked a motley crew, as indeed it was. Men from different battalions knew different drill. Some from the less combatant corps knew no drill at all. They resembled a "leave draft," and nobody can realise how undisciplined disciplined men can appear, who has not seen a draft of men from various units marching from the boat to a rest camp. The men are individuals. They trail along like a football crowd. They have no pride in their appearance, because they cannot feel they are on parade. They are only a crowd, not a company or a regiment. Corporate pride and feeling are absent. The company was composed of drafts. Before it could fight it must be made a company. The men described themselves with admirable humour in this song, to the tune "The Church's one foundation"—

> *We are Fred Karno's army, the Ragtime A.S.C.,*
> *We do not work, we cannot fight, what ruddy use are we?*
> *And when we get to Berlin, the Kaiser he will say—*
> *'Hoch, hoch, mein Gott!*
> *What a ruddy rotten lot*
> *Are the Ragtime A.S.C.!'*

The company lived in a rambling hospice, built round a large courtyard. The original inhabitants consisted of nuns and thirty or forty aged and infirm men, who, from their habits and appearance, we judged to be consumptives.

The nuns were friendly but fussy. They allowed the officers to use a large kitchen, but resented the intrusion of any but officers' mess cooks, and in putting forward claims for alleged damages and thefts the good nuns did not lag behind their less pious sisters in the village. We were grateful to them for their courtesy and kindliness; yet it cannot be said that any senior officer in the company ever went out of his way to meet the Mother Superior. She possessed a tactless memory.

The consumptives had a large room to themselves. It stank abominably. Where they slept at night was a mystery. They died in the room next to my bedchamber.

The door of my room was inscribed *Notre Dame des Douleurs*, and the room justified its title. All operations planned in it were cancelled. The day after I had first slept in it I fell ill. Colonel Elles, with Lieutenant-Colonel Burnett, came to see me in my bed. I had not shaved, and my temperature made me slightly familiar. I could never keep the room warm of nights. Once, when I was suffering from a bad cold, I put out my hand sleepily for my handkerchief, and, without thinking, tried to blow my nose. It was a freezing night, and I still have the scar.

The majority of the men had wire beds, made by stretching wire-mesh over a wooden frame; but the rooms were draughty. We made a sort of dining-hall in a vast barn, but it was cold and dark.

In these chilly rooms and enormous barns the official supply of fuel did not go far. The coal trains from the "*Mines des Marles*" often rested for a period in Blangy sidings. I am afraid that this source was tapped unofficially, but the French naturally complained, strict orders were issued, and our fires again were low. It was necessary to act, and to act with decision. I obtained a lorry from the battalion, handed it over to a promising subaltern, and gave him stern instructions to return with much coal. Late in the afternoon he returned, on foot. The lorry had broken down six miles away. Three tons of coal made too heavy a load in frosty weather. The lorry was towed in, and once again we were warm.

I did not ask for details, but a story reached my ears that a subaltern with a lorry had arrived that same morning at a certain Army coal dump. He asked urgently for two tons of coal. The Tanks were carrying out important experiments: coal they must have or the experiments could not be continued. Permission was given at once—he would return with the written order, which the Tanks had stupidly forgotten to give him. A little gift at the dump produced the third ton. To a Heavy Gunner the story needs no comment.

The mess was a dining-hall, medieval in size, with an immense open fireplace that consumed much coal and gave out little heat. We placed a stove in the middle of the hall. The piping was led to the upper part of the fireplace, but in spite of Jumbo's ingenuity it was never secure, and would collapse without warning. The fire smoked badly.

As the hall would seat at least fifty, we specialised in weekly guest-nights, and the reputation of the company for hospitality was unequalled. In those days canteens met all reasonable needs: the allotment system had not been devised; a worried mess-president, commissioned with threats to obtain whisky, was not offered fifty bars of soap in lieu. And we bought a piano that afterwards became famous. Luckily, we had an officer, nicknamed Grantoffski, who could play any known tune from memory.

Our mess was so large that we were asked to entertain temporarily several officers from other units of the Tank Corps in process of formation. Several of these guests came from the central work- shops of the Tank Corps at Erin, and later returned our hospitality by doing us small services.

One engineer, who remained with the Tank Corps for a few weeks only, told us a remarkable story. We were talking of revolvers and quick shooting and fighting in America. Suddenly to our amazement he became fierce.

"Do you see my hand? You wouldn't think it, but it's nearly useless—all through a Prussian officer. It was in Louisiana, and he went for me although I was unarmed. I caught his knife with my bare hand—it cut to the bone—I jerked back his wrist and threw him. My pal had a Winchester. He pushed it into the brute's face, smashed it all up, and was just going to pull the trigger when I knocked it away. But the sinews of my hand were cut and there was no doctor there. . . . I've been after that Prussian ever since. I'm going to get him—oh yes, don't you fear. I'm going to get him. How do I know he is still alive? I heard the other day. He is on the other side. I've pursued him for five years, and now I'm going to get him!"

He was a Scots engineer, a sturdy red-faced fellow with twinkling eyes and a cockney curl to his hair.

The mess was a pleasant place, and training proceeded smoothly, because no company commander ever had better officers. My second-in-command was Haigh, a young and experienced regular from the infantry. He left me after the second battle of Bullecourt, to instruct the Americans. My officers were Swears, an "old Tanker," who was instructing at Bermicourt, Wyatt, and "Happy Fanny," Morris, Puttock, Davies,. Clarkson, Macilwaine, Birkett, Grant, King, Richards, Telfer, Skinner, Sherwood, Head, Pritchard, Bernstein, Money, Talbot, Coghlan—too few remained long with the company. Of the twenty I have mentioned, three had been killed, six wounded, three transferred, and two invalided before the year was out.

Training began in the middle of December and continued until the middle of March. Prospective tank-drivers tramped up early every morning to the Tank Park or "Tankodrome"—a couple of large fields in which workshops had been erected, some trenches dug, and a few shell-craters blown. The Tankodrome was naturally a sea of mud. Perhaps the mud was of a curious kind—perhaps the mixture of petrol and oil with the mud was poisonous. Most officers and men working in the Tankodrome suffered periodically from painful and ugly sores, which often spread over the body from the face. We were never free from them while we were at Blangy.

The men were taught the elements of tank driving and tank maintenance by devoted instructors, who laboured day after day in the mud, the rain, and the snow. Officers' courses were held at Bermicourt. Far too few tanks were available for instruction, and very little driving was possible.

"Happy Fanny" toiled in a cold and draughty out-house with a couple of 6-pdrs. and a shivering class. Davies, our enthusiastic Welsh footballer, supervised instruction in the Lewis gun among the draughts of a lofty barn in the Hospice.

The foundation of all training was drill. As a very temporary soldier I had regarded drill as unnecessary ritual, as an opportunity for colonels and adjutants to use their voices and prance about on horses. "Spit and polish "seemed to me as antiquated in a modern war as pipeclay and red coats. I was wrong. Let me give the old drill-sergeant his due. There is nothing in the world like smart drill under a competent instructor to make a company out of a mob. Train a man to respond instantly to a brisk command, and he will become a clean, alert, self-respecting soldier.

We used every means to quicken the process. We obtained a bugle. Our bugler was not good. He became careless towards the middle of his calls, and sometimes he erred towards the finish. He did not begin them always on quite the right note. We started with twenty odd calls a day. Everything the officers and the men did was done by bugle-call. It was very military and quite effective. All movements became brisk. But the bugler became worse and worse. Out of self-preservation we reduced the number of his calls. Finally he was stopped altogether by the colonel, whose headquarters were at the time close to our camp.

Our football team helped to bring the company together. It happened to excel any other team in the neighbourhood. We piled up enormous scores against all the companies we played. Each successive victory made the men prouder of the company, and more deeply contemptuous of the other companies who produced such feeble and ineffective elevens. Even the money that flowed into the pockets of our more ardent supporters after each match strengthened the belief in the superiority of No. 2 Company. The spectators were more than enthusiastic. Our C.S.M. would run up and down the touchline, using the most amazing and lurid language.

Towards the middle of February our training became more ingenious and advanced. As painfully few real tanks were available for instruction, it was obviously impossible to use them for tactical schemes. Our friendly Allies would have inundated the claims officer if tanks had carelessly manoeuvred over their precious fields. In consequence the authorities provided dummy tanks.

Imagine a large box of canvas stretched on a wooden frame, without top or bottom, about six feet high, eight feet long, and five feet wide. Little slits were made in the canvas to represent the loopholes of a tank. Six men carried and moved each dummy, lifting it by the cross-pieces of the framework. For our sins we were issued with eight of these abortions.

We started with a crew of officers to encourage the men, and the first dummy tank waddled out of the gate. It was immediately surrounded by a mob of cheering children, who thought it was an imitation dragon or something out of a circus. It was led away from the road to avoid hurting the feelings of the crew and to safeguard the ears and morals of the young. After colliding with the corner of a house, it endeavoured to walk down the side of the railway cutting. Nobody was hurt, but a fresh crew was necessary. It regained the road when a small man in the middle, who had been able to see nothing, stumbled and fell. The dummy tank was sent back to the carpenter for repairs.

We persevered with those dummy tanks. The men hated them. They were heavy, awkward, and produced much childish laughter. In another company a crew walked over a steep place and a man broke his leg. The dummies became less and less mobile. The signallers practised from them, and they were used by the visual training experts. One company commander mounted them on wagons drawn by mules. The crews were tucked in with their Lewis guns, and each contraption, a cross between a fire-engine and a triumphal car in a Lord Mayor's Show, would gallop past targets which the gunners would recklessly endeavour to hit.

Finally, these dummies reposed derelict in our courtyard until one by one they disappeared, as the canvas and the wood were required for ignobler purposes.

We were allowed occasionally to play with real tanks. A sham attack was carried out before hilltops of generals and staff officers, who were much edified by the sight of tanks moving. The total effect was marred by an enthusiastic tank commander, who, in endeavouring to show off the paces of his tank, became badly ditched, and the tank was for a moment on fire. The spectators appeared interested.

On another day we carried out experiments with smoke-bombs. Two gallant tanks moved slowly up a hill against trenches. When the tanks drew near, the defenders of the trenches rushed out, armed with several kinds of smoke-producing missiles. These they hurled at the tanks, and, growing bolder, inserted them into every loophole and crevice of the tanks. At length the half-suffocated crews tumbled out, and maintained with considerable strength of language that all those who had approached the tanks had been killed, adding that if they had only known what kind of smoke was going to be used they would have loaded their guns to avoid partial asphyxiation.

In addition to these open-air sports, the senior officers of the battalion carried out indoor schemes under the colonel. We planned numerous attacks on the map. I remember that my company was detailed once to attack Serre. A few months later I passed through this "village," but I could only assure myself of its position by the fact that there was some brick-dust in the material of the road.

By the beginning of March the company had begun to find itself. Drill, training, and sport had each done their work. Officers and men were proud of their company, and were convinced that no better company had ever existed. The mob of men had been welded into a fighting instrument. My sergeant-major and I were watching another company march up the street. He turned to me with an expression of slightly amused contempt.

"They can't march like us, sir!"

CHAPTER 3

Before the First Battle
(MARCH AND APRIL 1917.)

In the first months of 1917 we were confident that the last year of the war had come. The Battle of the Somme had shown that the strongest German lines were not impregnable. We had learned much: the enemy had received a tremendous hammering; and the success of General Gough's operations in the Ancre valley promised well for the future. The French, it was rumoured, were undertaking a grand attack in the early spring. We were first to support them by an offensive near Arras, and then we would attack ourselves on a large scale somewhere in the north. We hoped, too, that the Russians and Italians would come to our help. We were told that the discipline of the German Army was loosening, that our blockade was proving increasingly effective, and we were encouraged by stories of many novel inventions. We possessed unbounded confidence in our Tanks.

Late in February the colonel held a battalion conference. He explained the situation to his company commanders and the plan of forthcoming operations.

As the result of our successes in the Ancre valley, the German position between the Ancre and Arras formed a pronounced salient. It was determined to attack simultaneously at Arras and from the Ancre valley, with the object of breaking through at both points and cutting off the German inside the salient.

Colonel Elles had offered two battalions of tanks. He was taking a risk. Officers and crews were only half-trained. Right through the period of training real tanks had been too scarce. Improved tanks were expected from England, but none had arrived, and he decided to employ again the old Mark I. tank which had been used in the operations on the Somme in the previous year. The two battalions selected were "C" and "D."

When we examined the orders for the attack in detail, I found that my company was destined to go through with the troops allotted to the second objective and take Mercatel and Neuville Vitasse. It should have been a simple enough operation, as two conspicuous main roads penetrated the German lines parallel with the direction of my proposed attack.

On March 9th I drove to Arras in my car with Haigh, my second-in-command, and Jumbo, my reconnaissance officer. We went by St Pol and the great Arras road. The Arras road is a friend of mine. First it was almost empty except for the lorry park near Savy, and, short of Arras, it was screened because the Germans still held the Vimy Ridge. Then before the Arras battle it became more and more crowded—numberless lorries, convoys of huge guns and howitzers, smiling men in buses and tired men marching, staff-cars and motor ambulances, rarely, a wagon with slow horses, an old Frenchman in charge, quite bewildered by the traffic.

When the battle had begun, whole divisions, stretching for ten miles or more, came marching along it, and the ambulances streamed back to the big hospital at St Pol. I saw it for the last time after the Armistice had been signed, deserted and unimportant, with just a solitary soldier here and there standing at the door of a cottage. It is an exposed and windy road. The surface of it was never good, but I have always felt that the Arras road was proud to help us. It seemed ever to be saying: "Deliver Arras from shell and bomb; then leave me, and I shall be content to dream again." . . .

We drove into Arras a little nervously, but it was not being shelled, and, hungry after a freezing ride, we lunched at the Hôtel de Commerce.

This gallant hotel was less than 2500 yards from the German

trenches. Across the street was a field battery in action. The glass of the restaurant had been broken, the upper stories had been badly damaged, the ceiling of the dining-room showed marks of shrapnel. Arras was being shelled and bombed every night, and often by day; German aeroplanes flew low over the town and fired down the streets. The hotel had still carried on ever since the British had been in Arras and before. The proprietress, a little pinched and drawn, with the inevitable scrap of fur flung over her shoulders, presided at the desk. Women dressed in the usual black waited on us. The lunch was cheap, excellently cooked, and well served—within easy range of the enemy field-guns.

After the battle the hotel was put out of bounds, for serving drinks in forbidden hours. Indeed, A.P.M.'s have no souls. It reopened later, and continued to flourish until the German attack of April 1918, when the enemy shelling became too insistent. The hotel has not been badly hit, and, if it be rebuilt, I beseech all those who visit the battlefields of Arras to lunch at the Hôtel de Commerce—in gratitude It is in the main street just by the station.

We motored out of Arras along a road that was lined with newly-made gun-pits, and, arriving at a dilapidated village, introduced ourselves to the divisional staff. We discussed operations, and found that much was expected of the tanks. After a cheery tea we drove home in the bitter cold.

On the 13th March we again visited the division. I picked up the G.S.O. 3 of the division, called on a brigadier, with whom I expected to work, and then drove to the neighbourhood of the disreputable village of Agny. We peeped at the very little there was to be seen of the enemy front line through observation posts in cottages and returned to Arras, where we lunched excellently with the colonel of an infantry battalion. I left Jumbo with him, to make a detailed reconnaissance of the Front. . . .

The Arras battle would have been fought according to plan, we should have won a famous victory, and hundreds of thousands of Germans might well have been entrapped in the Arras salient, if the enemy in his wisdom had not retired. Unfortu-

30

nately, at the beginning of March he commenced his withdrawal from the unpleasant heights to the north of the Ancre valley, and, once the movement was under way, it was predicted that the whole of the Arras salient would be evacuated. This actually occurred in the following weeks; the very sector I was detailed to attack was occupied by our troops without fighting. Whether the German had wind of the great attack that we had planned, I do not know. He certainly made it impossible for us to carry it out.

As soon as the extent of the German withdrawal became clear, my company was placed in reserve. I was instructed to make arrangements to support any attack at any point on the Arras front.

The Arras sector was still suitable for offensive operations. The Germans had fallen back on the Hindenburg Line, and this complicated system of defences rejoined the old German line opposite Arras. Obviously the most practical way of attacking the Hindenburg Line was to turn it—to fight down it, and not against it. Our preparations for an attack in the Arras sector and on the Vimy Ridge to the north of it were far advanced. It was decided in consequence to carry out with modifications the at-tack on the German trench system opposite Arras and on the Vimy Ridge. Operations from the Ancre valley, the southern re- entrant of the old Arras salient, were out of the question. The Fifth Army was fully occupied in keeping touch with the enemy.

On the 27th March my company was suddenly transferred from the Third Army to the Fifth Army. I was informed that my company would be attached to the 5th Corps for any operations that might occur. Jumbo was recalled from Arras, fuming at his wasted work, and an advance party was immediately sent to my proposed detraining station at Achiet-le-Grand.

On the 29th March I left Blangy. My car was a little unsightly. The body was loaded with Haigh's kit and my kit and a collaps-ible table. On top, like a mahout, sat Spencer, my servant. It was sleeting, and there was a cold wind. We drove through St Pol and along the Arras road, cut south through Habarcq to Beaumetz, and plunged over appalling roads towards Bucquoy. The roads became worse and worse. Spencer was just able to cling on, groaning at every bump.

Soon we arrived at our old rear defences, from which we had gone forward only ten days before. It was joyous to read the notices, so newly obsolete—"This road is subject to shell-fire"—and when we passed over our old support and front trenches, and drove across No Man's Land, and saw the green crosses of the Germans, the litter of their trenches, their signboards and their derelict equipment, then we were triumphant indeed. Since March 1917 we have advanced many a mile, but never with more joy. Remember that from October 1914 to March 1917 we had never really advanced. At Neuve Chapelle we took a village and four fields, Loos was a fiasco, and the Somme was too horrible for a smile.

On the farther side of the old German trenches was desolation. We came to a village and found the houses lying like slaughtered animals. Mostly they had been pulled down, like card houses, but some had been blown in. It was so pitiful that I wanted to stop and comfort them. The trees along the roads had been cut down. The little fruit-trees had been felled, or lay half- fallen with gashes in their sides. The ploughs rusted in the fields. The rain was falling monotonously. It was getting dark, and there was nobody to be seen except a few forlorn soldiers.

We crept with caution round the vast funnel-shaped craters that had been blown at each cross-road, and, running through Logeast Wood, which had mocked us for so many weeks on the Somme, we came to Achiet-le-Grand.

Ridger, the town commandant, had secured the only standing house, and he was afraid that it had been left intact for some devilish purpose. Haigh and Grant of my advance party were established in a dugout. So little was it possible in those days to realise the meaning of an advance, that we discovered we had only two mugs, two plates, and one knife between us.

In the morning we got to work. A supply of water was arranged for the men; there was only one well in the village that had not been polluted. We inspected the ramp by which the tanks would detrain, selected a tankodrome near the station, wired in a potential dump, found good cellars for the men, and began the construction of a mess in . the remains of a small brick stable. Then Haigh and I motored past the derelict factory of Bihucourt and through the outskirts of Bapaume to the ruins of Behagnies, on the Bapaume-Arras road. After choosing sites for an advanced camp and tankodrome, we walked back to Achiet-le-Grand across country, in order to reconnoitre the route for tanks from the station to Behagnies.

After lunch, Haigh, Jumbo, and I motored to Ervillers, which is beyond Behagnies, and, leaving the car there, tramped to Mory. Jumbo had discovered in the morning an old quarry, hidden by trees, that he recommended as a half-way house for the tanks, if we were ordered to move forward; but the enemy was a little lively, and we determined to investigate further on a less noisy occasion.

That night we dined in our new mess. We had stretched one tarpaulin over what had been the roof, and another tarpaulin took the place of an absent wall. The main beam was cracked, and we feared rain, but a huge blazing fire comforted us—until

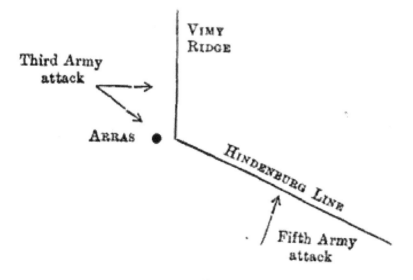

one or two slates fell off with a clatter. We rushed out, fearing the whole building was about to collapse. It was cold and drizzling. We stood it for five minutes, and then, as nothing further happened, we returned to our fire. . . .

In some general instructions I had received from the colonel, it was suggested that my company would be used by the 5th Corps for an attack on Bullecourt and the Hindenburg Line to the east and west of the village. It will be remembered that the attack at Arras was designed to roll up the Hindenburg Line, starting from the point at which the Hindenburg Line joined the old German trench system. General Gough's Fifth Army, consisting of General Fanshawe's 5th Corps and General Birdwood's Corps of Australians, lay south-east of Arras and on the right of the Third Army. The Fifth Army faced the Hindenburg Line, and, if it attacked, it would be compelled to attack frontally.

The disadvantages of a frontal attack on an immensely strong series of entrenchments were balanced by the fact that a successful penetration would bring the Fifth Army on the left rear of that German Army, which would be fully occupied at the time in repelling the onset of our Third Army.

The key to that sector of the Hindenburg Line which lay opposite the Fifth Army front was the village of Bullecourt.

In the last week of March the Germans had not taken refuge in their main line of defence, and were still holding out in the villages of Croisilles, Ecoust, and Noreuil.

We were attacking them vigorously, but with no success and heavy casualties. On the morning of the 31st March Jumbo and I drove again to Ervillers and walked to Mory, pushing forward down the slope towards Ecoust. There was a quaint feeling of insecurity, quite unjustified, in strolling about "on top." We had an excellent view of our shells bursting on the wire in front of Ecoust, but we saw nothing of the country we wanted to reconnoitre—the approaches to Bullecourt. Ecoust was finally captured at the sixth or seventh attempt by the 9th Division on April 1st.

In the afternoon I paid my first visit to the 5th Corps, then at Acheux, twenty miles back. I motored by Bapaume and Albert over the Somme battlefield. The nakedness of it is now hidden by coarse grass and rough weeds, but in March of 1917 it was bare. There was dark-brown mud for mile after mile as far as the eye could see—mud churned and tortured until the whole surface of the earth was pitted with craters. Mud overwhelmed the landscape. Trees showed only against the sky; dead men, old equipment, derelict tanks blended with the mud. At Le Sars bits of walls and smashed beams lay embedded in the mud. At Pozières the mud held a few mud-coloured bricks. I was glad when I came to Albert.

We took the Doullens road and found the corps well housed in the *château* at Acheux. I announced the imminent arrival of my tanks, but the news did not kindle the enthusiasm I had expected. The 5th Corps had already used tanks and knew their little ways. After tea I consulted with the lesser lights of the staff. Satisfactory arrangements were made for supplies, rations, and accommodation, and I demanded and obtained the use of a troop of Glasgow Yeomanry, on the plea that they were required to cover the tracks of my tanks. I wanted a horse to ride.

I decided to return by Puisieux-le-Mont. It was apparent that the Albert-Bapaume road would soon become uncomfortably crowded. I wanted to reconnoitre the only alternative route, and at the same time to inspect the village of Serre, which, on paper, I had so often and so violently attacked.

Never have I endured a more ghastly ride. In comparison with the country on either side of the Puisieux road, the Somme battlefield from the highway between Albert and Bapaume was serenely monotonous. After Mailly-Mailly the road became a rough track, narrow and full of unfilled shell-holes. Crazy bridges had been thrown across the trenches. The sun was setting in a fiery sky, and a reddish light tinged the pitiful tumbled earth, and glittered for a moment on the desolate water of the shell-holes. The crumbling trenches were manned with restless dead. In the doubtful light I thought a dead German moved. He lay on his back, half-sunken in the slimy mud, with knees drawn up, and blackened hand gripping a rusty rifle. Mercifully I could not see his face, but I thought his arms twitched.

It grew darker, and so narrow was the track that I might have been driving over the black mud of the battlefield. A derelict limber half-blocked the road, and, swerving to avoid it, we barely missed the carcass of a horse, dead a few days. Our progress was slow. Soon we lit the lamps. The track was full of horrible shadows, and big dark things seemed to come down the road to meet us—shattered transport or old heaps of shells. On either side of the car was the desert of mud and waterlogged holes and corpses, face downward under the water, and broken guns and mortars, and little graves, and mile-long strands of rusty wire. Everywhere maimed ghosts were rustling, and the plump rats were pattering along the trenches.

It is unwise to go through a battlefield at night. If they make the Somme battlefield a forest, no man will be brave enough to cross it in the dark.

We came to lights in the ruins of a village, and I stopped for a pipe and a word with my driver. . . .

My tanks arrived at Achiet-le-Grand just after dawn on April 1st. We had taken them over from the central workshops at Erin, and had drawn there a vast variety of equipment. The tanks had been driven on to the train by an Engineer officer. The railway journey had been delayed as usual, and the usual expert—this time a doctor—had walked along the train, when shunted at Doullens, and had pointed out to his companion the "new monster tanks."

In the morning we hauled off the sponson-trolleys—their use will be explained later—but we thought it wiser to wait until dusk before we detrained the tanks.

Tanks travel on flat trucks, such as are employed to carry rails. They are driven on and off the train under their own power, but this performance requires care, skill, and experience. A Mk. 1 or a Mk. 4 tank is not too easy to steer, while the space between the track and the edge of the truck is alarmingly small. With two exceptions, my officers had neither experience nor skill.

It was an anxious time—not only for the company commander. The office of the R.T.O., at the edge of the ramp, was narrowly missed on two occasions. Very slowly and with infinite care the tanks were persuaded to leave the train and move down the road to the tankodrome we had selected. Then it began first to sleet and then to snow, while an icy wind rose, until a blizzard was lashing our faces.

In the old Mark 1 tank it was necessary to detach the sponsons, or armoured "bow-windows," on either side before the tank could be moved by rail. This was no easy matter. The tank was driven into two shallow trenches. A stout four-wheeled trolley was run alongside, and a sort of crane was fitted, to which slings were secured. The sponson was girt about with these slings, the bolts which secured the sponson to the body of the tank were taken out, and the sponson was lowered on to the trolley.

My men, of whom the majority were inexperienced, carried out the reverse process on a dark night in a blizzard. Their fingers were so blue with cold that they could scarcely handle their tools. The climax was reached when we discovered that we should be compelled to drill new holes in several of the sponsons, because in certain cases the holes in the sponsons did not correspond with the holes in the tanks.

If the men never had a harder night's work, they certainly never worked better. Half the tanks fitted their sponsons and reached Behagnies by dawn. The remainder, less one lame duck, were hidden in Achiet-le-Grand until darkness once more allowed them to move.

Every precaution was taken to conceal the tanks from the enemy. My troop of Glasgow Yeomanry, under the direction of Talbot, who had been a sergeant-major in the Dragoons, rode twice over the tracks which the tanks had made in order to obliterate them by hoof-marks. At Behagnies the tanks were drawn up against convenient hedges and enveloped in tarpaulins and camouflage nets. In spite of our efforts they appeared terribly obvious as we surveyed them anxiously from one point after another.

Our subtle devices were soon tested. An enterprising German airman flew down out of the clouds and darted upon two luckless observation balloons to right and left of us. He set them both on fire with tracer bullets, came low over our camp, fired down the streets of Bapaume, and disappeared into the east. The sporting instinct of my men responded to the audacity of the exploit, and they cheered him; but for the next twenty-four hours I was wondering if the camouflage of my tanks had been successful, or if the attention of the airman had been concentrated solely on the balloons. Presumably we were not spotted, for while at Behagnies we were neither shelled nor bombed.

The preparations for my first essay in tank-fighting were beginning to bear fruit. Eleven tanks lay within two short marches of any point from which they were likely to attack, and my crews were busy overhauling them. One crippled tank was hidden at Achiet-le-Grand, but the mechanical defect which had developed in her must have escaped the notice of central workshops. Cooper[1] was engaged night and day in taking up supplies and making forward dumps. The corps had provided us with a convoy of limbered wagons drawn by mules—the forward roads were not passable for lorries—and the wretched animals had little rest.

We were ordered to be ready by the 6th, and the order meant a fight against time. Tanks consume an incredible quantity of petrol, oil, grease, and water, and it was necessary to form dumps of these supplies and of ammunition at Mory Copse, our half-way house, and at Noreuil and Ecoust. Night and day the convoy trekked backwards and forwards under Cooper or Talbot. Mules cast their shoes, the drivers were dog-tired, the dumps at Noreuil and Ecoust were shelled, both roads to Mory were blocked by the explosion of delayed mines,—in spite of all difficulties the dumps were made, and on the morning of the battle the convoy stood by loaded, ready to follow the tanks in the expected break through.

---

1. Major R. Cooper, M.C., Royal Fusiliers, had replaced Captain K. Haigh, M.C.

Haigh had ridden forward to Ecoust with a handful of Glasgow yeomen in order to keep an eye on the dump and reconnoitre the country between Ecoust and the Hindenburg Line. He started in the afternoon, joining an ammunition column on the way. They approached the village at dusk. The enemy was shelling the road and suspected battery positions short of the first houses. The column made a dash for it at full gallop, but a couple of shells found the column, killing a team and the drivers.

Haigh and his men wandered into a smithy and lit a small fire, for it was bitterly cold. The shelling continued, but the smithy was not hit. They passed a wretched night, and at dawn discovered a cellar, where they made themselves comfortable after they had removed the bodies of two Germans.

The reconnaissances were carried out with Haigh's usual thoroughness. Tank routes and observation posts were selected—"lying-up" places for the tanks were chosen. Everything was ready if the tanks should be ordered to attack Bullecourt from the direction of Ecoust.

On April 4th I was introduced to the Higher Command. The 5th Corps had moved forward from Acheux to the ruined *château* at Bihucourt. There I lunched with the general, and drove with him in the afternoon to an army conference at Fifth Army Headquarters in Albert. The block of traffic on the road made us an hour late, and it was interesting to see how an army commander dealt with such pronounced, if excusable, unpunctuality in a corps commander.

The conference consisted of an awe-inspiring collection of generals seated round a table in a stuffy room decorated with maps. The details of the attack had apparently been settled before we arrived, but I understood from the army commander's vigorous summary of the situation that the Third Army would not attack until the 7th. The greatest results were expected, and the Fifth Army would join in the fray immediately the attack of the Third Army was well launched. As far as I was concerned, my tanks were to be distributed along the fronts of the Australian and 5th Corps.

The conference broke up, and the colonel and I were asked to tea at the *château*. It was a most nervous proceeding, to drink tea in the company of a bevy of generals; but the major-general on my right was hospitality itself, and the colonel improved the occasion by obtaining the promise of some more huts from the major-general, who was engineer-in-chief of the army. Eventually we escaped, and the colonel[2] drove me back to Behagnies, where battalion headquarters lay close by my camp.

On the night of the 5th, as soon as it was dusk, my tanks moved forward. One by one they slid smoothly past me in the darkness, each like a patient animal, led by his officer, who flashed directions with an electric lamp. The stench of petrol in the air, a gentle crackling as they found their way through the wire, the sweet purr of the engine changing to a roar when they climbed easily on to the road—and then, as they followed the white tape into the night, the noise of their engines died away, and I could hear only the sinister flap-flap of the tracks, and see only points of light on the hillside.

Tanks in the daytime climbing in and out of trenches like performing elephants may appeal to the humour of a journalist. Stand with me at night and listen. There is a little mist, and the dawn will soon break. Listen carefully, and you will hear a queer rhythmical noise and the distant song of an engine. The measured flap of the tracks grows louder, and, if you did not know, you would think an aeroplane was droning overhead. Then in the half-light comes a tired officer, reading a map, and behind him another, signalling at intervals to a grey mass gliding smoothly like a snake.

And so they pass, one by one, with the rattle of tracks and the roar of their exhaust, each mass crammed with weary men, hot and filthy and choking with the fumes. Nothing is more inexorable than the slow glide of a tank and the rhythm of her tracks. Remember that nothing on earth has ever caused more deadly fear at the terrible hour of dawn than these grey sliding masses

2. Now Brigadier-General J. Hardress Lloyd, D.S.O.

crammed with weary men. . . .

My tanks were safely camouflaged in the old quarry at Mory Copse before dawn on April 6th. I joined them in the morning, riding up from the camp at Behagnies on a troop-horse I had commandeered from my troop of Glasgow Yeomanry. The quarry was not an ideal hiding-place, as it lay open to direct though distant observation from the German lines; but the tanks were skilfully concealed by the adroit use of trees, undergrowth, and nets, the hill surmounted by the copse provided an excellent background, and we were compelled to make a virtue of necessity as the open downs in the neighbourhood of Mory gave not the slightest cover.[3] The village itself was out of the question: the enemy were shelling it with hearty goodwill.

We lay there comfortably enough, though unnecessary movement by day and the use of lights at night were forbidden. No enemy aeroplane came over, but a few shells, dropping just beyond the copse on a suspected battery position, disturbed our sleep. The tanks were quietly tuned, the guns were cleaned, and officers were detailed to reconnoitre the tank routes to Ecoust and Noreuil.

The offensive was postponed from day to day, and we were growing a little impatient, when at dawn on April 9th the Third Army attacked.

It had been arranged at the last Army Conference that the Fifth Army would move when the offensive of the Third Army was well launched. My tanks were to be distributed in pairs along the whole front of the army, and to each pair a definite objective was allotted. I had always been averse to this scattering of my command. The Hindenburg Line, which faced us, was notoriously strong. Bullecourt, the key to the whole position, looked on the map almost impregnable. The artillery of the Fifth Army was to the best of my knowledge far from overwhelming, and gunners had told me that good forward positions for the guns were difficult to find.

I realised, of course, that an officer in my subordinate position

---

3. Paget, the Corps Camouflage Officer, was of the greatest assistance.

knew little, but I was convinced that a surprise concentration might prove a success where a formal attack, lightly supported by a few tanks scattered over a wide front, might reasonably fail. I planned for my own content an attack in which my tanks, concentrated on a narrow front of a thousand yards and supported as strongly as possible by all the infantry and guns available, should steal up to the Hindenburg Line without a barrage. As they entered the German trenches down would come the barrage, and under cover of the barrage and the tanks the infantry would sweep through, while every gun not used in making the barrage should pound away at the German batteries.

I was so fascinated by my conception that on the morning of the 9th I rode down to Behagnies and gave it to the colonel for what it was worth. He approved of it thoroughly. After a hasty lunch we motored down to the headquarters of the Fifth Army.

We found General Gough receiving in triumph the reports of our successes on the Third Army front opposite Arras.

"We want to break the Hindenburg Line with tanks. General," said the colonel, and very briefly explained the scheme.

General Gough received it with favour, and decided to attack at dawn on the following morning. He asked me when my tanks would require to start. The idea of an attack within twenty-four hours was a little startling—there were so many preparations to be made; but I replied my tanks should move at once, and I suggested air protection. General Gough immediately rang up the R.F.C., but their general was out, and, after some discussion, it was decided that my tanks would have sufficient time to reach the necessary position if they moved off after dusk. We drove at breakneck speed to the *château* near, which was occupied by the Australian Corps, and were left by General Gough to work out the details with the brigadier-general of the General Staff.

The colonel allowed me to explain the scheme myself. All my suggestions were accepted; but the concentration of men and guns that I had imagined in my dreams was made impossible by the fact that General Gough had ordered the attack for the morrow.

I took the colonel's car and tore back to Behagnies. I wrote out my orders while Jumbo, helped by two reconnaissance officers who were attached to us for instruction, rapidly marked and coloured maps for the tank commanders. My orders reached Swears, who was in charge at Mory Copse, by 6.30 p.m., and by 8 p.m. the tanks were clear of the quarry.

After dark I walked down the Bapaume road and presented myself at the headquarters of the Australian Division, with which my tanks were operating. It was a pitch-black night. The rain was turning to sleet.

Divisional Headquarters were in "Armstrong" or small canvas huts, draughty and cold. I discussed the coming battle with the staff of the Division and Osborne, the G.S.O. 2 of the corps. We turned in for a snatch of sleep, and I woke with a start—dreaming that my tanks had fallen over a cliff into the sea. At midnight I went to the door of the hut and looked out. A gale was blowing, and sleet was mingled with snow. After midnight I waited anxiously for news of my tanks. It was a long trek for one night, and, as we had drawn them so recently, I could not guarantee, from experience, their mechanical condition. There was no margin of time for any except running repairs.

At one o'clock still no news had come. The tanks had orders to telephone to me immediately they came to Noreuil, and from Noreuil to the starting-point was at least a ninety-minutes' run.

By two o'clock everybody was asking me for information. Brigade Headquarters at Noreuil had neither seen tanks nor heard them, but they sent out orderlies to look for them in case they had lost their way. At Noreuil it was snowing hard, and blowing a full gale.

My position was not pleasant. The attack was set for dawn. The infantry had already gone forward to the railway embankment, from which they would "jump off." In daylight they could neither remain at the embankment nor retire over exposed ground without heavy shelling. It was half-past two. I was penned in a hut with a couple of staff officers, who, naturally enough, were irritated and gloomy. I could do nothing.

The attack was postponed for an hour. Still no news of the tanks. The faintest glimmerings of dawn appeared when the telephone-bell rang. The Australian handed me the receiver with a smile of relief.

"It's one of your men," he said.

I heard Wyatt's tired voice.

"We are two miles short of Noreuil in the valley. We have been wandering on the downs in a heavy snowstorm. We never quite lost our way, but it was almost impossible to keep the tanks together. I will send in a report. The men are dead- tired."

"How long will it take to get to the starting-point?" I asked.

"An hour and a half at least," he replied wearily.

"Stand by for orders."

It was 1¼ hours before zero. The men were dead-tired. The tanks had been running all night. But the Australians were out on the railway embankment and dawn was breaking.

I went to see the general, and explained the situation briefly.

"What will happen to your tanks if I put back zero another hour and we attack in daylight? "he asked.

"My tanks will be useless," I replied. "They will be hit before they reach the German trenches—particularly against a background of snow."

He looked at his watch and glanced through the window at the growing light.

"It can't be helped. We must postpone the show. I think there is just time to get the boys back. Send B. to me."

I called up Wyatt and told him that the men were to be given a little sleep. The officers, after a short rest, were to reconnoitre forward. I heard orders given for the Australians to come back from the railway embankment—later I learned that this was done with practically no casualties—then I stumbled down the road to tell the colonel.

I found him shaving.

"The tanks lost their way in a snowstorm and arrived late at Noreuil. The attack was postponed."

He looked grave for a moment, but continued his shaving.

"Go and have some breakfast," he said cheerily. "You must be hungry. We'll talk it over later."

So I went and had some breakfast. . . .

Chapter 4

The First Battle of Bullecourt
(April 11, 1917.)

Later in the morning we heard from Jumbo, who had returned from Noreuil, the full history of the weary trek in the
blizzard.

The tanks had left Mory Copse at 8 p.m. under the guidance
of Wyatt. In the original plan of operations it had been arranged
that Wyatt's section should attack from Noreuil and the remaining sections from Ecoust So Wyatt was the only section commander who had reconnoitred the Noreuil route.

No tape had been laid. We had not wished to decorate the
downs with broad white tape before the afternoon of the day
on which the tanks would move forward. On the other hand,
we had not calculated on such a brief interval between the receipt of orders and the start of the tanks. An attempt to lay tape
in front of the tanks was soon abandoned: the drivers could not
distinguish it, and Wyatt was guiding them as well as he could.

Soon after they had set out the blizzard came sweeping over
the downs, blocking out landmarks and obscuring lamps. The
drivers could not always see the officers who were leading their
tanks on foot. Each tank commander, blinded and breathless,
found it barely possible to follow the tank in front. The pace was
reduced to a mere crawl in order to keep the convoy together.

Though Wyatt never lost his way, he wisely proceeded with
the utmost caution, checking his route again and again. Our line
at the time consisted of scattered posts—there were no trench-

es—and on such a night it would have been easy enough to lead the whole company of tanks straight into the German wire.

The tanks came down into the valley that runs from Vaulx-Vraucourt to Noreuil two miles above Noreuil. The crews were dead-tired, but they would have gone forward willingly if they could have arrived in time. The rest of the story I have told.

The blizzard confounded many that night. The colonel told me later he had heard that a whole cavalry brigade had spent most of the night wandering over the downs, hopelessly lost. I cannot vouch for the story myself.

In the afternoon (April 10) I was called to a conference at the headquarters of the Australian Division. General Birdwood was there, Major-General Holmes, who commanded the Division with which we were to operate, Brigadier-General Rosenthal, commanding the artillery of the corps, sundry staff officers, the colonel, and myself.

The conference first discussed the situation on the front of the Third Army. The initial advance had been completely successful, but the German forces were far from defeat, and were continuing to offer a most determined and skilful resistance. We certainly had not broken through yet. The battle, however, was still in its earliest stages; the situation had not crystallised; there was still hope that the enormous pressure of our offensive might cause the enemy line to crumble and disappear.

It had been decided, in consequence, to proceed with the postponed attack on Bullecourt, but to overhaul the arrangements which had been improvised to meet an emergency. The original idea of a stealthy and silent attack, led by tanks and supported by a bombardment rather than a barrage, was abandoned after some discussion, and the conference agreed to return to more classical methods.

Two infantry brigades would attack and pierce the Hindenburg Line on the front immediately to the east of Bullecourt. The attack was to be led by tanks under cover of a barrage and a heavy bombardment. Emphasis was laid on the necessity for strong counter-battery work. The right attacking brigade would

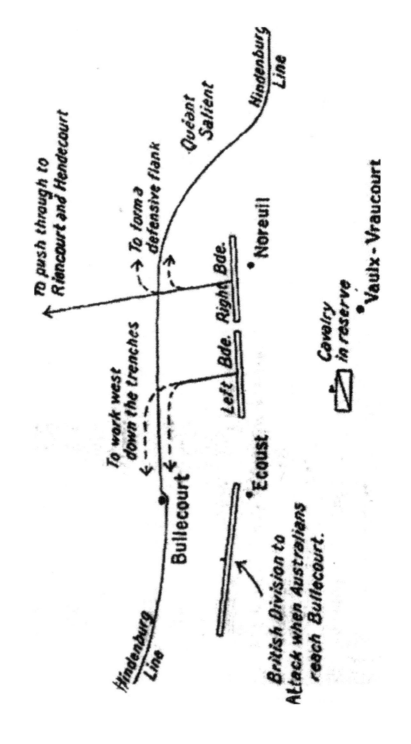

To push through to
Riencourt and Hendecourt

→ To form a
defensive flank

Quéant
Salient

Hindenburg
Line

Right Bde.

• Noreuil

Left Bde.

To work west
down the trenches

Bullecourt

Hindenburg
Line

Cavalry
in reserve

• Vaulx - Vraucourt

• Ecoust

British Division to
Attack when Australians
reach Bullecourt.

form a defensive flank in the direction of Quéant, and at the same time endeavour to press through to Riencourt and Hendecourt. The left brigade would work its way down the German trenches into Bullecourt itself. Immediately the village was reached, the British division on the left would extend the front of the attack westwards.

My tanks were detailed to co-operate very closely with the infantry. The right section (Wyatt's) were given three duties: first, to parade up and down the German wire immediately to the right of the front of the attack; second, to remain with the infantry in the Hindenburg Line until the trenches had been successfully "blocked" and the defensive flank secured; third, to accompany the infantry in their advance on Riencourt and Hendecourt.

The centre section (Field's) were required to advance between the two brigades and plunge into the Hindenburg Line. This movement was made necessary by the decision to attack not on a continuous front but up two slight spurs or shoulders. The Hindenburg Line itself lay just beyond the crest of a slope, and these almost imperceptible shoulders ran out from the main slope at right angles to the line. It was thought that the depression between them would be swept by machine-gun fire, and it was decided in consequence to leave the attack up the depression to the tanks alone.

My left section (Swears') were to precede the infantry of the left Australian brigade. They were to obtain a footing in the Hindenburg Line and then work along it into Bullecourt. Whether, later, they would be able to assist the British infantry in their attack on the trenches to the west of Bullecourt was a matter for their discretion.

The atmosphere of the conference was cheerless. It is a little melancholy to revive and rebuild the plan of an attack which has been postponed very literally at the last moment. The conference was an anticlimax. For days and nights we had been completing our preparations. The supreme moment had come, and after hours of acute tension had passed without result. Then again, tired and without spirit, we drew up fresh plans. War is never romantic because emergencies, which might be adventures, come only when the soldier is stale and tired.

We hurried back to the camp at Behagnies and composed fresh orders, while Jumbo remarked his maps and reshuffled his aeroplane photographs. At dusk Jumbo and I started out in the car for Noreuil, but at Vaulx-Vraucourt we decided to leave the car as the road was impossible. It was heavy with mud and slush and we were far from fresh. We passed Australians coming up and much transport—in places the road was almost blocked. After an hour or more we came to the valley above Noreuil, full of new gun-pits. Our tanks lay hidden against the bank at the side of the road, shrouded in their tarpaulins. My men were busily engaged in making them ready. One engine was turning over very quietly. It was bitterly cold, and the snow still lay on the downs.

We struggled on to a ruined house at the entrance to the village. One room or shed—it may have been a shrine—constructed strongly of bricks, still stood in the middle of the wreckage. This my officers had made their headquarters. I gave instructions for all the officers to be collected, and in the meantime walked through the street to one of the two brigade headquarters in the village.

This brigade was fortunate in its choice, for it lay safe and snug in the bowels of the earth. An old brewery or factory possessed whole storeys of cellars, and the brigade office was three storeys down.

Haigh and Swears were discussing operations with the brigadier. They were all under the illusion that the postponed attack would take place as originally planned, and bitter was the disappointment when I told them that the orders had been changed. I gave the general and his brigade-major a rough outline of the new scheme, and took Swears and Haigh back with me to the ruins.

All my officers were assembled in the darkness. I could not see their faces. They might have been ghosts: I heard only rustles and murmurs. I explained briefly what had happened. One or two of them naturally complained of changes made at such a late hour. They did not see how they could study their orders, their maps, and their photographs in the hour and a half that remained to them before it was time for the tanks to start. So, again, I set out carefully and in detail the exact task of each tank. When I had finished, we discussed one or two points, and then my officers went to their tanks, and I returned to brigade head-quarters, so that I might be in touch with the colonel and the Division should anything untoward happen before zero.

The night passed with slow feet, while my tanks were crawl-ing forward over the snow. The brigade-major rewrote his or-ders. Officers and orderlies came in and out of the cellar. We had some tea, and the general lay down for some sleep. There was a rumour that one of the tanks had become ditched in climbing out of the road. I went out to investigate, and learned that Mor-ris's tank had been slightly delayed. It was, unfortunately, a clear cold night.

When I returned to the cellar the brigade staff were making ready for the battle. Pads of army signal forms were placed con-veniently to hand. The war diary was lying open with a pencil beside it and the carbons adjusted. The wires forward to battal-ion headquarters were tested. Fresh orderlies were awakened.

Apparently there had been little shelling during the early part of the night. Noreuil itself had been sprinkled continu-ously with shrapnel, and one or two 5.9's had come sailing over. Forward, the railway embankment and the approaches to it had been shelled intermittently, and towards dawn the Germans be-gan a mild bombardment, but nothing was reported to show that the enemy had heard our tanks or realised our intentions.

I received messages from Haigh that all my tanks were in position, or just coming into position, beyond the railway em-bankment. Zero hour was immediately before sunrise, and as the minutes filed by I wondered idly whether, deep down in the earth, we should hear the barrage. I was desperately anxious that the tanks should prove an overwhelming success. It was impossible not to imagine what might happen to the infantry if the tanks were knocked out early in the battle. Yet I could not help feeling that this day we should make our name.

We looked at our watches—two minutes to go. We stared at the minute-hands. Suddenly there was a whistling and rustling in the distance, and a succession of little thumps, like a dog that hits the floor when it scratches itself. The barrage had opened. Constraint vanished, and we lit pipes and cigarettes. You would have thought that the battle was over. We had not blown out our matches when there was a reverberating crash overhead. Two could play at this game of noises.

Few reports arrive during the first forty minutes of a battle. Everybody is too busy fighting. Usually the earliest news comes from wounded men, and naturally their experiences are limited. Brigade headquarters are, as a rule, at least an hour behind the battle. You cannot often stand on a hill and watch the ebb and flow of the fight in the old magnificent way.

At last the reports began to dribble in and the staff settled down to their work. There were heavy casualties before the German wire was reached. The enemy barrage came down, hot and strong, a few minutes after zero. . . . Fighting hard in the Hindenburg trenches, but few tanks to be seen. . . . The enemy are still holding on to certain portions of the line. . . . The fighting is very severe. . . . Heavy counter-attacks from the sunken road at L. 6 b. 5.2. The news is a medley of scraps.

Soon the brigadier is called upon to act. One company want a protective barrage put down in front of them, but from another message it seems probable that there are Australians out in front. The brigadier must decide.

One battalion asks to be reinforced from the reserve battalion. Is it time for the reserve to be thrown into the battle? The brigadier must decide. They have run short of bombs. An urgent message for fresh supplies comes through, and the staff captain hurries out to make additional arrangements.

There is little news of the tanks. One report states that no tanks have been seen, another that a tank helped to clear up a machine-gun post, a third that a tank is burning.

At last R., one of my tank commanders, bursts in. He is grimy, red-eyed, and shaken.

"Practically all the tanks have been knocked out, sir!" he reported in a hard excited voice.

Before answering I glanced rapidly round the cellar. These Australians had been told to rely on tanks. Without tanks many casualties were certain and victory was improbable. Their hopes were shattered as well as mine, if this report were true. Not an Australian turned a hair. Each man went on with his job.

I asked R. a few questions. The brigade-major was listening sympathetically. I made a written note, sent off a wire to the colonel, and climbed into the open air.

It was a bright and sunny morning, with a clear sky and a cool invigorating breeze. A bunch of Australians were joking over their breakfasts. The streets of the village were empty, with the exception of a "runner," who was hurrying down the road.

The guns were hard at it. From the valley behind the village came the quick cracks of the 18-pdrs., the little thuds of the light howitzers, the ear-splitting crashes of the 60-pdrs., and, very occasionally, the shuddering thumps of the heavies. The air rustled and whined with shells. Then, as we hesitated, came the loud murmur, the roar, the overwhelming rush of a 5.9, like the tearing of a giant newspaper, and the building shook and rattled as a huge cloud of black smoke came suddenly into being one hundred yards away, and bricks and bits of metal came pattering down or swishing past.

The enemy was kind. He was only throwing an occasional shell into the village, and we walked down the street in comparative calm.

When we came to the brick shelter at the farther end of the village we realised that our rendezvous had been most damnably ill-chosen. Fifty yards to the west the Germans, before their retirement, had blown a large crater where the road from Ecoust joins the road from Vaulx-Vraucourt, and now they were shelling it persistently. A stretcher party had just been caught. They lay in a confused heap half-way down the side of the crater. And a few yards away a field-howitzer battery in action was being shelled with care and accuracy.

We sat for a time in this noisy and unpleasant spot. One by one officers came in to report. Then we walked up the sunken road towards the dressing station. When I had the outline of the story I made my way back to the brigade headquarters in the cellar, and sent off a long wire. My return to the brick shelter was, for reasons that at the time seemed almost too obvious, both hasty and undignified. Further reports came in, and when we decided to move outside the village and collect the men by the bank where the tanks had sheltered a few hours before, the story was tolerably complete.

All the tanks, except Morris's, had arrived without incident at the railway embankment. Morris ditched at the bank and was a little late. Haigh and Jumbo had gone on ahead of the tanks. They crawled out beyond the embankment into No Man's Land and marked out the starting-line. It was not too pleasant a job. The enemy machine-guns were active right through the night, and the neighbourhood of the embankment was shelled intermittently. Towards dawn this intermittent shelling became almost a bombardment, and it was feared that the tanks had been heard.[1]

Skinner's tank failed on the embankment. The remainder crossed it successfully and lined up for the attack just before zero. By this time the shelling had become severe. The crews waited inside their tanks, wondering dully if they would be hit before they started. Already they were dead-tired, for they had had little sleep since their long painful trek of the night before.

Suddenly our bombardment began—it was more of a bombardment than a barrage—and the tanks crawled away into the darkness, followed closely by little bunches of Australians.

On the extreme right Morris and Puttock of Wyatt's section were met by tremendous machine-gun fire at the wire of the Hindenburg Line. They swung to the right, as they had been ordered, and glided along in front of the wire, sweeping the para-

---

1. We learned later that they had been heard.

pet with their fire. They received as good as they gave. Serious clutch trouble developed in Puttock's tank. It was impossible to stop since now the German guns were following them. A brave runner carried the news to Wyatt at the embankment. The tanks continued their course, though Puttock's tank was barely moving, and by luck and good driving they returned to the railway, having kept the enemy most fully occupied in a quarter where he might have been uncommonly troublesome.

Morris passed a line to Skinner and towed him over the embankment. They both started for Bullecourt. Puttock pushed on back towards Noreuil. His clutch was slipping so badly that the tank would not move, and the shells were falling ominously near. He withdrew his crew from the tank into a trench, and a moment later the tank was hit and hit again.

Of the remaining two tanks in this section we could hear nothing. Davies and Clarkson had disappeared. Perhaps they had gone through to Hendecourt. Yet the infantry of the right brigade, according to the reports we had received, were fighting most desperately to retain a precarious hold on the trenches they had entered.

In the centre Field's section of three tanks were stopped by the determined and accurate fire of forward field-guns before they entered the German trenches. The tanks were silhouetted against the snow, and the enemy gunners did not miss.

The first tank was hit in the track before it was well under way. The tank was evacuated, and in the dawning light it was hit again before the track could be repaired.

Money's tank reached the German wire. His men must have "missed their gears." For less than a minute the tank was motionless, then she burst into flames. A shell had exploded the petrol tanks, which in the old Mark 1 were placed forward on either side of the officer's and driver's seats. A sergeant and two men escaped. Money, best of good fellows, must have been killed instantaneously by the shell.

Bernstein's tank was within reach of the German trenches when a shell hit the cab, decapitated the driver, and exploded in the body of the tank. The corporal was wounded in the arm, and Bernstein was stunned and temporarily blinded. The tank was filled with fumes. As the crew were crawling out, a second shell hit the tank on the roof. The men under the wounded corporal began stolidly to salve the tank's equipment, while Bernstein, scarcely knowing where he was, staggered back to the embankment. He was packed off to a dressing station, and an orderly was sent to recall the crew and found them still working stubbornly under direct fire.

Swears' section of four tanks on the left were slightly more fortunate.

Birkett went forward at top speed, and, escaping the shells, entered the German trenches, where his guns did great execution. The tank worked down the trenches towards Bullecourt, followed by the Australians. She was hit twice, and all the crew were wounded, but Birkett went on fighting grimly until his ammunition was exhausted and he himself was badly wounded in the leg. Then at last he turned back, followed industriously by the German gunners. Near the embankment he stopped the tank to take his bearings. As he was climbing out, a shell burst against the side of the tank and wounded him again in the leg. The tank was evacuated. The crew salved what they could, and, helping each other, for they were all wounded, they made their way back painfully to the embankment. Birkett was brought back on a stretcher, and wounded a third time as he lay in the sunken road outside the dressing station. His tank was hit again and again. Finally it took fire, and was burnt out.

Skinner, after his tank had been towed over the railway embankment by Morris, made straight for Bullecourt, thinking that as the battle had now been in progress for more than two hours the Australians must have fought their way down the trenches into the village. Immediately he entered the village machine-guns played upon his tank, and several of his crew were slightly wounded by the little flakes of metal that fly about inside a Mk. 1 tank when it is subjected to really concentrated machine-gun fire.

No Australians could be seen. Suddenly he came right to the edge of an enormous crater, and as suddenly stopped. He tried to reverse, but he could not change gear. The tank was absolutely motionless. He held out for some time, and then the Germans brought up a gun and began to shell the tank. Against field-guns in houses he was defenceless so long as his tank could not move. His ammunition was nearly exhausted. There were no signs of the Australians or of British troops. He decided quite properly to withdraw. With great skill he evacuated his crew, taking his guns with him and the little ammunition that remained. Slowly and carefully they worked their way back, and reached the railway embankment without further casualty.

The fourth tank of this section was hit on the roof just as it was coming into action. The engine stopped in sympathy, and the tank commander withdrew his crew from the tank.

Swears, the section commander, left the railway embankment, and with the utmost gallantry went forward into Bullecourt to look for Skinner. He never came back.

Such were the cheerful reports that I received in my little brick shelter by the cross-roads. Of my eleven tanks nine had received direct hits, and two were missing. The infantry were in no better plight. From all accounts the Australians were holding with the greatest difficulty the trenches they had entered. Between the two brigades the Germans were clinging fiercely to their old line. Counter-attack after counter-attack came smashing against the Australians from Bullecourt and its sunken roads, from Lagnicourt and along the trenches from the Quéant salient. The Australians were indeed hard put to it.

While we were sorrowfully debating what would happen, we heard the noise of a tank's engines. We ran out, and saw to our wonder a tank coming down the sunken road. It was the fourth tank of Swears' section, which had been evacuated after a shell had blown a large hole in its roof.

When the crew had left the tank and were well on their way to Noreuil, the tank corporal remembered that he had left his "Primus" stove behind. It was a valuable stove, and he did not wish to lose it. So he started back with a comrade, and later they were joined by a third man. Their officer had left to look for me and ask for orders. They reached the tank—the German gunners were doing their very best to hit it again—and desperately eager not to abandon it outright, they tried to start the engine. To their immense surprise it fired, and, despite the German gunners, the three of them brought the tank and the "Primus" stove safe into Noreuil. The corporal's name was Hayward. He was one of Hamond's men.

We had left the brick shelter and were collecting the men on the road outside Noreuil, when the colonel rode up and gave us news of Davies and Clarkson. Our aeroplanes had seen two tanks crawling over the open country beyond the Hindenburg trenches to Riencourt, followed by four or five hundred cheering Australians. Through Riencourt they swept, and on to the large village of Hendecourt five miles beyond the trenches. They entered the village, still followed by the Australians. . . .[2]

What happened to them afterwards cannot be known until the battlefield is searched and all the prisoners who return have been questioned. The tanks and the Australians never came back. The tanks may have been knocked out by field-guns. They may have run short of petrol. They may have become "ditched." Knowing Davies and Clarkson, I am certain they fought to the last—and the tanks which later were paraded through Berlin were not my tanks. . . .

We rallied fifty-two officers and men out of the one hundred and three who had left Mory or Behagnies for the battle. Two men were detailed to guard our dump outside Noreuil, the rescued tank started for Mory, and the remaining officers and men marched wearily to Vaulx-Vraucourt, where lorries and a car were awaiting them.

I walked up to the railway embankment, but seeing no signs of any of my men or of Davies' or Clarkson's tanks, returned to Noreuil and paid a farewell visit to the two brigadiers, of whom

2. An airman who flew over the battlefield is inclined to doubt this story. We must wait for the official history.

one told me with natural emphasis that tanks were "no damned use." Then with Skinner and Jumbo I tramped up the valley towards Vraucourt through the midst of numerous field-guns. We had passed the guns when the enemy began to shell the crowded valley with heavy stuff, directed by an aeroplane that kept steady and unwinking watch on our doings.

Just outside Vaulx-Vraucourt we rested on a sunny slope and looked across the valley at our one surviving tank trekking back to Mory. Suddenly a "5.9" burst near it. The enemy were searching for guns. Then to our dismay a second shell burst at the tail of the tank. The tank stopped, and in a moment the crew were scattering for safety. A third shell burst within a few yards of the tank. The shooting seemed too accurate to be unintentional, and we cursed the aeroplane that was circling overhead.

There was nothing we could do. The disabled tank was two miles away. We knew that when the shelling stopped the crew would return and inspect the damage. So, sick at heart, we tramped on to Vaulx-Vraucourt, passing a reserve brigade coming up hastily, and a dressing station to which a ghastly stream of stretchers was flowing.

We met the car a mile beyond the village, and drove back sadly to Behagnies. When we came to the camp, it was only ten o'clock in the morning. In London civil servants were just beginning their day's work.

The enemy held the Australians stoutly. We never reached Bullecourt, and soon it became only too clear that it would be difficult enough to retain the trenches we had entered. The position was nearly desperate. The right brigade had won some trenches, and the left brigade had won some trenches. Between the two brigades the enemy had never been dislodged. And he continued to counter-attack with skill and fury down the trenches on the flanks—from the sunken roads by Bullecourt and up the communication trenches from the north.

In the intervals his artillery pounded away with solid determination. Bombs and ammunition were running very short, and to get further supplies forward was terribly expensive work, for all the approaches to the trenches which the Australians had won were enfiladed by machine-gun fire. Battalions of the reserve brigade were thrown in too late, for we had bitten off more than we could chew; the Germans realised this hard fact, and redoubled their efforts. The Australians suddenly retired. The attack had failed.

A few days later the Germans replied by a surprise attack on the Australian line from Noreuil to Lagnicourt. At first they succeeded and broke through to the guns; but the Australians soon rallied, and by a succession of fierce little counter-attacks drove the enemy with great skill back on to the deep wire in front of the Hindenburg Line. There was no escape. Behind the Germans were belts of wire quite impenetrable, and in front of them were the Australians. It was a cool revengeful massacre. The Germans, screaming for mercy, were deliberately and scientifically killed.

Two of my men, who had been left to guard our dump of supplies at Noreuil, took part in this battle of Lagnicourt. Close by the dump was a battery of field howitzers. The Germans had broken through to Noreuil, and the howitzers were firing over the sights; but first one howitzer and then another became silent as the gunners fell. My two men had been using rifles. When they saw what was happening they dashed forward to the howitzers, and turning their knowledge of the tank 6-pdr. gun to account, they helped to serve the howitzers until some infantry came up and drove back the enemy. Then my men went back to their dump, which had escaped, and remained there on guard until they were relieved on the following day.

The first battle of Bullecourt was a minor disaster. Our attack was a failure, in which the three brigades of infantry engaged lost very heavily indeed; and the officers and men lost, seasoned Australian troops who had fought at Gallipoli, could never be replaced. The company of tanks had been, apparently, nothing but a broken reed. For many months after the Australians distrusted tanks, and it was not until the battle of Amiens, sixteen months later, that the Division engaged at Bullecourt were fully converted. It was a disaster that the Australians attributed to the tanks. The tanks had failed them—the tanks "had let them down."

The Australians, in the bitterness of their losses, looked for scapegoats and found them in my tanks, but my tanks were not to blame. I have heard a lecturer say that to attack the Hindenburg Line on a front of fifteen hundred yards without support on either flank was rash. And it must not be forgotten that the attack ought to have been, and in actual fact was, expected. The artillery support was very far from overwhelming, and the barrage, coming down at zero, gave away the attack before my tanks could cross the wide No Man's Land and reach the German trenches.

What chances of success the attack possessed were destroyed by the snow on the ground, the decision to leave the centre of the attack to the tanks alone, the late arrival of the reserve brigade, and the shortage of bombs and ammunition in the firing line. These unhappy circumstances fitted into each other. If the snow had not made clear targets of the tanks, the tanks by themselves might have driven the enemy out of their trenches in the centre of the attack. If the first stages of the attack had been completely successful, the reserve brigade might not have been required. If the Australians had broken through the trench system on the left and in the centre, as they broke through on the left of the right brigade, bombs would not have been necessary.

It is difficult to estimate the value of tanks in a battle. The Australians naturally contended that without tanks they might have entered the Hindenburg Line. I am fully prepared to admit that the Australians are capable of performing any feat, for as storm troops they are surpassed by none. It is, however, undeniable that my tanks disturbed and disconcerted the enemy. We know from a report captured later that the enemy fire was concentrated on the tanks, and the German Higher Command instanced this battle as an operation in which the tanks compelled the enemy to neglect the advancing infantry. The action of the tanks was not entirely negative. On the right flank of the right brigade, a weak and dangerous spot, the tanks enabled the

Australians to form successfully a defensive flank.

The most interesting result of the employment of tanks was the break-through to Riencourt and Hendecourt by Davies' and Clarkson's tanks, and the Australians who followed them. With their flanks in the air, and in the face of the sturdiest opposition, half a section of tanks and about half a battalion of infantry broke through the strongest field-works in France and captured two villages, the second of which was nearly five miles behind the German line. This breakthrough was the direct forefather of the breakthrough at Cambrai.

My men, tired and half-trained, had done their best. When General Elles was told the story of the battle, he said in my presence, "This is the best thing that tanks have done yet."

The company received two messages of congratulation. The first was from General Gough—

> The Army Commander is very pleased with the gallantry and skill displayed by your company in the attack today, and the fact that the objectives were subsequently lost does not detract from the success of the tanks.

The second was from General Elles—

> The General Officer Commanding Heavy Branch M.G.C. wishes to convey to all ranks of the company under your command his heartiest thanks and appreciation of the manner in which they carried out their tasks during the recent operations, and furthermore for the gallantry shown by all tank commanders and tank crews in action.

The company gained two Military Crosses, one D.C.M., and three Military Medals in the first Battle of Bullecourt.

CHAPTER 5

The Second Battle of Bullecourt
(MAY 3, 1917.)

When the First Battle of Bullecourt had been fought in the office as well as in the field, when all the returns and reports had been forwarded to the next higher authority, and all the wise questions from the highest authority had been answered yet more wisely, we obtained lorries and made holiday in Amiens.

It was my first visit, and I decided whenever possible to return. It rained, but nobody minded. We lunched well at the Restaurant des Huîtres in the Street of the Headless Bodies. It was a most pleasant tavern—two dainty yellow-papered rooms over a mean shop. The girls who waited on us were decorative and amusing, the cooking was magnificent, and the Chambertin was satisfying. Coming from the desolate country we could not want more. We tarried as long as decorum allowed, and then went out reluctantly into the rain to shop. We bought immense quantities of fresh vegetables—cauliflowers, Brussels sprouts, new potatoes, and a huge box of apples, also a large "*paté de canard*," as recommended by Madame de Sévigne. A shampoo enabled us to consume chocolate and cakes. We put our last packages in the car and drove back in the evening.

At Behagnies we made ourselves comfortable, now that the strain was removed of preparing against time for a battle. Our tents mysteriously increased and multiplied. Odd tarpaulins were fashioned into what were officially termed "temporary structures." My orderly-room was cramped. I gave a willing officer the loan of a lorry, and in the morning I found an elaborate canvas cottage "busting into blooth" under the maternal solicitude of my orderly-room sergeant. The piano, which for several days was ten miles nearer the line than any other piano in the district, was rarely silent in the evenings.

Only a 6-inch gun, two hundred yards from the camp, interrupted our rest and broke some of our glasses. It was fine healthful country of downs and rough pasture. We commandeered horses from our troop of Glasgow Yeomanry, and spent the afternoons cantering gaily. Once I went out with the colonel, who was riding the famous horse that had been with him through Gallipoli, but to ride with an international polo-player has its disadvantages. Luckily, my old troop-horse was sure-footed enough, and if left to his own devices even clambered round the big crater in the middle of Mory.

A few days after the first battle. Ward's[1] company detrained at Achiet-le-Grand and trekked to Behagnies. They came from the Canadians at Vimy Ridge, and were full of their praises. The Canadians left nothing to chance. Trial "barrages" were put down, carefully watched and "thickened up" where necessary. Every possible plan, device, or scheme was tried—every possible preparation was made. The success of the attack was inevitable, and the Germans, whose aeroplanes had been busy enough, found their way to the cages without trouble, happy to have escaped.

Ward's company, filled with the unstinted rations of the Canadians, who had thought nothing of giving them a few extra sheep, were gallant but unsuccessful. The ground was impossible and the tanks "ditched." They were dug out, hauled out, pulled out, one way or another under a cruel shelling, but they never came into the battle. It was naturally a keen disappointment to Ward, and he and his company at Behagnies were spoiling for a fight.

The third company of the battalion under Haskett-Smith had been fighting in front of Arras with great dash and astonishingly

1 Major R. O. C. Ward, D.S.O., killed at Trescaut in November while leading his tanks forward.

few casualties. "No. 10" was a lucky company, and deserved its luck, until the end of the war. In sections and in pairs the tanks had helped the infantry day after day. At Telegraph Hill they had cleared the way, and again near Heninel. The company was now resting at Boiry, and we drove over to see Haskett-Smith and congratulate him on his many little victories.

It will be remembered that there were two phases to the battle of Arras. In the first phase we gained success after success. The enemy wavered and fell back. At Lens he retired without cause. Then his resistance began to stiffen, and we were fought to a standstill. Men and guns were brought by the enemy from other parts of the front, and the German line became almost as strong as it had been before the battle, while we were naturally handicapped by the difficulty of bringing up ammunition and supplies over two trench systems and a battlefield.

In the second phase we attacked to keep the Germans busy, while the French hammered away without much success away to the south. This second phase was infinitely the deadlier. We made little headway, and our casualties were high. We had not yet begun our big attack of the year. We were losing time and losing men.

The left flank of the German Armies engaged rested on the

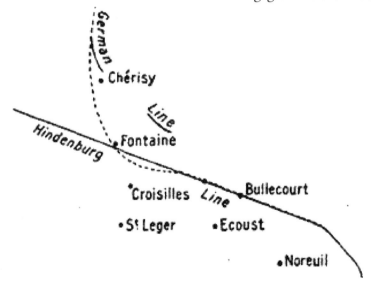

Hindenburg Line. As the Germans retired, their left flank withdrew down the Hindenburg Line, until, at the end of April, it rested on the Hindenburg Line at Fontaine-lez-Croisilles. West of Fontaine the Hindenburg Line was ours, and east of it German.

Ward's company and mine were concerned with the "elbow" from Chérisy to Bullecourt. Ward's company was detailed to renew the attack on Bullecourt, and a section of mine under Haigh was allotted to the Division which was planning to attack Fontaine itself At first it was decided to clear the Hindenburg Line in front of Fontaine by a preliminary operation, but the picture of two lone tanks working down the trenches in full view of German gunners on higher ground did not appeal to the colonel, and nothing came of it. The grand attack, the Second Battle of Bullecourt, was scheduled for May 3rd.

On 29th April Cooper and I went reconnoitring. It was a blazing hot day, with just enough wind. First we drove to St Leger—a pleasant half-ruined village, surrounded by German horse lines under the trees, where the Glasgow Yeomanry had been badly shelled in the days before the first battle, when we were attacking Croisilles and Ecoust. We visited Haigh's section, who had come up overnight from Behagnies,—they were snugly hidden under the railway embankment,—then, putting on our war- paint, we strolled up the hill to the right. It was most open warfare for the guns. They were drawn up on the reverse side of the hill, with no particular protection. Most of them were firing. The gun crews who were not on duty were sitting in the sun smoking or kicking a football about.

Further back our big guns were carrying out a sustained bombardment, and in the course of it experimenting with "artillery crashes," at that time a comparatively new form of "frightfulness." There is some particular point, an emplacement, or perhaps an observation post, which you want to destroy utterly and without question. Instead of shelling it for a morning with one or two guns, you concentrate on it every gun and howitzer that will bear, and carefully arrange the timing, so that all the shells arrive together.

It is extravagant but effective—like loosing off a ship's broadside. The noise of the shells as they come all together through the air, whining and grumbling loudly and more loudly, is wonderfully exhilarating. We employed the "artillery crash" in the Loos salient with the 16th Division during the summer of '16, but we had not too many shells then.

The Germans were firing little and blindly as we struck across to the Hindenburg Line, having planned to walk alongside it, as far as we might, down towards Fontaine. The enemy, however, suddenly conceived a violent dislike to their old trenches and some batteries near. So we dropped first into a shell-hole, and then, jumping into the trench, found a most excellent concrete machine- gun emplacement, where we sat all at our ease and smoked, praising the careful ingenuity of the German engineer.

We saw much from a distance, but little near, and returned along the upper road by Mory Copse.

Cooper and I made another expedition on the 30th, driving to Heninel and walking up the farther side of the Hindenburg Line. We pushed forward to the ridge above Chérisy and Fontaine, but we could see little of the enemy lines on account of the convexity of the slope. Gunner officers were running about like ants searching for positions and observation posts.

On the way back to the car we were resting and looking at our maps when we saw a characteristic example of the iron nerves of the average soldier. A limbered wagon was coming along a rough track when a small shell burst on the bank a few yards behind the wagon. Neither the horses nor the drivers turned a hair. Not the slightest interest was taken in the shell. It might never have burst.

On the night of the first of May Haigh's section moved forward from St Leger. The night had its incidents. Mac's baggage rolled on to the exhaust-pipe and caught fire,—it was quickly put out and no harm done, except to the baggage. The tanks stealthily crossed the Hindenburg Line by an old road and crept to the cover of a bank. Close by was a large clump of "stink" bombs, Very lights, and similar ammunition. Just as the first tanks were passing a shell exploded the dump. It was a magnificent display of deadly fireworks, and the enemy, as usual, continued to shell the blaze. There is no spot on earth quite so unpleasant as the edge of an exploding dump. Boxes of bombs were hurtling through the air and exploding as they fell. Very lights were streaming away in all directions. "Stink" bombs and gas bombs gave out poisonous fumes. Every minute or two a shell dropping close added to the uproar and destruction. With great coolness and skill the crews, led and inspired by Haigh, brought their tanks past the dump without a casualty.

Mac's tank had been delayed by the burning of his kit. When he arrived on the scene the pandemonium had died down, and the great noisy bonfire was just smouldering. Mac's tank came carefully past, when suddenly there was a loud crackling report. A box of bombs had exploded under one of the tracks and broken it. There was nothing to be done except send post-haste for some new plates and wait for the dawn.

When, on the afternoon of the 2nd, the colonel and I went up to see Haigh, the mechanics were just completing their work, and Mac's tank was ready for the battle a few hours after the plates had arrived.

Ward had moved his tanks forward to Mory Copse, where we had hidden ourselves before the trek through the blizzard to the valley above Noreuil. He was to work with the division detailed to attack the stronghold of Bullecourt. The front of the grand attacks had widened. On the 3rd of May the British armies would take the offensive from east of Bullecourt to distant regions north of the Scarpe. This time the Australians were without tanks.

I had given Haigh a free hand to arrange what he would with the brigade to which he was attached, and, not wishing to interfere with his little command, I determined to remain at Behagnies until the battle was well under way, and content myself with a scrutiny of his plans.

It was agreed that his section should "mother" the infantry, who were attacking down the Hindenburg Line, by advancing alongside the trenches and clearing up centres of too obstinate resistance. I endeavoured to make it quite clear to the divisional commander that no very great help could be expected from a few tanks operating over ground broken up by a network of deep and wide trenches.

At 3.45 a.m. the barrage woke me. I might perhaps have described the tense silence before the first gun spoke, and the mingled feelings of awe, horror, and anxiety that troubled me; but my action in this battle was essentially unheroic. Knowing that I should not receive any report for at least an hour, I cursed the guns in the neighbourhood, turned over and went to sleep.

The first messages began to arrive about 5.30 a.m. All the tanks had started to time. There was an interval, and then real news dribbled in. The Australians had taken their first objective— the front trench of the Hindenburg system. We had entered the trenches west of Bullecourt. Soon aeroplane reports were being wired through from the army. A tank was seen here in action; another tank was there immobile. Two tanks had reached such-and- such a point.

With what tremulous excitement the mothers and fathers and wives of the crews would have seized and smoothed out these flimsy scraps of pink paper! "Tank in flames at L. 6. d. 5. 4." That might be Jimmy's tank. No, it must be David's! Pray God the airman has made a mistake! We, who had set the stage, had only to watch the play. We could not interfere. Report after report came in, and gradually we began, from one source or another, to build up a picture of the battle.

The division attacking Bullecourt could not get on. Furious messages came back from Ward. His tanks were out in front, but the infantry "could not follow." His tanks were working up and down the trenches on either side of Bullecourt. One tank had found the Australians and was fighting with them. Tanks went on, returned, and went forward again with consummate gallant-ry, but the infantry could not get forward. They would advance a little way, and then, swept by machine-gun fire, they would dig in or even go back.

One of his officers, commonly known as "Daddy," was sent back in Ward's car. "Daddy" was dirty, unshorn, and covered with gore from two or three wounds. He was offered breakfast or a whisky-and-soda, and having chosen both, told us how he had found himself in front of the infantry, how the majority of his crew had been wounded by armour- piercing bullets, how finally his tank had been disabled and evacuated by the crew, while he covered their withdrawal with a machine-gun.

These armour-piercing bullets caused many casualties that day. We were still using the old Mark 1 Tank, which had fought on the Somme, and the armour was not sufficiently proof.

Bullecourt remained untaken, though the Australians clung desperately to the trenches they had won. The British infantry returned to the railway embankment. The attack had not been brilliant. It required another division to reach the outskirts of the village, but the division which failed on the 3rd of May became a brilliant shock-division under other circumstances, just as "Harper's Duds" became the most famous division in France.

Ward's company was lucky. Several of his tanks "went over" twice, one with a second crew after all the men of the first crew had been killed or wounded. The majority of his tanks rallied, and only one, the tank which had fought with the Australians, could not be accounted for when Ward, wrathful but undismayed, returned to battalion headquarters at Behagnies.

Meanwhile little news had come from Haigh. Twice I motored over to the headquarters of the division with which his tanks were operating, but on each occasion I heard almost nothing. The attack was still in progress. The situation was not clear. The air reports gave us scant help, for the airmen, unaccustomed to work with tanks, were optimistic beyond our wildest dreams, and reported tanks where no tank could possibly have been. I had given such careful orders to my tank commanders not to get ahead of the infantry, that with the best wish in the world I really could not believe a report which located a tank two miles within the German lines.

At last I drove up to see Haigh. I remember the run viv-idly, because four 9.2-in. howitzers in position fifty yards off the road elected to fire a salvo over my head as I passed, and at the same moment an ambulance and a D.R. came round the corner in front of us together. Organ, my driver—I had hired his car at Oxford in more peaceful days—was, as always, quite undis-turbed, and by luck or skill we slipped through. I left the car by the dressing station outside the ruins of Heninel, which the enemy were shelling stolidly, and walked forward.

A few yards from Haigh's dugout was a field-battery which the enemy were doing their best to destroy. Their "best" was a "dud" as I passed, and I slipped down, cheerfully enough, into the gloom. Haigh was away at brigade headquarters, but I gath-ered the news of the day from Head, whose tank had not been engaged.

The tanks had left the neighbourhood of the destroyed dump well up to time. It had been a pitch-black night at first, and the tank commanders, despite continual and deadly machine-gun fire and some shelling, had been compelled to lead their tanks on foot. They had discovered the "going" to be appalling, as, in-deed, they had anticipated from their reconnaissances.

When our barrage came down, Mac's tank was in position one hundred and fifty yards from it. The enemy replied at once, and so concentrated was their fire that it seemed the tank could not survive. Twice large shells burst just beside the tank, shaking it and almost stunning the crew, but by luck and good driving the tank escaped.

The tank moved along the trench in front of our infantry, firing drum after drum at the enemy, who exposed themselves fearlessly, and threw bombs at the tank in a wild effort to de-stroy it. The gunners in the tank were only too willing to risk the bombs as long as they were presented with such excellent targets.

Mac was driving himself, for his driver fell sick soon after they had started. The strain and the atmosphere were too much for his stomach. You cannot both drive and vomit.

The tank continued to kill steadily, and our infantry, who had been behind it at the start, were bombing laboriously down the trenches. Suddenly the tank came to a broad trench running at right angles to the main Hindenburg Line. The tank hesitated for a moment. That moment a brave German seized to fire a trench-mortar point-blank. He was killed a second later, but the bomb exploded against the track and broke it. The tank was completely disabled. It was obviously impossible to repair the track in the middle of a trench full of Germans.

The crew continued to kill from the tank, until our infantry arrived, and then, taking with them their guns and their ammunition, they dropped down into the trench to aid the infantry. One man of them was killed and another mortally wounded. The infantry officer in command refused their assistance and ordered them back, thinking, perhaps, that they had fought enough. They returned wearily to their headquarters without further loss, but by the time I had arrived, Mac had gone out again to see if the attack had progressed sufficiently to allow him to repair his tank. He came in later disappointed. The fight was still raging round his tank. The German who fired the trench-mortar had done better than he knew. The disabled tank was the limit of our success for the day.

The second tank was unlucky; it set out in the darkness, and, reaching its appointed place by "zero," plunged forward after the barrage. The tank reached the first German trench. None of our infantry was in sight. The ground was so broken and the light so dim that the tank commander thought he might have overshot his mark. Perhaps the infantry were being held up behind him. He turned back to look for them, and met them advancing slowly. He swung again, but in the deceptive light the driver made a mistake, and the tank slipped sideways into a trench at an impossible angle. Most tanks can climb out of most trenches, but even a tank has its limitations. If a tank slips sideways into a certain size of trench at a certain angle, it cannot pull itself out unless it possesses certain devices which this Mark 1 lacked. The tank was firmly stuck and took no part in the day's fighting.

The third tank ran into the thick of the battle, escaping by a succession of miracles the accurate fire of the German gunners. It crashed into the enemy, who were picked troops, and slaughtered them. The Germans showed no fear of it. They stood up to it, threw bombs and fired long bursts at it from their machine-guns. They had been issued with armour-piercing bullets, and the crew found to their dismay that the armour was not proof against them. Both gunners in one sponson were hit. The corporal of the tank dragged them out of the way—no easy matter in a tank—and manned the gun until he in his turn was wounded. Another gunner was wounded, and then another. With the reduced crew and the tank encumbered by the wounded, the tank was practically out of action. The tank commander broke off the fight and set out back.

While I was receiving these reports in the dugout, Haigh had returned from brigade headquarters. The news was not good. The infantry could make little or no impression on the enemy defences. When attacking troops are reduced to bombing down a trench, the attack is as good as over, and our attack had by now degenerated into a number of bombing duels in which the picked German troops, who were holding this portion of their beloved Hindenburg Line, equalled and often excelled our men.

Wretched Head, whose tank was in reserve, was waiting most miserably to know whether he would be called upon to start out alone and retrieve the battle. It would have been a desperate and fool- hardy undertaking for one tank to attack in broad daylight, and I instructed Haigh strongly to urge this view. Luckily the brigade commander had never admired tanks, and now that his attack had failed, he distrusted them. Head's tank was not used that day.

The Germans were still trying to silence that plucky battery above the dugout. So, praising the skill and labour of the enemy, I crawled along the gallery, which runs the length of the Hindenburg Line, and came out into the open beyond the danger area.

I found my car intact, for my driver, in a proper spirit of respect for Government property, had moved to the shelter of a bank. The road was full of "walking wounded." I had the privilege of giving two officers a lift in my car. They belonged to battalions which had attacked north of Fontaine, At first, they told me, the attack went well, but apparently the enemy had retired to counter-attack the more effectively. Our battalions, diminished and disorganised by the time they had reached their first objective, were overwhelmed and sent reeling back with very heavy casualties to the trenches they had left at "zero."

Apparently the grand attack of the third of May was a costly failure. North of Chérisy we advanced a little, but later we were compelled to withdraw. The Australians had entered the Hindenburg Line, and there they remained with a magnificent obstinacy which it is difficult to match in all the records of the war. Whether our attack, in spite of its failure, was successful in occupying the attention of Germans, who might otherwise have been assisting their comrades elsewhere in holding up the French, is a question which a humble company commander would not dare to answer.

The tanks had done their part. It was not the fault of Ward's gallant company that Bullecourt remained inviolate. His tanks did all that it was possible to do. At Fontaine, Haigh's section killed more than their share of Germans. We were satisfied that we had shown our usefulness. We prayed now with all our hearts that in the big battle of the summer we might be sent forward in mass on good ground in improved tanks after further training.

CHAPTER 6

Rest and Training
(MAY AND JUNE 1917.)

We thought that we should remain in camp at Behagnies for a couple of months or more, and train. The prospect pleased us mightily. It was true that we were no longer alone. When we had selected the site for our camp, we had been able to choose from the whole countryside, but now the downs resembled some great fair. Horse lines stretched to the horizon. The German light railway had been repaired, and busy little trains were forming a large ammunition dump a few hundred yards away from the camp on the road between Behagnies and Ervillers, the next village towards Arras. Balloon sections, water-lorry companies, well-boring companies, all sorts and conditions of army troops, were moving up and occupying the waste spaces.

But the air was glorious; the country was open, clean, and unshelled; there were trenches to practise on and good ground for manoeuvres; our camp was comfortable, and, after our recent exertions, we did not look forward to the troubles of a move. Haskett-Smith's company had joined us from Boiry, and our workshops were being set up with much care among the ruins. So the battalion, after fighting on the fronts of three armies, once again was complete, though, to our sorrow, Colonel Hardress Lloyd had left us to form a brigade, and a stranger from our particular rivals, "C" Battalion, had taken his place.

There were rumours, too, that we should soon be asked to assist in an attack on the Quéant salient, immediately to the west of the Bullecourt trenches and east of the front on which we attacked in November. It was reported that Tank head-quarters had been most favourably impressed with the country, which was in fact singularly adapted to the use of tanks. The going was hard and good. Natural obstacles could be neglected. We determined at the first definite hint to take time by the forelock and spend some summer days in close reconnaissance.

Our hopes were blighted early. The authorities soon decided that the Behagnies area was not suitable for training. It was becoming too crowded. The trenches were to be kept in good repair for defensive purposes, and might be used only by cavalry, who, to the unconcealed amusement of us mechanical folk, would go galloping through lanes in the wire and over carefully-prepared crossings. We were ordered to Wailly, a day's trek distant. We began to pack up, and I took Cooper over in my car to see our new habitation.

Wailly is a shelled village on the edge of the old trench system from which the Germans had retired in March. From Arras it is the next village to Agny, whence, according to the original plan of battle made before the enemy withdrawal, my tanks should have set out for Mercatel and Neuville Vitasse. Naturally, there are plenty of trenches just outside the village, and Tank headquarters had decided to set up a driving-school. When we arrived, some of my men were putting up Nissen huts for the school, and close by there was a park of practice-tanks. One company of a new battalion, fresh out from England, was already installed in tents. We nosed round the village.

It had rained. You could smell the earth and the new grass. There were little green copses and orchards behind broken walls. The fruit-trees were in blossom, white with rare pink buds. Under the trees and in out-of-the-way nooks and corners in dilapidated houses and old barns tiny bunches of oats were sprouting, liquid-green shoots, where the horses had been. There was rhubarb in the gardens, and the birds were singing.

The French at one time used to hold this sector, and their notices still remained in the village. Some pictures had been done on plaster, which *Messieurs les Militaires* were asked to protect; but time and weather had erased them, until nothing was left except the fine scrawl of the artist's signature, the title *Mont St Michel*, and some patches of red and brown.

The church must have been ugly with its stucco and imitation woodwork, but in its death it was a pleasant place for meditation—the white plaster with scraps of blue-and-gold, the plum-coloured brickwork laid bare, and the fresh tender grass clustered on every cornice.

Our camping-ground was a green slope between two derelict trenches, half-way up a hill—a clean and healthy site away from the road, but near enough for convenience. We looked down from it on the village, which had a friendly air, because the cottages, despite the shelling, were at least recognisable, and not mere rubbish-heaps like those in the country which the enemy had laid waste. . . .

We moved on the 10th. A company of tanks moves luxuriously. If there is no room on the lorries for any article of virtue, it goes on the tank. The equipment officer or the company commander need not be as inexorable as the quartermaster of an infantry battalion, for he is not haunted with a vision of transport fully loaded and much baggage still piled by the roadside. Each officer, for instance, carried at this period a rough wire bed on the roof of his tank, with a chair and perhaps a table. The additional weight did not affect the tank, while the additional comfort did affect the officer. The only danger was from fire. These superfluities, if carelessly lashed, would slip on to the red-hot exhaust-pipe. Again, if we moved a short way, the lorries could easily make a second journey. If we moved a long way, we moved by train, and usually, but not always, the train possessed facilities. Later, we became more Spartan and strenuous.[1]

We arrived without incident at Wailly—the tanks had trekked across country—and proceeded to re-erect the tents and struc-

---

1. This paragraph was written in the comfortable days before the lorries disappeared into battalion or brigade "pools," In the spring of 1918, when movement was necessarily hurried, my company had to do without—higher formations had so much of value to move.

tures which we had collected at Behagnies. The men were glad to return to the edge of civilisation. They had not seen a civilian for two months.

Training commenced at once, but before we had moved my company had begun to melt away. There were dumps at Montenescourt to be collected: the material had not been required in the Arras battle. There were new battalions arriving in France who would need camps. The driving-school wanted a few men. Brigade headquarters wanted a few men, and, naturally, battalion headquarters could not be content with its exiguous establishment. My hopes of thorough training dwindled with my company. Soon I was left with under a third of my men. I was scarcely able to collect a few scratch crews to drive the tanks which had been allotted to us for practice.

This scattering of my company was intensely disappointing. My drivers were only half-trained before the first battle of Arras, and most of them were to continue half-trained until we returned to Wailly in October; for in the third battle of Ypres we drove either along straightforward tracks or over appalling roads. Moreover, when a driver is driving in action or into action he dare not go beyond what he knows. He cannot experiment, find out what the tank can do, and discover the best way to do it.

Our tanks were most useful in allowing my new officers to learn by teaching. The old German front trench was a fearsome place in which it was easy enough to become ditched, and it was good for these officers to spend a day in the hot sun extricating their charges.

The great event of the month was the Tank Cross-country Race.

The course lay over a sunken road with steep and crumbling banks, across a mile or so of rough grass intersected by some slight trenches, over our old trench system, back again across the open and the sunken road, and home along a tape carefully laid out in curves and. odd angles. Marks were allotted for style and condition as well as for speed. The sunken road was to be crossed where there was no recognised "crossing," if marks were not to be lost, and the tank had to take the tape between its tracks, twisting and turning without stopping and without touching the tape.

It was a gorgeous day. An excited crowd gathered in front of the tanks, which were drawn up in line. Officers walked up and down with field-glasses, slung racing style. The form of the runners was canvassed, and bets were made freely. Ward's tanks were the favourites. Ward had taken the greatest care in selecting and training his crews. He possessed a few really skilled drivers, and on the evening before the race his tanks had done remarkably well in a private trial. Haskett-Smith had refused to interrupt his training. His crews were to drive over the course as part of their afternoon's exercises. We had practised immediately before the race, and my men were as keen as they could be. As some of my best drivers were away I did not hope to win the Company championship—even with my best drivers present, Ward's men would have been the toughest of customers—but I hoped with one of my two best tanks to win the first prize.

The tanks started at minute intervals. The first tank took the sunken road with consummate skill. The second, looking for an unused crossing, tried to climb over a dugout which caved in. One tank blindly fouled another, and they slipped to the bottom of the road interlocked and unable to move. The rest were well away. At the turning-post there was a marvellous jumble of tanks. One fellow could not get his gears in and blocked the road, but the rest managed to nose their way through, sweeping against each other.

As the tanks crossed the sunken road on the return journey you felt the driver brace himself for the final test. The tank would come forward with the tape between its tracks. At the first curve it would barely hesitate before swinging. Ward, bubbling over with excitement, watched the tank breathlessly. She was just going to scrape the tape. No, by heaven, she's missed it! Another tank might stop—the gears had not been changed cleanly—amidst the scorn of the spectators. Luckily, the driver inside the tank could hear nothing that was said.

I should have liked to relate how the tanks came crawling along sponson to sponson, and how my tank won, but I must in fairness confess that Ward's company won an overwhelming victory. My favourite did not even start. He had been sent in the morning to instruct some infantry, and when he came to the starting-post a little late in the day, his engine was so hot that he dared not compete.

I strongly advise some enterprising gentleman to buy a few tanks cheap, and stage a cross-country race over give-and-take country. There is nothing quite like it. . . .

A few days later we were paraded to receive congratulatory cards, and an address from General Elles. It was a steaming hot day, without a breath of fresh air. The sun beat down unmercifully on our shrapnel helmets. As usual, we had to wait for half an hour or more, and in our hearts we cursed all inspections, generals, and suchlike things. The ceremony was fortunately not prolonged, and the address held us attentive. The general had taken a great risk in sending to the battle two half-trained battalions in old-fashioned tanks. He had been justified by results. We had shown our worth. By steady training we were to prepare ourselves for the next battle.

When the general spoke of "steady training," I thought of my company's ranks depleted by the call of innumerable "fatigues," and sighed. It was, of course, unavoidable—"fatigues" were not created for fun,—but I earnestly prayed that soon the Tank Corps might obtain by hook or by crook some Labour companies to put up their huts, and leave me my fighting men to train for the great battle.

It was all the fault of these new battalions, who wanted snug places prepared for them. . . .

Our life at Wailly was not all training, inspections, and fatigues. It was necessary, for instance, to celebrate certain domestic events which occur even in the most modern families. My car had disappeared for the time being, but a box-body or van was sufficient to carry us into the "Hôtel de Commerce" at Arras, and, later in the evening, to bring back a merry singing crew to the old cottage which was the section's mess. There, with the gramophone and Grantoffski at the piano, we poured out libations to the Fates, and completed the celebration of an event which cannot happen twice in the life of one man.

Even towards the end of May we played an occasional game of football, and in the stream which ran through the village there was a bathing-place near the bridge, overhung by willows. . . .

Although in the far distance we could just see a German balloon and Arras still was shelled, we were not unduly disturbed by the enemy. The days of concentrated night-bombing had not yet arrived. Only one venturesome plane, looking for Corps Headquarters, then at Bretencourt, the next village, bombed down the valley and sadly frightened the pet kid of our workshops by dropping a small bomb into the courtyard of their farm.

Johnson,[2] our workshops officer, replied by carrying out experiments with the child of his brain, "the unditching beam," a device whereby a tank was enabled in marshy ground or crumbly soil to lay a log in its path and pull itself through the slush or the soil. This device was of the utmost value. It saved innumerable tanks, and the lives of their crews. The invention was perfected by others, but the credit of the original idea belongs to Major Johnson, who first applied the unditching beam in its most elementary form to Ward's tanks before Vimy.

While we were basking in the sunshine at Wailly, and while one important officer was trying to cure the sweaty itch by taking strong sulphur baths, and feverishly sucking multitudinous oranges, the Tank Corps was expanded and reorganised.

The First Tank Brigade, under Colonel C. D. Baker-Carr, had consisted of "C" and "D" battalions. These two battalions had taken part in the recent battle. The Second Brigade, under Colonel Courage, was formed provisionally of "A" and "B" battalions. The arrival of new battalions, who had been raised and trained at home, made a Third Brigade necessary. "C" battalion was taken from the First Brigade and two new battalions from home, "E" and "G," added to it. The Third Brigade, under

2. Major P. Johnson, D.S.O.

Colonel J. Hardress Lloyd, D.S.O., was made up of "C," "F," and "I" battalions. "H "battalion was to join the Second Brigade in due course. That was the second stage in the growth of the Tank Corps—from twelve companies to twenty-seven.

We were not allowed to stop long at Wailly. Each battalion had to take its turn at training over the derelict trenches, and we had had our turn, although less than half of my drivers had been able to practice. Before we went into action at Ypres in the autumn, my drivers received no further training. In justice to the four battalions which were formed in France, I find it necessary to emphasise the handicaps under which they fought.

We had no desire to move our camp, particularly when we were told that we were to leave "standing" all those tents and "temporary structures "which we had so cunningly acquired. You can never persuade a soldier to believe that possession is not ten points of the law. Our "temporary structures," we would argue, belonged to us, because we won them by the subtlety of our brains and the sweat of our brows. That canvas orderly-room, for instance, would have been rotting in a deserted camp on the Somme if we had not sent a lorry and three stout men for it.

Those five extra tents belonged to us, because the Fifth Army forgot to recall them when we moved into the Third Army area. Those tarpaulins—well, everybody is justified in picking up anything that the garrison gunners may leave about,—it is only taking what they stole from somebody else. Still, there was no getting round the order, though it was remarkable how full the quartermaster's store became, how some of our tents and "temporary structures "seemed to change colour and shape in the night, and how neighbouring units, who had jeered at us because we had now to leave our well-gotten gains behind, began to lose a tarpaulin or two, an unoccupied tent, or portions of an outlying hut.

I do not intend to imply for a moment that my men ever took anything to which they had no right. Such an accusation would be a vile slander. Nothing of the sort ever came to my notice. I never once received an official complaint; or only once, when some coal disappeared from some trucks standing on the sidings at Blangy—and then none of my men were recognised; but I will say that neither of the two tank companies which I commanded in France was ever short of accommodation for more than a few days. My men were always perfectly capable of looking after themselves, and my own comfort was not neglected. We never allowed Government property to remain for long without a thoroughly efficient guard.

I went from Wailly by car on May 27th, a few days before my company, as I had been detailed to attend a course at Erin. I was sorry to leave the bright dilapidated village, the coarse grass, and the breathless, dusty trenches, the hot lanes, heavy with the scent of wild flowers on the banks, the masses of lilac in Bretencourt, and the old people slowly returning,—it is always the oldest people who return first.

I drove through delicious lanes to St Pol, and then by the lower road to Erin, a leafy village in the Tank Corps area, which extended along the valley of the Ternoise from St Pol to Hesdin. Erin was the "workshops" capital of this little state. There were the central workshops and the central stores with their vast hangars, their sidings, their light railways, their multitude of tanks, old and new, and their thousands of grinning Chinamen. There was the driving-school with its lecture huts, full of stripped engines carefully set out on scrubbed tables.

There were the experimental workshops, from which, later in the war, tanks with "mystery" engines would dash out and career madly about at incredible speeds until they broke down. In a quiet corner of the village were the trim cheerful huts of the Rest Camp, where men, too weary of the battle, sat in the sun, planted cabbages, or looked for something that had not been whitewashed. Add the Cinema, the Supper Club, hutting for a battalion, a good *château* and a Reinforcement Camp, which, finding itself strangely far forward, retired to the company of its brethren on the coast.

After I had reported at Erin, I drove through Bermicourt,

where Tank Corps Headquarters dwelt, to Humières, the immediate destination of my company. I was met by Cooper, my second-in-command, who was in charge of the company's advanced party. He reported well of the village, and in the quietude of dusk it seemed a most pleasant place. The mess-cook, however, had not arrived, and as we had no substitute, we drove into Hesdin, at that time an outpost of G.H.Q., and dined moderately well at the Hôtel de France.

My first impressions of Humières were confirmed. The village lay off the great highroad that runs from Arras and St Pol through Hesdin and Montreuil to the coast at Boulogne. All the cottages' have little shady gardens and hot orchards and rich meadows. Everywhere are big trees and more birds singing than I had ever heard before in one village. At first we determined to move our huts into a quiet orchard, carpeted with thick luscious grass, and two lazy cows for friendly company.

On three sides the orchard was enclosed with stout hedges of hawthorn. On the fourth it sloped down to some ploughland, and from our tents we should have looked over the bare countryside, misty in the heat. Finally, to avoid the work of moving, I chose to remain in a large double Armstrong hut, which stood under a row of great elms at the edge of a big grass field which we used as a parade- ground. Most of the officers and all the men were billeted in cottages and barns. In the farther end of the village was Haskett-Smith's company, Battalion Headquarters were at the *château*, where the Countess and her three daughters still remained, and Ward's company were at Eclimeux, a smaller village on the Blangy road. The tanks were packed in a tiny tankodrome just outside Eclimeux, too hot a walk from Humières in the sun.

I saw little of the village at first, for every morning I motorcycled down to Erin for my course. Nothing could have been more thorough. First we paraded, and then we disappeared into various huts, where we were lectured on the engine. In the afternoon we would go down to the hangar, and after a general description we would plunge into grease and oil, doing all those things which are required. Later we drove under the direction of an expert instructor. It was a senior officers' course, and we were all of us not entirely ignorant, but soon we realised how little we had known.

We drove over trenches and banks, and at night we learned the art of bringing a tank to its point of balance and keeping her poised there for a moment, so that she might slide easily down into the trench. We were initiated into the secrets of sweet gear-changing and all the arts and devices that a proper driver should know. It was most certainly a good course.

While I sweated inside a tank and inhaled noisome fumes and spoilt a pair of good gloves, my company had arrived at Humières. It was hardly a company. Although the company was "resting," my men were working hard. Some were still at Montenescourt clearing surplus dumps. Some were at Sautre-court putting up huts and taking them down again, when it was discovered that some cheaper land was available nearby.[3] Some marched down each morning to Central Workshops and assisted the Chinamen in their labours. Some went down to the coast on gunnery and physical training courses. For most of the time I had only forty to fifty in camp. But the huts at Sautrecourt were finally erected on a proper site, and my men at Montenescourt rejoined in time to make good a few of the casualties we sustained in our next action.

On the 4th June I accompanied Johnson, the battalion engineer, and Cozens, the adjutant, on an expedition to the north. We drove through Lillers and Bailleul to Ouderdom. I had not seen Bailleul since March 1915, when the 5th Divisional Cyclist Company, in which I had just received a commission, moved north to Ouderdom. Bailleul had not changed. It was still a clean and pleasant town, where you could buy fish. Tina, an almost legendary damsel, whose wit and beauty were known in five armies, had arisen and was about to disappear. The "Allies Tea Room" had opened. The lunatic asylum still held good baths that were open to officers twice a week. The "Faucon" was

---

3. The Tank Corps was always the very soul of economy.

as dingy as ever.

In June the back area of the salient was like a disturbed ant-heap. We were making every possible preparation for an attack, and apparently we did not mind in the very least whether or not the enemy knew all about it. The countryside was "stiff" with light railways, enormous dumps, fresh sidings, innumerable gun-pits, new roads, enlarged camps. No advertisement of the impending attack was neglected. The enemy, of course, realised what was happening, and acted accordingly. He had brought up a large number of long-range guns, and his aeroplanes flew over on every fine day. He had, too, the advantage of direct observation over all the forward area.

The results were unpleasant enough, even in June. Dumps would "go up" with a pleasing regularity. Camps and railheads were always being shelled. Bombing continued by day and by night. In front we destroyed the German trenches, breastworks and fortifications, and shelled their batteries. They retaliated in kind, and the unprejudiced observer would have found it difficult to award the prize. The enemy were scoring heavily with their gas shells.

We drove first to Ouderdom, a vast and enticing railhead, which the enemy shelled methodically each night, much to the annoyance of "B" Tank Battalion, who lived, for reasons of state, at the edge of the railhead. Their tanks were housed with disarming frankness in a series of canvas stalls surrounded by a high canvas screen. The whole erection was perhaps three-quarters of a mile in circumference. The tanks were so obviously concealed that the enemy never suspected their existence. The shells that dropped each night into the camp were the ordinary courtesies of warfare, although they did at last produce a move.

We had an excellent lunch with the Engineers of the battalion, Johnson expatiated on his new "underitching beam," we inspected certain novelties that had been fitted to the tanks, and then from a windmill on a hillock we watched the smoke of a "practice barrage." We drove on by Dranoutre, where in '14 I was despatch-rider to a brigade of the 5th Division, over the hill to the headquarters of "A" battalion in some pleasant woods, untroubled by the enemy. After drinks, salutations, and some "shop," we returned in the cool of the evening, stopping in the square at Hazebrouck for dinner and a good bottle of burgundy. It had been a fine day, with just enough sun. All the woods were fresh and green, and there was a purple sunset.

The Battle of Messines was fought four days later. The attack was a complete and overwhelming success. The whole of the Ridge, which for so many weary months had dominated our lines, was captured at a low cost. "A" and "B" battalions of tanks were useful but not indispensable. The ground was difficult and in places impossible. Many tanks became ditched. Certain tanks retrieved a local situation finely by the stout repulse of a strong counter-attack. We received the impression that, if the weather had been wet, tanks could not have been used. Although we did not realise it at the time, the battle of Messines was the first and only successful act in a tragedy of which the last act was never played.

An expedition to the Salient only sharpened our appreciation of the quiet and charm of Humières. What more could man want in the year of grace 1917 than to lie under the trees, sipping a cool drink, and watch Wright, the left-handed mainstay of our side, open his shoulders to a half-volley, or, when the sun had gone in, to stroll out and scrape together a lucky "6" instead of the usual "4"? We had no "seasons "at Humières. Each evening during the week we would play cricket, and on Sunday we would play a company of "F" battalion at football, and beat them by some outrageous score—12-love, I think it was—or, while we were indulging in the equivalent of a little net practice, the football enthusiasts would be crowded round the goal at the other end of the field. Whichever game we played, the company won most of its matches.

No self-respecting battalion would ever allow its period of rest to go by without battalion sports, and "D" battalion respected itself mightily. Our pet athletes started to train as soon as we reached Humières. After the Messines battle there was some doubt whether it might not be necessary to postpone the sports until after the next "show." Rumours of an immediate move came thick and fast, but the Fates were not so unkind, and our sports were held on the eve of things.

My company had prepared the way with a minor affair. The field was small and uneven, and in the longer races there were so many laps that, as our company wag exclaimed, it was a wonder the runners did not get giddy before they finished. If the times were doubtful, the enjoyment was unstinted, and after mess all the seats and the company piano were brought out into the open, and we sang songs until it was quite dark.

The battalion sports, a few days later, were a social event. An immense field positively sprouted with dark-blue flags, the colour of the battalion. There were pipes and drums from the 51st Division. The staff were conspicuously resplendent, while the Countess and her daughters were the centre of attraction. It was a splendid afternoon, although Battalion Headquarters won the cup. They would not have tried to win it, someone said, if they had not been able to drink out of it.

In the evening there was the usual entertainment of the "Follies" type under the direction of the "Old Bird." It was organised more or less on the spur of the moment. Supported by an issue of free beer it was an uproarious success, although it was sometimes not too easy to translate the jokes into French for the benefit of the Countess and her daughters.

It was a great night, and all the pipers were so satisfied with their refreshment that they could not ask for more; and if pipers of the 51st are incapable of asking for another drink, then they are incapable indeed, and a loading party must turn out to place them gently in the lorries. . . .

In the heavy heat of those long days it was easy to forget the war and the shadow of the battle, coming up wrathfully, like a thunderstorm. Little expeditions were as pleasurable as children's treats. The drowning of a bus driver at Merlimont Plage, where our gunnery school was among the dunes, gave me a swift run to the sea, and we called in at Boulogne "on the way back" for stores. Then there was always that old coaching hostelry at Hesdin, the Hôtel de France, which provided none too bad a dinner for those who were sick of the eternal roast-beef of the mess.

Finally, lest we should find life too monotonous, the new tank battalions were arriving from Bovington Camp in Dorset, which had always been held up to us in France as a very pattern of discipline, a haven of content, a perfect well of energy, a paradise where the senior officers and the tank engineers never thought of using any part or fitting of a tank, such as a clock, accumulators, or even a dynamo, for their own private purposes and the decoration of their huts.

As for the depot at Wareham, we pictured it as a place where thoroughly nice young officers spent laborious days and nights in fitting themselves for the noble tasks before them. Certainly these new battalions were beautiful to look upon. Their uniforms were new, they saluted smartly, and by a stupid and tactless blunder they were wearing on their sleeves the famous badge, representing a tank, which we had waited for so long.

I shall never cease to wonder at the patience of the British soldier. Here were four battalions of veteran volunteers, who, after they had spent hot and weary weeks removing vast dumps and erecting multitudinous huts, were given the privilege of watching these immaculate recruits, of whom many were conscripts, swaggering with their tank badges. I do not pretend that the course of the war was changed by this incident, and I do not wish for one moment to insinuate that these new battalions did not very soon prove themselves worthy of any badge.

It was, however, a pity that when there were not enough badges to go round, the men who had fought and volunteered were left badgeless. The badge at once became a thing without value, just as later the savour of the 1914 Star disappeared when fighting men first saw the ribbon on the chests of clerks at Boulogne. In any war there must always be some jealousy between men who fight and men who do safe though indispensable work behind the lines, between men who have borne the heat and burden of the day and those newly out from home.

Unfortunately these little jealousies were often accentuated by such blunders, and the fighting man felt that he was neglected. A baker and a bomber received the same medal, and the appalling state of the leave-trains was always attributed to the fact that the staff, who went on leave, with such tactless regularity, travelled to the coast by motorcar.

It was good to see Hamond, who had come back to France again in command of a company of "F" battalion, to plumb once more the depths of his vocabulary, and to hear his frank criticism of those set in authority. But the comments of these newcomers, or rather in Hamond's case, these returned wanderers, led us to doubt whether after all Bovington Camp was a better place than Humières.

So June passed in rich sunshine—all those glorious fighting days were wasted. The order came for us to draw new tanks, and we began to hurry our preparations for the most ghastly of all battles, the third battle of Ypres, in which the wounded fell into pits of slimy water and drowned slowly, screaming to their comrades for help, and the tanks, sticking in the mud and sinking sometimes till they were swallowed up, were compelled at last to fight precariously from destroyed roads.

CHAPTER 7

The Third Battle of Ypres
—Preparations
(JULY 1917.)

We had begun the year in confident anticipation of a "great battle," which was to give the enemy such a handsome blow that he would go reeling back towards his frontiers, and in the winter either ask for peace or lick his sores, until in the spring-time, with a concentration of every man and gun, we would crush him once and for all. Before Arras optimists had hoped that we might make an end of things that season, but the rumours abroad of delay in preparations, of the too slow provision of material and men, and of the breaking-up of the Russian Armies, sobered our prophecies.

Even with the great battle to which we pinned our faith, we should want another year. After Arras we were a little crestfallen: the second act of that battle had been so obviously a failure, and the grand attack of the French—a victory until it was fought—made curiously little progress. The taking of the Messines Ridge was encouraging, and for a time we cast covetous eyes on Lille; but, thinking it over, we began to rate Messines at its true value—a very notable but local success.

As early as March the good people of Amiens were whispering "Ypres," and the prognostications of the Amienois were always astonishingly correct. It was obvious to the merest amateur that the Salient was boiling with activity, and, as one fact after another was revealed, we could soon make a pretty shrewd guess at the probable course of events. The great battle was to take place in the neighbourhood of Ypres, and our hearts sank to our boots.

The Salient represented all that was most horrible in war. The veteran, experienced in the terrors of the Brickstacks or the Somme, would feel that he had something still to learn and suffer if he had not done his time in the Salient. The first and second battles, it was true, had been triumphs of defence, but triumphs so full of tragedy that a man cannot tell of them without bringing sorrow. It is not easy to forget the fruitless massacre of Hill 60, that ghastly morning when the 14th Division, never too lucky, were driven out of their trenches by liquid fire; that night when the choking Zouaves came back to the canal, and the moonlight shining through the green fumes of the gas shells in Boesinghe, and the troubled old French general in the *château* whose brigade-major was so pathetically insistent on the counter-attacks that would surely be put in hand at once, and the shell which blotted out my patrol. . . .

The thought of tanks in the Salient made those of us shiver a little who knew the country. The Salient had swallowed up so many reputations and made so few. With water everywhere just below the surface, and a heavy preliminary bombardment, the ground would be almost impassable for tanks, and if it rained . . . Surely, we felt, there could never have been a more hopeless enterprise! It was an ugly business.

Yet I must confess that in the eager hustle and stir of our preparations we became almost confident; those who had never seen the Salient made light of our fears; perhaps, after all, Johnson's "unditching beam" would see us through; they would never send the tanks to the Salient if they had not made sure. We allowed ourselves to be encouraged, and, hoping against hope, entered upon the battle.

Experiments certainly were made. One of my tanks, with a few others, were sent away to demonstrate how easy it was for tanks to cross dykes and ditches and wet ground. . . .

Several crews were taken from the battalion to form a special company, which was hedged round with mystery and secrecy. There was soon, however, a strong rumour in the camp that this company was destined to land at Ostend with an army under Rawlinson from England. As I had no desire to know more about the matter than was good for me, I did not take an early opportunity of going to Amiens to learn the truth. However, the secret was not too badly kept—I believe the doctor's daughter at Blangy knew nothing of it. I heard later—but I am sure my information must have been inaccurate—that the whole project was quite frankly discussed in the more discreet drawing- rooms of London...

Before the battle actually began we were told little but surmised much, and our surmises proved moderately correct. We were bidding for the coast....

There was something of a tragic experiment in the Battle of the Somme. We had hoped vaguely then that the German line might be broken or at least dangerously bent, but we had seen no glittering prize to grasp. And after the first few days when our tremendous and expensive assaults had created but a microscopic indentation, we realised in a spirit of grim fatalism that the battle must become, as indeed it did, a series of terrible mechanical attacks in an atmosphere of monstrous shelling.

We looked forward to the great battle of 1917 in a different spirit. Perhaps we knew more about it. Perhaps the early successes at Arras had encouraged us. Perhaps the mere companionship of our tanks infected us with optimism. We did feel that there was a cheerful breadth of conception about it—and we knew that we had guns innumerable and limitless ammunition....

In July 1917 the line from the coast to the Lys was divided into four sectors, each widely different from the others. First, there was the narrow front on the coast, where men fought among the sand-dunes. This sector we had just taken over and stiffened with guns. It was rumoured—I believe with truth—that here we would attack. If no attack was intended, it is difficult to account for the concentration of guns, infantry, and aeroplanes.

From the right flank of the coast sector practically to the left re-entrant of the Ypres Salient stretched the inundated area, where Belgians and Germans had looked through their field-glasses at each other since the early days of the war. Here it was almost impossible to attack.

Then came the infamous Salient, where for so many bitter months we had clung desperately to the skirts of the foothills. Our trenches were overlooked and water-logged; our approaches were observed and shelled mercilessly, and all the areas back to Poperinghe were shelled, while lately bombing by night had become more frequent and unpleasant. Now we were expecting to sweep over the hills, where the Germans lay, and out into the dead flat plains beyond. There were enormous difficulties ahead in this sector,—the Passchendaele Ridge, which stretched into the enemy lines, and the Houthulst Forest, set down in a marsh,—and the average soldier was inclined to reason it out that if the enemy had found it impossible to push us down into the plain we should find it as impossible to push him back over his hills and through his forest—yet as a matter of sober fact we were absurdly confident.

Finally, on the right there was the Messines Ridge, which we had just captured. From this ridge the enemy had been able to look into our lines. Without it we could not hope to attack from the Salient, for the attackers would have had the enemy sitting on a hill to their left rear. Now we had won it, and on a narrow front would give the Germans a taste of the Salient.

This, then, was the motive of the battle—to push through along the coast and at the Ypres Salient, forcing the German back from his edge of the floods by threatening his flanks. At the height of the operations a strong force equipped with tanks would land at Ostend, and once more the German Army would possess a vulnerable right flank.

This diagram will show roughly the outline of the operations, as we understood they would be:—

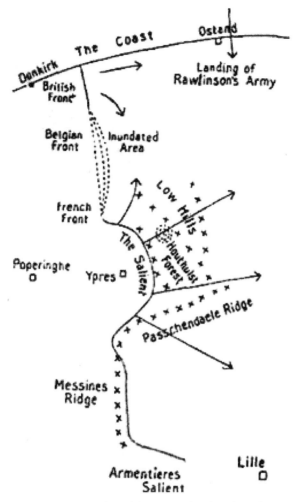

The Coast

Ostend

Dunkirk

British Front

Landing of Rawlinson's Army

Belgian Front

Inundated Area

French Front

Low Hills

Poperinghe

Ypres

The Salient

Houthulst Forest

Passchendaele Ridge

Messines Ridge

Armentières Salient

Lille

We had struck the first blow in the battle of Messines; the enemy struck the second. They made a sudden skilful attack on the coast sector, and, showing themselves, as always, masters of the local operation with a limited objective, did serious damage. A brigade was practically annihilated, a division was roughly handled, and all our preparations were put so badly out of gear that soon a number of big guns came trundling south to the Salient. . . .

In that little pocket-handkerchief of a tankodrome at Eclimeux we were making our preparations in our own small way for the grand battle. We had drawn a job lot of tanks, the majority of which had been much in use at the driving-school at Wailly. Some of them we had even taken over "*in situ*" at Wailly, where we made good in haste the damage done by successive classes. At this period of its existence the Tank Corps was always in a hurry. Everything was left to the last minute, and then there was a sudden scare. It did not please the men that they had to patch up tanks at the last minute before going north. Some tanks were in so poor a state that the brigade commander very properly refused to take them.

Leaving my men to work all day—by this time I had managed to scrape most of my company together again—I drove north on the 2nd July to see Jumbo, who had been sent on ahead to our destination, Oosthoek Wood, north of Vlamertinghe, which is the village half-way between Poperinghe and Ypres.

I found after a hot and dusty ride that the site of our proposed camp was on the northern edge of the wood, close by a siding and a very obvious ramp.

It was a part of the world which the German gunner found interesting. Jumbo was quite clear on the point, though Jumbo himself, revelling in the cool and shade of the woods after hot days forward on reconnaissance, did not turn a hair. The ramp and the northern edge of Oosthoek Wood were shelled nightly. There were two painfully fresh shell-holes in the middle of the area allotted to us, and "G" Battalion across the road were not sleeping at all. One night they actually left their camp, and I am afraid when they returned they found one or two little things were missing.

Anyway, at breakfast the next morning, Horobin, Jumbo's batman, had a broad smile. We found too, on examination, that the undergrowth had been thoroughly fouled by the constant succession of troops who had stayed for a night or so, and then had gone back to rest or forward to the line.

In short, I had no love for the place.

We took the opportunity of studying the approaches to the ramp, which mercifully was broad and strong and approached by a nearly straight stretch of rail. The route to the wood, in which we were instructed to hide our tanks, was only a couple of hundred yards long with no difficulties.

Before I left I was told that a shell had dropped into "C" Battalion lines and nearly wiped out Battalion Headquarters. I had never liked the Salient, and as I drove in the evening back to Humières, it seemed to me clear enough that I should like it even less. That night I dreamed of shells landing in the middle of foul undergrowth. A few days later I heard with more than a little relief that the brigade had decided to move the men's lines to the neighbourhood of La Lovie Château, north of Poperinghe. The tanks would remain under a small guard at Oosthoek, and the men would march or be carried down every day to work on them. The scheme had its disadvantages—it is always a nuisance to be too far from your tanks—but the decision was incontrovertibly right. Nothing can be more fretting to the nerves of man than this nagging gunfire at night, and somebody is always hit sooner or later, and the somebody cannot usually be replaced.

We discovered, when the battle had begun, that a prisoner, whom the Germans had taken while we were making our preparations, had informed the Germans, probably under pressure, that there were tanks at Oosthoek Wood. Knowing what they did, it is a little astonishing that the German gunners did not increase their nightly ration of shells, which merely disturbed the guard, who slept under the tanks when not on duty, and did not damage a tank.

A week before we moved my officers were seized with a fantastical idea, and, disdaining to comb their hair, like Spartans before the battle, cropped it almost to the skin. I have known similar outbursts of decapillation. Ward's officers once shaved off their moustaches before Bullecourt, and, when one subaltern indignantly refused to submit, his fellows painted a large moustache on the lower part of his back. Unfortunately he was wounded next day in the same spot. I have often wondered what the nurse must have thought. . . .

One fine morning—it was the 10th of July—my tanks pulled out of the little tankodrome, and did their best to block the street of Eclimeux. It was an annoying day: so many things went wrong, and we did not know how much time we might be given at the other end to put them right. The track led down the road, across some cornfields, and, leaving our old friends at Blangy on the left, beside the main road to Erin. Eventually all the tanks arrived, and were parked up in the vast enclosure, surrounded by a wall of canvas.

I remember that the entraining was poor. We took nearly forty minutes. Entraining and detraining provide searching tests of a tank's mechanical efficiency and the skill of a crew. If there is any flaw in the tuning, any clumsiness in the driver, driving on to a train will discover it. A tank dislikes a train. It slides on with grunts of obstinate dissatisfaction. If it ever wants to jib, it will jib then. Luckily we had no severe casualties, for to tow a "dud" tank on or off a train may be heartbreaking work. At last all the tanks were neatly covered with tarpaulins, the baggage was placed in the trucks, and the men were settling down and making themselves comfortable. Many months, full of hard fighting, were to pass before "D" Battalion, or what was left of it, returned to Erin. . . .

Cooper and I, in a car loaded, as usual, with kit, drove north through Heuchin and over the hills, and along the main road to Aire and lunch in a cool tea-room. Then on we went to Hazebrouck and Bailleul, and at last to Poperinghe, thick with troops. The sign of the Fifth Army, the Red Fox, was everywhere; and the Fifth Army was in those days known as the Army of Pursuit. Outside the town we passed the King of the Belgians, apparently riding alone—a fine unassuming figure of a man; and so we came to the copses near the *château* of La Lovie.

In a laudable attempt at hiding our camp, though the whole Salient was an open secret, we had pitched our tents among thick undergrowth and some saplings. Orders had been given that the undergrowth was not to be cleared, and life in consequence had its little difficulties. At first to walk about the camp at night was simply foolish, for, if you had the courage to leave your tent, you either plunged into a bush, collided with a tree, or tripped over tent-ropes decently hidden in the vegetation. But man cannot live in a forest without itching to make some clearance—it is the instinct of the pioneer,—and before we had been long in the copse I am afraid that one or two of the more tempting bushes had disappeared, paths had been trodden, and the inevitable "temporary structures" raised on what to all outward appearance had recently been young trees.

On the afternoon that we arrived we came to the decision that we disliked heat and aeroplanes. There was no shade, unless you lay at full length under a bush, and innumerable aeroplanes— "Spads"—were ascending and descending from an enormous aerodrome close by. The flying men were in the cheeriest mood, and endeavoured always to keep us amused by low and noisy flying.

I do not think that there is any aeroplane more consistently noisy than a "Spad."

At dusk we drove down to the ramp at Oosthoek Wood. The train backed in after dark. We brought off our tanks in great style, under the eye of the brigade commander, who was always present at these ceremonies. The enemy was not unkind. He threw over a few shells, but one only disturbed our operations by bursting on the farther side of the ramp and so frightening our company dog that we never saw her again.

There was no moon, and we found it difficult to drive our tanks into the wood without knocking down trees that made valuable cover. It was none too easy without lights, which we did not wish to use, to fasten the camouflage nets above the tanks on to the branches. The track of the tanks from the ramp to the wood was strewn with branches and straw.

By the time we had finished the night had fled, and it was in the fresh greyness of dawn that we marched the weary miles to the camp at La Lovie. The men were dog-tired, my guide was not certain of the road, though he never missed it, and I had never realised the distance. After an interminable tramp we staggered into camp. The men were given some hot breakfast, and then, as the sun rose, you would have heard nothing but snores. For our sins we had arrived in a "back area" of the Salient.

That was on the 11th of July: the next twenty days were crammed full of preparations.

Every morning the men marched down to the wood, wondering a little if the shelling during the night had done any damage—and Oosthoek Wood was shelled every night. Gradually the tanks were "tuned" to the last note of perfection, the new Lewis guns were fired, and finally the tanks were taken out on a cloudy day to a field close by and the compasses adjusted by "swinging." Names and numbers were painted. Experiments were made with the new and not very satisfactory form of "unditching gear." Supplies of water, petrol, and ammunition were taken on board. Everything that the crews could do was done.

We were told soon after we had arrived in the Salient that during the first stages of the great battle "D" Battalion would remain in reserve. There was, in consequence, no need for us to make any elaborate reconnaissances of our own trench system, because by the time that we were likely to come into action it was probable that we should be beyond trenches and operating in the open country.

If a tank company is ordered to attack with the infantry on the first day of a battle, no reconnaissance can be too detailed and patient, for on the night before the attack a tank can do untold mischief. There are wires, light railways, emplacements, communication trenches, dugouts to be avoided, and a specific spot to be reached at a given time. Tanks unfortunately are not allowed to roam wildly over the battlefield either before or during a battle.

The route that a tank will take from the moment it starts to move up on the night before the battle to the moment it rallies after the battle is only a few yards wide. It is chosen after the most painstaking examination of aeroplane photographs and the daily reconnaissance of the enemy country. To our own front line the route is taped, and forward it should be taped—in the mind's eye of the tank commander.

Nor was it necessary for us to "liaise" with the infantry. Immediately a tank company commander learns that he is "going over "with a certain battalion of infantry, he begins at once to establish the closest possible "liaison." The infantry officers are entertained and shown over the tanks. A demonstration is arranged, and if time permits a dress rehearsal of the attack is carried out in order that there may be a thorough understanding between the tanks and the infantry.

At the beginning of the Ypres battle combined tactics scarcely existed. The infantry attacked, the tanks helped, and the only question to be decided was whether the tanks went in front of the infantry or the infantry in front of the tanks. But even in July 1917 it was just as well to know personally the officers and men of the battalion concerned, although as late as September 1918 one divisional commander refused to tell his men that they would be attacking with tanks, in case they should be disappointed if the tanks broke down before the battle.

We had only to reconnoitre the routes to the canal, and make a general study of the sector in which we might be engaged.

Nothing, I suppose, sounds more elementary than to take a marked map and follow a tank route from a large wood to a canal which cannot be avoided.

In practice there are not a few little difficulties. First, it is necessary to extricate the tanks from the wood without knocking down the trees, which may later be required to shelter others from aeroplanes. This requires care and skill. Then the tanks proceed along a cart-track until the route crosses a main road by a camp, where it is necessary to swing sharply to avoid important wires and some huts. Beyond the main road we trek across a field or two until the track divides, and it is easy enough in the dark to bear to the right instead of to the left. Then there is a ditch to cross, with marshy banks—a good crossing in dry weather, but doubtful after rain—and we mark an alternative.

We come to a light railway, and this under no circumstances must be damaged. We arrange for it to be "ramped" carefully with sleepers, but it is just as well to carry a few spare sleepers in the tanks, because some heavy gunners live nearby. The track, which by this time is two feet deep in mud, again divides, and bearing to the right we find that an ammunition column has camped across it. So we suggest that tanks through horse lines at night may produce dire results, and a narrow passage is cleared. Another main-road crossing and a bridge—we are doubtful about that bridge, and walk down the stream until we come to something more suitable to our weight. Along the route we look for woods, copses, or ruins, so that, if a tank breaks down, we may know the best cover for the night: you cannot afford to leave a tank lying about in the open, however skilfully you may camouflage it.

I shall never forget those hot arduous days when we tramped in the moist heat over all the possible routes, plunging, after it had rained, through sticky mud often up to our knees, setting up little signposts wherever it was possible to make a mistake, and wondering whether the car would meet us at the other end.
. . .

The canal was a problem in itself. To live in a Salient under the eyes of the enemy is miserable enough, but when it is necessary to cross a canal to reach your own trenches life becomes intolerable.

The canal ran north and south from Ypres. It was an everyday canal, with dugouts in its banks and only three or four feet of mud and water at the bottom. It was crossed by a number of bridges, and on each the enemy gunners had been "registering" for two years, so that by July 1917 their fire had become moderately accurate. They knew it was necessary for us to cross the canal by a bridge, unless we went through Ypres, with the result that no man lingered on a bridge a moment longer than he must. Even our infantry, who would march steadily through a barrage, crossed the canal at the double, and yet were often caught.

With the tanks we determined to take no risks. Bridges might be—and often were—destroyed by a single shell, and it was decided to build two solid embankments. Immediately the sappers started the enemy discovered what was happening, and shelled the work without mercy by day and by night and dropped bombs, but resolutely the work went forward. Gang after gang of men were swept out of existence, but the sappers just set their teeth and hung on, until a few days before the battle the two embankments were well and properly built, and the little graveyard by divisional headquarters was nearly filled.

In those days the German gunners gave us no peace. It was a magnificent duel between the two artilleries. The enemy knew, of course, that we were about to attack, and they determined that, if shells could spoil our preparations, our preparations should be spoiled. I believe we lost ten thousand men in the three weeks before the battle. We were consoled only by the thought that the enemy was getting as much as he gave. It was pleasant, for instance, to find a long gun, whose sole object in life was to drop shells on the station at Roulers from dusk to dawn, particularly after a chance shell in Poperinghe had spoiled a little dinner at "Skindles," or a salvo into St Jean had distinctly delayed an important reconnaissance on a sweltering day. And the shelling of the canal was beyond a joke.

As I was a little anxious about the embankments, I decided to reconnoitre, for my own peace of mind, a passable route through the outskirts of Ypres round the "dead end" of the canal. It was a typical day. Cooper and I motored to within a mile, and then, leaving our car under the shelter of some trees, walked boldly ahead along the road to the "dead end." There was no shelling near—it was a pleasant quiet morning. We noticed, however, that the enemy had been active very recently. The road was covered with fresh branches and dirt. The shell-holes were suspiciously new. We crossed two bridges, and, having satisfied ourselves that they would easily bear tanks, we walked down to the quayside and stopped for a moment to light our pipes, with mutual congratulations that we had chosen such a calm morning.

We did not then know the neighbourhood. We barely heard a shell before it dropped neatly on the farther bank. We decided to push on down the canal, but a little barrage drove the inhabitants of the canal into their dugouts. Finally, the salvos of H.E. shrapnel made the quayside a place to be avoided, and we retired hastily into a strong shelter where some jolly gunners offered us tea. They belonged to a 6-inch howitzer battery a little distance away, and already they had lost two-thirds of their men, and two of their howitzers had received direct hits.

We waited for twenty minutes. There is nothing more difficult, and at the same time more easy, than to take cover until a "strafe "stops. Probably, if you walk straight on, as you intended, you will not only be just as safe as you are under cover, but you will add to your self-respect and rise in the estimation of your fellow-prisoners. On the other hand, there is no hurry, and the enemy cannot go on forever. Why not wait until he stops? Still, as a major you should set a good exam.ple, and not take any notice of a few shells. Yes, but they are large shells, and you are perfectly certain that the last one fell exactly on the road. Now, if we had been there

Twice we started and twice we were driven in. Then at last we made up our minds that the shelling was dying down, and we began to walk back over the bridges, which had been hit at least twice since we had crossed them. I heard something come very, very quickly, and I do not mind confessing that I ducked. It exploded in the back of the house which we were passing. We walked a little more rapidly, and strained our ears for the next. We just heard it, and this time we flung ourselves down, and the dirt and bits of things came pattering down on to us. I looked at Cooper. There was agreement in his eye. We ran for our lives. . . . That was our final reconnaissance on the 28th July.

After mess on the 30th, I strolled out with Cooper to the corner of the main road. It was dusk, and the coolness was sweet. We waited, and then battalion after battalion came swinging round the corner, where guides stood with lanterns. Some of the men were whistling, a few were singing, and some, thinking of the battle or their homes, had set faces. Soon it became too dark to distinguish one man from another, and I thought it as well. What did it matter if one man was singing and another brooding over the battle to come? They were shadowy figures, dark masses, just so many thousand infantrymen marching to the battle, just so many units to kill or be killed. One grave is the same as any other, and one infantryman should be the same as any other; for it is difficult to endure war, and at the same time to think of the fear, the love, the songs, the hope, the courage, the devices of the individual men who fight. There is nothing noble, glorious, or romantic in war, unless you forget the souls of the men. . . .

The squealing mules with their clattering limbers plunged round the corner, and we returned to our tents. It was hard to sleep. In a few hours there was a momentary silence. Then right along the line an uneasy drone broke the stillness—the weary tank crews had started their engines, and the barrage fell with a crash on the German trenches.

CHAPTER 8

The Third Battle of Ypres—St Julien
(AUGUST 1917.)

The opening moves of the battle were not too fortunate. The first objectives were gained on the left and in the centre, but the cost was high. The Welsh Division in particular suffered heavily: the enemy had learned through treachery the Welsh plan of attack. On the right we made little impression on the western end of the Passchendaele Ridge. Once the first great onrush was over, we reverted to the old siege tactics—to blow a trench system to pieces and then to occupy it under cover of a thick barrage. The rain came down, and the whole battlefield, torn up already by our guns, became impassable.

We advanced more slowly. The enemy brought up every spare gun, and the artilleries hammered away mechanically day and night, while the wretched infantry on either side lay crouched in flooded shell-holes. The preliminary bombardments became longer, and the objectives of the infantry more limited. Soon the attacks ominously began to fail—at Hooge and Polygon Wood attack after attack had broken on the enemy defences. "Pill-boxes," little forts of concrete, proved at first almost impregnable. The enemy could congratulate themselves that they had brought to a standstill the great British attack of the year.

That was the first stage. Then there were changes in command and in tactics. The Second Army extended its front to the north, and Plumer began slowly to solve the problem with the aid of a little fine weather. Tactics were adapted to the nature of the ground and the character of the enemy defences. Tanks were at last permitted to use the roads. The Australians were "put in" on the Passchendaele Ridge. Once again the vast creaking machine began to move slowly forward, but very slowly. We reached the outskirts of the Houthulst Forest; we crawled along the top of the ridge and to the north of it. At last we were within reach of Passchendaele itself, and we had hopes of Roulers. . . .

It was too late. The weather definitely had broken: the Italians were pouring back to the Piave: the Russians had left us to ourselves. November had come, and to distract the enemy's attention we made a strong little effort down at Cambrai. When the copse of Passchendaele finally was taken, we were occupied with other things.

We had forced the enemy back at Ypres six or seven miles in three and a half months. Our casualties, I believe, had amounted to a quarter of a million. The Salient had indeed preserved its reputation, and that grim spirit who broods over the hills beyond Ypres must have smiled maliciously when in a few months we were again compelled to withdraw our lines.

In the third battle of Ypres the reputation of the Tank Corps was almost destroyed. When we went south to Cambrai we must have left behind us two or three hundred derelict tanks sinking by degrees into the mud. The fighting virtues of the crews could not be questioned, for the gallantry of the corps was amazing. Time after time the men started out to fight in the full knowledge that unless some miracle intervened they must stick in the mud—and either spend hours under a deadly fire endeavouring to extricate their tanks or fight on, the target of every gun in the neighbourhood, until they were knocked to pieces.

There was the famous tank "Fray Bentos," which went out in front of our infantry and "ditched." The crew fought for seventy-two hours, bombed, shelled, and stormed by day and by night, until, when all of them were wounded, they gave up hope that the infantry ever would reach them and crawled back to our own lines.

At last it was decided that the tanks might use the roads. This must not be misunderstood. A civilian could search for a road in the forward area and not recognise it when he came to it. The roads had been shelled to destruction, like everything else in that ghastly, shattered country, but they possessed at least some sort of foundation which prevented the tanks from sinking into the mud.

Operating on the roads, we had one or two little successes—a mixed company of "G" Battalion surprised and captured a few pill-boxes at a ridiculously low cost, and later the 10th Company, "D" Battalion, carried out a splendid feat in moving from St Julien, assisting the infantry to capture half the village of Poelcapelle and some strong points near, and then returning to St Julien with all tanks intact and two men wounded.

It would require a partial historian to assert that the tanks seriously affected the course of the battle. Every action was a deadly gamble, and soon the infantry realised as transparently as the stout- hearted crews that, in the Salient, a company of tanks, however skilfully driven and gallantly fought, could not be relied upon at need. And the divisions, which came up in the later stages of the battle, had only to use their eyes. It is not very encouraging to pass a succession of derelict tanks.

Luckily for the future of the corps, the infantryman was generous enough to attribute at least part of our failures to the appalling ground. The average infantry officer[1] could not understand why on earth tanks had ever been brought to the Salient. We made the most of our successes and said nothing of our failures. Then came the battle of Cambrai, and those poor old battered derelicts, rusting in the mud, were forgotten. . . . After all, not only the tanks failed in the Third Battle of Ypres. . . .

I have given this little picture of the battle in order that the reader, spoon-fed on journalese, may not come to my story under the delusion that this tragic battle was a glorious victory. The details of operations he may find elsewhere: a proper history of the tank corps may soon be written: the careful critic may find

---

1. The regimental officer always appreciated our difficulties, praised our achievements, and sympathised with us in our misfortunes.

my dates inaccurate. I want to give the atmosphere in which we fought, and this battle was a gloomy, bitter business. . . .

On the 31st July, the first day of the battle, it began to rain, and it rained until August 6th, and then it rained again. We, who were in corps reserve, had nothing to do except to wait restlessly in our camp—we might receive orders to move up at any moment, if the enemy line gave any indication of breaking; but, although on our corps front we had successfully reached our first objectives, and the Pilkem Ridge, from which we had been driven by gas in April '15, was once more in our hands, the German defence remained intact. It was clear that the enemy, who, like us, had made every possible preparation, must once again be thrown back by sheer force. And the continual downpour made the task day by day more difficult. The more it rained, the more necessary a prolonged preliminary bombardment became, and a lengthy bombardment made the ground increasingly unsuitable for the use of infantry and tanks. It was an altogether vicious circle.

The necessity, however, for a series of siege attacks with limited objectives relieved the tension for us, and the rain, which gravely hindered all preparations, postponed indefinitely the day on which my company, the reserve company of the reserve battalion, would come into action. We again made a thorough overhaul of our tanks, and fearing that the officers and men might become stale, I granted generous leave out of camp.

The war for us consisted in watching the arrival of prisoners at the Army Cage, which was just round the corner; in putting out our lights when the enemy 'planes came over; in reconnoitring once again our routes forward; in making little expeditions to neighbouring towns when the strain of waiting became too insistent. . . .

There was no hate in our hearts for the gangs of prisoners who, on the morning and afternoon of every attack, poured miserably along the Poperinghe road. They looked such wretched, sullen outcasts. Even the pride of the officers—a quaint ridiculous dignity—was a little pitiful. When the gangs halted by the roadside, just by the camp, it was impossible at first to prevent our men from giving them tea and cigarettes, though later this practice was sternly forbidden. In some ways we treated these prisoners well.

When we drew biscuits instead of bread, we would always say that a fresh batch of prisoners must have arrived. But the Cage itself rapidly became a swamp, and we sympathised, in spite of ourselves, with the poor devils lying out in the mud. I used to wonder in the following year whether those of our men who were taken prisoner looked so unutterably woebegone as these Germans, or whether, perhaps, they bore themselves more bravely. . . .

The bombing at night, even back at La Lovie, was an infernal nuisance. During August it rapidly developed, and it reached its height towards the middle of September. We possessed, apparently, no means of defence against it. The "Archies" seemed useless. Machine-gun fire was effective only when the 'planes flew daringly low. The enemy came over when he liked, and we could not understand why he did not show himself more frequently.

We in our camp were only annoyed—never damaged, and we began to treat it all rather as a joke. Then the two Casualty Clearing Stations on the railway were bombed. Several nurses, moving quietly among the screaming wounded, were killed. We hoped that it was a terrible mistake, but the hospitals were deliberately bombed a second time, and the ghastly scenes were repeated. I do not know whether in very shame we invented some shadow of excuse, but it was rumoured at this time that, in our nightly shelling of Roulers Station, a shell had dropped into the German hospital nearby, and that the enemy were now retaliating. I do not vouch for this explanation, and it is quite, probably an invention.

The heavy rain had made the reconnaissance of approach routes to Ypres and the canal the hardest labour. The tracks had been churned up by passing tanks until they were knee-deep in mud—not the slimy, oozy kind, but the damp spongy mud which sticks. In spite of the rain it was a month of close muggy days, and these tramps through the steaming odorous mud were a very sore infliction. But the routes were so various, wandering, and difficult that the most thorough reconnaissance was necessary. At any rate we acquired a knowledge of the countryside, and the more we saw of it the less we loved it.

Once the country must have been rough heath, with big woods, isolated clumps of firs, and everywhere stagnant pools and dirty streams. Then the painstaking natives took hold of it and determined to make a living out of it. They cultivated and cultivated with meticulous care. In the back areas hops, corn, turnips, beans, market gardens, all in their enclosures, came right up to the roads and the woods, but forward all the country was returning to heath. Little cottages or farms lined the roads or stood at the corners of the fields, while, farther back again, the main roads were fringed with queer temporary bungalows or shelters, where the *evacués* eked out a livelihood by selling food, cigarettes, vegetables, or bad beer to the troops, or by making coarse lace.

Now fill every wood with camps and every open space with dumps or parks, cover the country with such a close network of railways that there is a level-crossing every three hundred yards along any road, and block all the roads with transport. Further forward there are guns everywhere—behind cottages, in houses, along hedges, camouflaged in the open. . .

The country seemed out of proportion. The fields were so small, the hedges so numerous, the roads so narrow. . . . It was a battlefield over allotments, cultivated on a marshy heath.

Cooper and I would go beyond the canal and gaze at the villages which we might attack. It has always fascinated me to see the inviolate country—the pleasant green fields and nice red houses behind the enemy line that must, when we advance, become a brown shell-pocked desert and shapeless heaps of rubble. In the old trench battles we achieved victory only by destruction. The houses and fields stood terrified at our advance, praying that it would be stopped, so that they could be spared. We looked through our glasses at Passchendaele and Westroosebeke, standing on the ridge. It was a clear day and the villages might have been in Surrey. By the end of November they were nothing but a few bricks and stones lying about in the mud.

These little expeditions forward to convenient Observation Posts had their excitements. The canal was curiously the frontier of the war. On this side of the canal it was peaceful enough save for a deafening railway-gun, a super-heavy howitzer, or a chance shell from the enemy. On that side it seemed that all the guns in the world were packed together, and the enemy, when he became annoyed, shelled the whole area indiscriminately. We had one particularly bad day. . . .

By the last week in August it had been found impossible for tanks successfully to operate over the open country of the Salient, and they were tied strictly to the remains of roads. . . .

On the front which concerned my battalion we had driven the enemy back over the Pilkem Ridge into the valley of the Hannebeek, and at the foot of the further slopes he was holding out successfully in a number of "pill-boxes" and concreted ruins.

St Julien itself was ours, a little village along the main road to Poelcapelle at the crossing of the stream. Beyond, the ground was so ravaged with shell-fire that it had become a desert stretch of shell-holes, little stagnant pools, with here and there an odd hedge or a shattered tree. The enemy defences, which consisted of strong points skilfully linked up by fortified shell-holes, overlooked the opposite slope, and our guns were compelled to remain behind the shelter of the Pilkem crest.

A few of the strong points on the west of the main road, notably the "Cockroft," had already been cleared by a mixed company of "G" Battalion in a successful little action. The tanks, using the roads for the first time, had approached the forts from the rear, and the garrisons in their panic had surrendered almost without a fight.

Ward's company had made a similar attack along the road running east from the village. On the day before the action the enemy had spotted his tanks, which were "lying up" on the western slope of the Pilkem Ridge, and had attempted to destroy them with a hurricane bombardment of 5.9's; but a tank has as many lives as a cat, and only three or four were knocked out, though the flanks of the remainder were scarred and dented with splinters.

The action itself was typical of many a tank action in the Salient. The tanks slipped off the road and became irretrievably ditched, sinking into the marsh. They were knocked out by direct hits as they nosed their way too slowly forward. One gallant tank drew up alongside a "pill-box," stuck, and fought it out. We never quite knew what happened, but at last the tank caught fire. The crew never returned.

The road out of St Julien was littered with derelicts, for tanks of another battalion, endeavouring by that road to reach another part of the battlefield, had met their fate.

It was therefore with mixed feelings that I received the order to get ready a section with a view to co-operating with the infantry in an attack on the same front.

I had already moved my company without incident to the canal, where they remained peacefully, camouflaged under the trees.

I selected for the enterprise Wyatt's section, which, it will be remembered, had fought on the extreme right at the first battle of Bullecourt, His four tanks were at this time commanded by Puttock, Edwards, Sartin, and Lloyd. It was a good section.

First, we consulted with the G. S.O.I, of the Division, which lived in excellent dugouts on the banks of the canal. The infantry attack was planned in the usual way—the German positions were to be stormed under cover of the thickest possible barrage.

We were to attack practically the same positions which Ward's company had so gallantly attempted to take. The direct road, perhaps luckily, was blocked by derelicts. A rough diagram will make the position clear:—

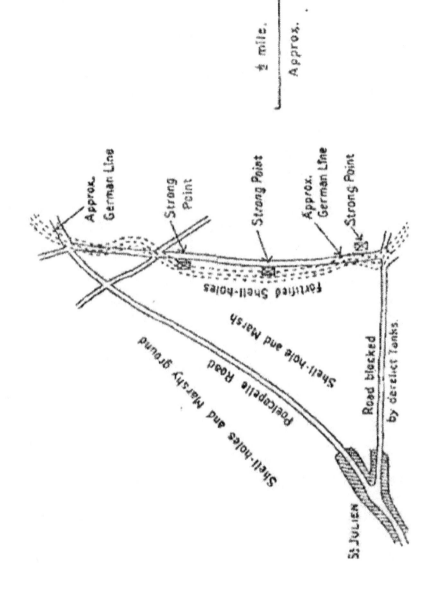

Approx. German Line

Strong Point

Strong Point

Approx. German Line

Strong Point

Fortified Shell-holes

Shell-hole and Marsh

Shell-holes and Marshy ground

Poelcapelle Road

Road blocked

by derelict Tanks.

St. JULIEN

½ mile.

Approx.

It will be obvious that, since my tanks could not leave the road, and the direct road was blocked, it had become necessary to use the main road across the enemy front and attack the strong points down the road from the north. Further, the tanks could not move out of St Julien before "zero" in case the noise of their engines should betray the coming attack. We were reduced, in consequence, to a solemn crawl along the main road in sight of the enemy after the battle had commenced.

We decided boldly to spend the night before the battle at St Julien. We had realised by then that the nearer we were to the enemy the less likely we were to be shelled. And the idea of a move down the road into St Julien actually on the night before the battle was not pleasant. No margin of time would be left for accidents, mechanical or otherwise.

Cooper, Wyatt, and I carried out a preliminary reconnaissance into the outskirts of St Julien on a peaceful day before coming to our decision. The sun was shining brightly after the rain, and the German gunners were economising their ammunition after an uproar on the night before, the results of which we saw too plainly in the dead men lying in the mud along the roadside. Wyatt made a more detailed reconnaissance by night and planned exactly where he would put each tank.

On the night of the 25th/26th August Wyatt's section moved across the canal and up along a track to an inconspicuous halting-place on the western side of the crest. It was raining, and, as always, the tracks were blocked with transport. An eager gunner endeavoured to pass one of the tanks, but his gun caught the sponson and slipped off into the mud. It was a weary, thankless trek.

On the following night the tanks crawled cautiously down the road into St Julien with engines barely turning over for fear the enemy should hear them. The tanks were camouflaged with the utmost care.

The enemy aeroplanes had little chance to see them, for on the 27th it rained. A few shells came over, but the tanks were still safe and whole on the night before the battle, when a storm of wind and rain flooded the roads and turned the low ground beyond the village, which was treacherous at the best of times, into a slimy quagmire.

Before dawn on the 28th the padre walked from ruin to ruin, where the crews had taken cover from shells and the weather, and administered the Sacrament to all who desired to partake of it. The crews stood to their tanks. Then, just before sunrise, came the whine of the first shells, and our barrage fell on the shell-holes in which the enemy, crouched and sodden, lay waiting for our attack. The German gunners were alert, and in less than two minutes the counter-barrage fell beyond the village to prevent reinforcements from coming forward. Big shells crashed into St Julien. The tanks swung out of their lairs in the dust and smoke, and, moving clear of the village, advanced steadily in the dim light along the desolate road, while the padre and Wyatt slipped back through the counter-barrage to brigade head-quarters.

It was lonely on the Poelcapelle Road, with nothing for company but shells bursting near the tanks. After the heavy rain the tanks slipped about on the broken setts, and every shell-hole in the road was a danger—one lurch, and the tank would slide off into the marsh.

Very slowly the tanks picked their way. Three tanks reached the cross-roads. The fourth, Lloyd's, scraped a tree-trunk, and the mischief was done. The tank sidled gently off the road and stuck, a target for the machine-gunners. Two of the crew crept out, and the unditching beam was fixed on to the tracks. The tank heaved, moved a few inches, and sank more deeply. Another effort was made, but the tank was irretrievably ditched, half a mile from the German lines.

Three tanks turned to the right at the first cross-roads, and, passing through our infantry, enfiladed the shell-holes occupied by the enemy. The effect of the tanks' fire could not be more than local, since on either side of the road were banks about four to five feet in height. The enemy were soon compelled to run back from the shell-holes near the road, and many dropped into the mud; but machine-gun fire from the shell-holes, which the guns of the tanks could not reach effectively, prevented a further advance.

One tank moved south down the track towards the strong points, but found it blocked by a derelict tank which the enemy had blown neatly into two halves. My tank remained there for an hour, shooting at every German who appeared. Then the tank commander tried to reverse in order to take another road, but the tank, in reversing, slid on to a log and slipped into a shell-hole, unable to move. One man was mortally wounded by a splinter.

The barrage had passed on and the infantry were left floundering in the mud. The enemy seized the moment to make a counter-attack, two bunches of Germans working their way forward from shell-hole to shell-hole on either side of the tank. Our infantry, already weakened, began to withdraw to their old positions.

The tank commander learned by a runner, who on his adventurous little journey shot two Germans with his revolver, that the second tank was also ditched a few hundred yards away on another road. This tank, too, had cleared the shell-holes round it, and, bolting the garrison of a small strong point near it with its 6-pdr. gun, caught them as they fled with machine-gun fire.

There was nothing more to be done. The tanks were in full view of the German observers, and the enemy gunners were now trying for direct hits. The tanks must be hit, sooner or later. The infantry were withdrawing. The two wretched subalterns in that ghastly waste of shell-holes determined to get their men away before their tanks were hit or completely surrounded. They destroyed what was of value in their tanks, and carrying their Lewis guns and some ammunition, they dragged themselves wearily back to the main road.

The remaining tank, unable to move forward as all the roads were now blocked, cruised round the triangle of roads to the north of the strong points. Then a large shell burst just in front of the tank and temporarily blinded the driver. The tank slipped off the road into the mud, jamming the track against the trunk

of a tree. All the efforts of the crew to get her out were in vain.
. . .

Meanwhile, we had been sitting drearily near Divisional Headquarters on the canal bank, in the hope that by a miracle our tanks might succeed and return. The morning wore on, and there was little news. The Germans shelled us viciously. It was not until my tank commanders returned to report that we knew the attack had failed.

When the line had advanced a little, Cooper and I went forward to reconnoitre the road to Poelcapelle and to see our derelicts. Two of the tanks had been hit. A third was sinking into the mud. In the last was a heap of evil-smelling corpses. Either men who had been gassed had crawled into the tank to die, or more likely, men who had taken shelter had been gassed where they sat. The shell-holes nearby contained half-decomposed bodies that had slipped into the stagnant water. The air was full of putrescence and the strong odour of foul mud. There was no one in sight except the dead. A shell came screaming over and plumped dully into the mud without exploding. Here and there was a little rusty wire, climbing in and out of the shell-holes like noisome weeds. A few yards away a block of mud- coloured concrete grew naturally out of the mud. An old entrenching tool, a decayed German pack, a battered tin of bully, and a broken rifle lay at our feet. We crept away hastily. The dead never stirred.

CHAPTER 9

The Third Battle of Ypres—
The Poelcapelle Road
(SEPTEMBER AND OCTOBER 1917.)

For three weeks there was no big offensive, though the artill-eries continued their pitiless duel without a break, and the mis-erable infantry, tormented by bombs and shells as they crouched in their water- logged holes, or staggering dully over the mud in a series of little local attacks, which too often failed, could scarcely have realised that there was a distinct lull in the battle. We were pulling ourselves together for another enormous effort. The guns were pushed forward, and more guns arrived. Tired Divisions were taken out and new Divisions took their place with reduced fronts. There were new groupings, new tactics. ... A possible month of fighting weather remained. We might still make something of this tragic struggle.

My company had returned from the canal, as it was not likely that we should be wanted again in the near future, and were liv-ing in shameless comfort at La Lovie. The rain had stopped—we always had bright sunshine in the Salient, when we were not ready to attack. If it had not been for the growl of the guns, an occasional shell in Poperinghe while we were bargaining for greengages, or the perseverance of the enemy airmen, who dropped bombs somewhere in the neighbourhood each fine night, we might have forgotten the war completely. There were walks through the pine-woods, canters over the heath, thrilling football matches against our rivals, little expeditions to Bailleul for fish, or Cassel for a pleasant dinner in the cool of the evening. And I fell in with Susie.

She was a dear, graceful little woman, with timid, liquid brown eyes, black hair, a pleasant mouth, and the most marvellous teeth. Our friendship began one night when, returning from mess, I found her sitting on my bed.

It is better to be frank. She was half a German—at least we all thought so, because, if she had no dachshund blood in her, she had no other strain in her that we could recognise.

Then there was the Brigade barber across the way, who came from Bond Street. He had been given his own little shop, and he possessed such a store of the barber's polite conversation that to listen was to become home-sick. Sometimes, as we were in Flanders, he would flavour his stories a little fully, ending always with a half-apology—

"A topic, sir, I can assure you, that I should scarcely have approached, if it had not been for my eighteen months in the ranks."

His little deprecating cough was pure joy. . . .

On the 19th the weather broke again, and it rained heavily. On the 20th we delivered an attack in the grand style, with every man and gun available. For a few days we were full of hope. The enemy could not resist our sheer strength, and their line bent and almost broke. We threw in division after division, attacking day after day. We thrust him back to the fringes of the Houthulst Forest. We crawled along the Passchendaele Ridge, and on the 26th we captured Zonnebeke. Then slowly and magnificently the Germans steadied themselves, and once more the attacks died down with the enemy line still in being. But the Great General Staff must have had a terrible fright.

Ward's company had been engaged between the Poelcapelle Road and Langemarck. Much to my disgust I had been compelled to hand over to him two of my best tanks. His company did excellent work, though, as had become customary in the Salient, only a few of his tanks returned. One tank particularly distinguished itself by climbing a barricade of logs, which had been built to block the road a few hundred yards south of Poelcapelle, and slaughtering its defenders.

At the end of September we had driven back the enemy, on the front with which I was principally concerned, to a position immediately in front of Poelcapelle—that is, just over a mile N.E. of the cross-roads near which Wyatt's section had fought at the end of August. Our progress in a month, though we thought it to be satisfactory at the time, had not been astonishingly rapid. It was determined to clear Poelcapelle as soon as possible, since, while the Germans held it, we were greatly handicapped in attacking either the S.E. edge of the Houthulst Forest or the Passchendaele Ridge itself from the north-west. Further, the only two main roads in the neighbourhood passed through the village.

Marris, who had succeeded Haskett-Smith in the command of No. 10 Company, was instructed to assist the infantry in the attack. His company had just returned from Wailly, where they had greatly improved their driving by hard practice over the derelict trenches. They had suffered few casualties at Arras, and, as they had not previously been engaged in the Salient, they were fresh and keen.

The attack was scheduled for October 4th. Marris brought down his tanks into St Julien and camouflaged them in the ruins. St Julien, though still easily within close field-gun range, was now respectably "behind the line." It was only shelled once or twice a night, and during the day on state occasions. It could not hope entirely to escape—the bridge across the Hannebeek was too important—but it became the place at which you left the car if you wanted to reconnoitre forward.

The attack was incredibly successful. Of Marris's twelve tanks, eleven left St Julien and crawled perilously all night along the destroyed road. At dawn they entered the village with the infantry and cleared it after difficult fighting. One section even found their way along the remains of a track so obliterated by shell-fire that it scarcely could be traced on the aeroplane photographs, and "bolted" the enemy from a number of strong points. Then, having placed the infantry in possession of their objectives, the tanks lurched back in the daylight. It was a magnificent exhibition of good driving, which has never been surpassed, and was without doubt the most successful operation in the Salient carried out by tanks.

Unfortunately the tanks could not remain in the village. By midday every German gun which could bear had been turned upon it, and by dusk the enemy had forced their way back into the ruins at the farther end of the long street.

It soon became clear that we should be required to finish the job. The weather, of course, changed. A few days of drying sun and wind were followed by gales and heavy rain. The temperature dropped. At night it was bitterly cold.

On the 6th, Cooper and I made a little expedition up the Poelcapelle Road. It was in a desperate condition, and we felt a most profound respect for the drivers of No. 10 Company. The enemy gunners had shelled it with accuracy. There were great holes that compelled us to take to the mud at the side. In places the surface had been blown away, so that the road could not be distinguished from the treacherous riddled waste through which it ran. To leave the road was obviously certain disaster for a tank. Other companies had used it, and at intervals derelict tanks which had slipped off the road or received direct hits were sinking rapidly in the mud. I could not help remembering that the enemy must be well aware of the route which so many tanks had followed into battle.

We were examining a particularly large shell-hole, between two derelict tanks, when the enemy whose shells had been falling at a reasonable distance, began to shell the road. . . .

Two sections of my tanks—Talbot's and Skinner's—had moved forward once more from the canal, and were safely camouflaged in St Julien by dawn on the 8th. All the tank commanders and their first drivers had reconnoitred the road from St Julien to the outskirts of Poelcapelle. The attack was to be made at 5.20 a.m. on the 9th. The tanks were ordered to enter

Poelcapelle with the infantry and drive the enemy out of the houses which they still held.

I was kept at La Lovie until dusk for my final instructions. I started in my car, intending to drive to Wieltje, two miles from St Julien, but Organ was away, and I found to my disgust that my temporary driver could not see in the dark. Naturally, no lights were allowed on the roads, and the night was black with a fluster of rain. After two minor collisions on the farther side of Vlamertinghe I gave up the car as useless, and tramped the two and a half miles into Ypres. The rain held off for an hour, and a slip of moon came out to help me.

I walked through the pale ruins, and, though the enemy had ceased to shell Ypres regularly, fear clung to the place. For once there was little traffic, and in the side streets I was desperately alone. The sight of a military policeman comforted me, and, leaving the poor broken houses behind, I struck out along, the St Jean road, which the enemy were shelling, to remind me, perhaps, that there could still be safety in Ypres.

It began to rain steadily and the moon disappeared. I jumped into an empty ambulance to escape from the rain and the shells, but beyond St Jean there was a bad block in the traffic; so, leaving the ambulance, I wormed my way through the transport, and, passing the big guns on the near side of the crest which the enemy had held for so many years, I splashed down the track into St Julien. I only stumbled into one shell-hole, but I fell over a dead mule in trying to avoid its brother. It was a pitch-black night.

We had decided to use for our headquarters a perfectly safe "pill-box," or concreted house in St Julien, but when we arrived we discovered that it was already occupied by a dressing station. We could not stand upon ceremony—we shared it between us.

Soon after I had reached St Julien, weary, muddy, and wet, the enemy began to shell the village persistently. One shell burst just outside our door. It killed two men and blew two into our chamber, where, before they had realised they were hit, they were bandaged and neatly labelled.

My crews, who had been resting in our camp by the canal, arrived in the middle of the shelling, and, paying no attention to it whatever, began to uncover their tanks and drive them out from the ruins where they had been hidden. Luckily nobody was hurt, but the shelling continued until midnight.

By 10 p.m. the tanks had started on the night's trek, with the exception of one which had been driven so adroitly into a ruin that for several hours we could not extract it. By midnight the rain had stopped and the moon showed herself—but with discretion.

Very slowly the seven tanks picked their way to Poelcapelle. The strain was appalling. A mistake by the leading tanks, and the road might be blocked. A slip—and the tank would lurch off into the mud. The road after the rain would have been difficult enough in safety by daylight. Now it was a dark night, and, just to remind the tanks of the coming battle, the enemy threw over a shell or two.

One tank tried to cross a tree-trunk at the wrong angle. The trunk slipped between the tracks and the tank turned suddenly. The mischief was done. For half an hour S. did his best, but on the narrow slippery road he could not swing his tank sufficiently to climb the trunk correctly. In utter despair he at last drove his tank into the mud, so that the three tanks behind him might pass.[1]

About 4 a.m. the enemy shelling increased in violence and became a very fair bombardment. The German gunners were taking no risks. If dawn were to bring with it an attack, they would see to it that the attack never developed. By 4.30 a.m. the enemy had put down a barrage on every possible approach to the forward area. And the Poelcapelle Road, along which tanks had so often endeavoured to advance, was very heavily shelled. It was anxious work, out in the darkness among the shells, on the destroyed road. . . .

In the concrete ruins we snatched a little feverish sleep in a

---

1. S. entirely retrieved his reputation as a skilful and gallant tank commander by attacking a field-gun single-handed at Flesquieres on November 20th.

sickly atmosphere of iodine and hot tea. A few wounded men, covered with thick mud, came in, but none were kept, in order that the station might be free for the rush on the morning of the battle.

By four the gunnery had become too insistent. I did not expect Talbot to send back a runner until just before "zero," but the activity of the guns worried me. The Poelcapelle Road was no place for a tank on such a night. Still, no news was good news, for a message would have come to me if the tanks had been caught.

We went outside and stood in the rain, looking towards the line. It was still very dark, but, though the moon had left us in horror, there was a promise of dawn in the air.

The bombardment died down a little, as if the guns were taking breath, though far away to the right a barrage was throbbing. The guns barked singly. We felt a weary tension; we knew that in a few moments something enormously important would happen, but it had happened so many times before. There was a deep shuddering boom in the distance, and a shell groaned and whined overhead. That may have been a signal. There were two or three quick flashes and reports from howitzers quite near, which had not yet fired. Then suddenly on every side of us and above us a tremendous uproar arose; the ground shook beneath us; for a moment we felt battered and dizzy; the horizon was lit up with a sheet of flashes; gold and red rockets raced madly into the sky, and in the curious light of the distant bursting shells the ruins in front of us appeared and disappeared with a touch of melodrama. ...

We went in for a little breakfast before the wounded arrived.
. . .

Out on the Poelcapelle Road, in the darkness and the rain, seven tanks were crawling very slowly. In front of each tank the officer was plunging through the shell-holes and the mud, trying hard not to think of the shells. The first driver, cursing the darkness, peered ahead or put his ear to the slit, so that he could hear the instructions of his commander above the roar of the engine. The corporal "on the brakes" sat stiffly beside the driver. One man crouched in each sponson, grasping the lever of his secondary gear, and listening for the signals of the driver, tapped on the engine-cover. The gunners sprawled listlessly, with too much time for thought, but hearing none of the shells.

S. was savagely attempting to unditch the tank which he had purposely driven into the mud.

The shells came more rapidly—in salvos, right on the road, on either side of the tanks. The German gunners had decided that no tank should reach Poelcapelle that night. The tanks slithered on doggedly—they are none too easy to hit. . . .

Suddenly a shell crashed into the third tank, just as it was passing a derelict. The two tanks in front went on. Behind, four tanks were stopped. The next tank was hit on the track.

It was a massacre. The tanks could not turn, even if they had wished. There was nothing for it but to go on and attempt to pass in a rain of shells the tanks which could not move, but each tank in turn slipped off into the mud. Their crews, braving the shells, attached the unditching beams—fumbling in the dark with slippery spanners, while red-hot bits flew past, and they were deafened by the crashes—but nothing could be done. The officers withdrew their men from the fatal road and took cover in shell-holes. It was a stormy cheerless dawn.

The first two tanks, escaping the barrage, lurched on towards Poelcapelle. The first, delayed by an immense crater which the enemy had blown in the road, was hit and caught fire. The crew tumbled out, all of them wounded, and Skinner, brought them back across country. The second, seeing that the road in front was hopelessly blocked—for the leading tank was in the centre of the fairway—turned with great skill and attempted vainly to come back. By marvellous driving she passed the first derelict, but in trying to pass the second she slipped hopelessly into the mud. . . .

The weary night had passed with its fears, and standing in front of the ruin we looked down the road. It was bitterly cold, and tragedy hung over the stricken grey country like a mist.

First a bunch of wounded came, and then in the distance we saw a tank officer with his orderly. His head was bandaged and he walked in little jerks, as if he were a puppet on a string. When he came near he ran a few steps and waved his arms. It was X., who had never been in action before.

We took him inside, made him sit down, and gave him a drink of tea. He was badly shaken, almost hysterical, but pulling himself together and speaking with a laboured clearness, he told us what had happened. His eyes were full of horror at the scene on the road. He kept apologising—his inexperience might lead him to exaggerate—perhaps he ought not to have come back, but they sent him back because he was wounded; of course, if he had been used to such things he would not have minded so much—he was sorry he could not make a better report. We heard him out and tried to cheer him by saying that, of course, these things must happen in war. Then, after he had rested a little, we sent him on, for the dressing station was filling fast, and he stumbled away painfully. I have not seen him since.

The crews had remained staunchly with their tanks, waiting for orders. I sent a runner to recall them, and in an hour or so they dribbled in, though one man was killed by a chance shell on the way. Talbot, the old dragoon, who had fought right through the war, never came back. He was mortally wounded by a shell which hit his tank. I never had a better section-commander.

We waited until late in the morning for news of Skinner, who had returned across country. The dressing station was crowded, and a batch of prisoners, cowed and grateful for their lives, were carrying loaded stretchers along trench-board tracks to a light railway a mile distant. Limbers passed through and trotted toward the line. Fresh infantry, clean and obviously straight from rest, halted in the village. The officers asked quietly for news. At last Cooper and I turned away and tramped the weary muddy miles to the canal. The car was waiting for us, and soon we were back at La Lovie. I reported to the colonel and to the brigade commander. Then I went to my hut, and, sitting on my bed, tried not to think of my tanks. Hyde, the mess-waiter, knocked at the door—

"Lunch is ready, sir, and Mr King has got some whisky from the canteen, sir!"

I shouted for hot water. . . .

The great opportunity had gone by. We had failed, and to me the sense of failure was inconceivably bitter. We began to feel that we were dogged by ill-fortune: the contrast between the magnificent achievement of Marris's company and the sudden overwhelming disaster that had swept down on my section was too glaring. And we mourned Talbot. . . .

During the next few days we made several attempts to salve our tanks or clear the road by pulling them off into the mud, but the shells and circumstances proved too much for individual enterprise. In the following week, after the enemy at last had been driven beyond Poelcapelle, I sent Wyatt's section forward to St Julien, and, working under the orders of the Brigade Engineer, they managed to clear the road for the passage of transport, or, with luck and good driving, of tanks.

Later, there was a grandiose scheme for attacking Passchendaele itself and Westroosebeke from the north-west through Poelcapelle. The whole Brigade, it was planned, would advance along the Poelcapelle and Langemarck Roads and deploy in the comparatively unshelled and theoretically passable country beyond. To us, perhaps prejudiced by disaster, the scheme appeared fantastic enough: the two roads could so easily be blocked by an accident or the enemy gunners; but we never were able to know whether our fears were justified, for the remains of the Tank Corps were hurriedly collected and despatched to Wailly. . . .

The great battle of the year dragged on a little longer. In a few weeks the newspapers, intent on other things, informed their readers that Passchendaele had fallen. The event roused little comment or interest. Now, if we had reached Ostend in September . . . but it remains to be seen whether or not tanks can scale a sea-wall.

CHAPTER 10

The Battle of Cambrai—Flesquieres
(NOVEMBER 4TH TO 20TH, 1917.)

From La Lovie in the Salient I went on leave. I was recalled by wire on the 4th November to discover that, during my absence, the battalion had moved south to our old training-ground at Wailly. The apathy and bitter disappointment, caused by our misfortunes on the Poelcapelle Road, had disappeared completely, and the company, scenting a big mysterious battle, was as eager and energetic as if it had just disembarked in France.

For once the secret was well kept. The air was full of rumours, but my officers knew nothing. It was not until I saw the colonel that I learnt of the proposed raid on Cambrai, and discovered to my great joy that we were to attack in company with the Fifty-first Division.

This Division of Highland Territorials had won for itself in the course of a year the most astounding reputation. Before Beaumont Hamel in November '16 it had been known as "Harper's Duds." Since that action it had carried out attack after attack with miraculous success, until at this time it was renowned throughout the British Armies in France as a grim and terrible division, which never failed. The Germans feared it as they feared no other.

We trained with this splendid division for ten days, working out the plans of our attack so closely that each platoon of Highlanders knew personally the crew of the tank which would lead it across No Man's Land. Tank officers and infantry officers attended each other's lectures and dined with each other. Our camp rang at night with strange Highland cries. As far as was humanly possible within the limits of time, we discussed and solved each other's difficulties, until it appeared that at least on one occasion a tank and infantry attack would in reality be "a combined operation."

The maps and plans which we used in these pleasant rehearsals were without names, but although this mystery added a fillip of romance to our strenuous preparations, we were met by a curious difficulty—we did not dare to describe too vividly the scene of the coming battle for fear the area should be recognised. There was a necessary vagueness in our exhortations. . . .

One fine day Cooper, Jumbo, and I motored over to this nameless country. We passed through the ruins of Bapaume and came to the pleasant village of Metz-en-Couture on the edge of the great Havrincourt Wood. Leaving our car, we walked over the clean grassy hills to the brand-new trench system, then lightly held by the Ulster Division.

It was a country of bare downs, occasional woods, sunken roads, plentiful villages, surprising chalk ravines, and odd disconnected mounds, and the key to it was Bourlon Wood.

You will remember that on the east of the Bullecourt front was the Quéant Salient. Beyond it the German defences then ran suddenly to the south in order to obtain the protection of the enormous, unfinished Canal du Nord. By Havrincourt village, which was set conspicuously on the side of a hill, the Canal met Havrincourt Wood, and the enemy line turned again to the east, skirting the fringes of the wood and continuing cleverly at the foot of a range of low chalk hills. A rough diagram may make this clear, (see next page) and will enable you to connect this battle with the lesser battles of Bullecourt.

The front which concerned my brigade extended from Havrincourt to east of Flesquieres. Havrincourt itself was defended on the west by the canal, and on the south by a ravine and the outlying portions of the great wood. In front of the German trenches the trees had been cut down, so that the approach was difficult and open. East of Havrincourt the German trenches were completely hidden from view by the lie of the ground. This method of siting trenches was much favoured by the Germans at the time. Clearly it prevented direct observation of fire. Further, it compelled tanks to start on their journey across No Man's Land, unable to see the trenches which they were about to attack.

The trenches on the slope immediately behind the enemy first line were in full view, and the roads, buildings, patches of chalk, distinctively-shaped copses, would provide useful landmarks, if they were not hidden by the smoke of battle.

Apart from its natural defences the Hindenburg System was enormously strong. In front of it there were acres of low wire. The trenches were wide enough to be serious obstacles to tanks. Machine-gun posts, huge dugouts, long galleries, deep communication trenches, gun-pits—the whole formed one gigantic fortification more than five miles in depth.

Yet we came back from our reconnaissance in the firm belief that tanks could break through this fortification without any difficulty at all. The ground was hard chalk, and no amount of rain could make it unfit for our use. Natural and artificial obstacles could be surmounted easily enough or avoided. Given sufficient tanks and the advantage of surprise, there was no earthly reason why we should not go straight through to Cambrai.

What could stop us? The wire? It did not affect us in the slightest. The trenches? They were a little wide, but we knew how to cross them. Guns? There were not many, and few would survive the duel with our own artillery. Machine-guns or armour-piercing bullets? The Mk. 4 tank was practically invulnerable. If the infantry were able to follow the tanks, the tanks would see them through the trench systems. In open country it would be for commonsense and the cavalry, until the enemy filled the gap with his reserves.

We were only troubled by the thought of Bourlon Wood, which, from its hill, dominated the whole countryside between Havrincourt and Cambrai. But Bourlon Wood was only a mat-

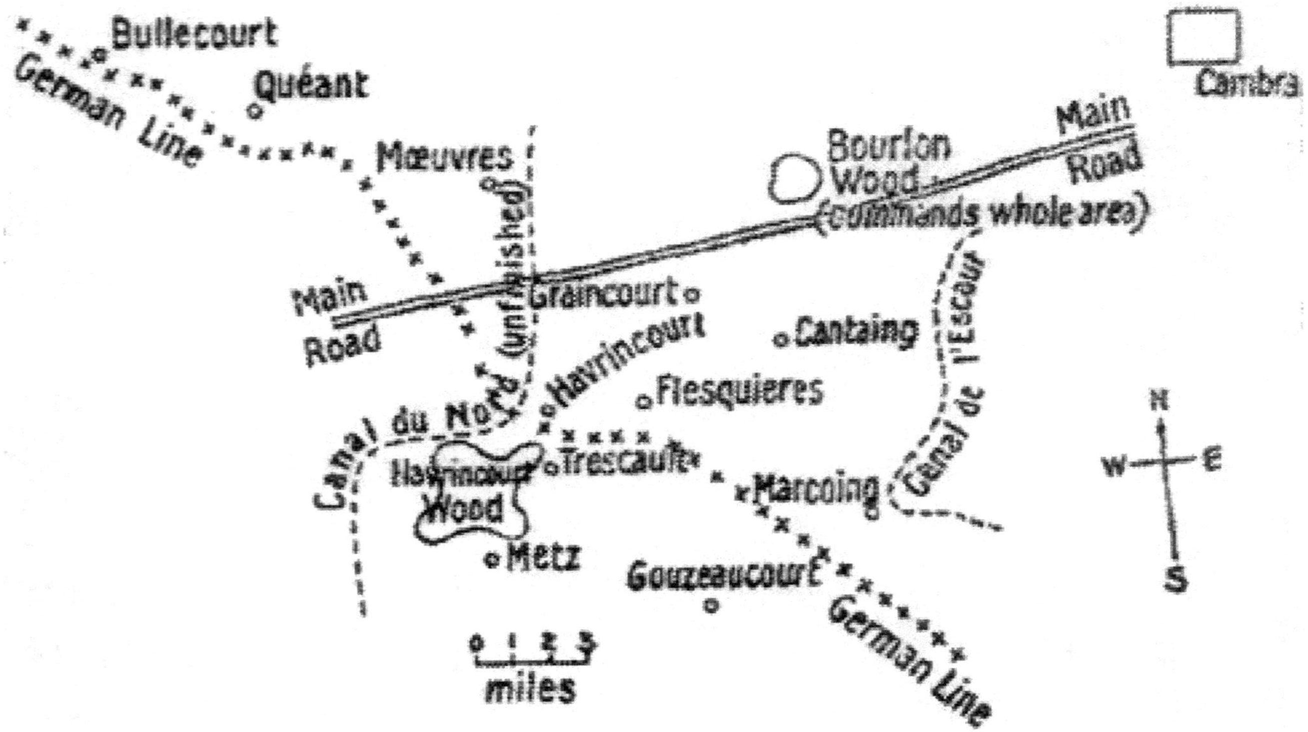

Cambrai

Main Road

Bourlon Wood
(commands whole area)

Canal de l'Escaut

Cantaing

Flesquières

Marcoing

German Line

Gouzeaucourt

Graincourt

Havrincourt

Trescault

Metz

Havrincourt Wood

Canal du Nord (unfinished)

Main Road

Mœuvres

Quéant

Bullecourt

German Line

N E W S

0 1 2 3 miles

ter of 7000 yards behind the German lines. If we were to break through at all, we should take the wood in our stride on the first day.

Jumbo expressed our feelings admirably—

"Unless the Boche catches on before the show, it's a gift!"

We returned to Wailly bubbling over with enthusiasm. The last rehearsals were completed, and our future comrades, the 6th Black Watch and the 8th Argyll and Sutherland Highlanders, appeared implicitly to trust us. We tuned our engines and practised with the wily "fascine."

Fascine is the military term for "faggot." Each of our fascines was a huge bundle of brushwood, weighing over one ton. By an ingenious mechanism it could be hoisted on to the roof of the tank. When a dangerously wide trench was reached, the driver pulled a rope, the fascine gently rolled off the tank into the trench, and the tank crossed at its ease. It was a simple device that produced an astonishing amount of bad language. Entraining was hideously complicated. Dropping the fascine on to the truck in front of the tank requires care and precision, while obviously if a fascine refuses to be picked up again, tanks are prevented from coming off the train. . . .

At dawn on the 13th we arose and trekked a matter of five miles to Beaumetz Station, where, after an excellent and hilarious lunch at the local *estaminet*, we entrained successfully for an unknown destination, although it took a little time to arrange the fascines on the trucks so that they would not fall off in the tunnels.

I watched the trains pull out from the ramps. The lorries had already started for our next halting-place. We were clear of

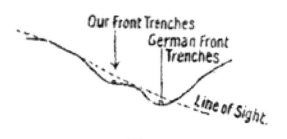

Wailly. I motored down to the neighbourhood of Albert, and at dusk my car was feeling its way through a bank of fog along the road from Bray to the great railhead at Le Plateau, at the edge of the old Somme battlefield.

It was a vast confusing place, and even a major in the Tank Corps felt insignificant among the multitudinous rails, the slow dark trains, the sudden lights. Tanks, which had just detrained, came rumbling round the corners of odd huts. Lorries bumped through the mist with food and kit. Quiet railwaymen, mostly American, went steadily about their business.

I found a hut with a fire in it and an American, who gave me hot coffee and some wonderful sandwiches, made of sausage and lettuce, and there I sat, until, just after midnight, word came that our train was expected. We walked to the ramp, and at last after an interminable wait our train glided in out of the darkness. There was a slight miscalculation, and the train hit the ramp with a bump, carrying away the lower timbers, so that it could not bear the weight of tanks.

Wearily we tramped a mile or so to another ramp. This time the train behaved with more discretion. The tanks were driven off into a wood, where they were carefully camouflaged; the cooks set to work and produced steaming tea; officers and men made themselves comfortable. Then we set off in our car again. The mist still hung heavily over the Somme battlefield and we continually lost our way. It was dawn before a desperately tired company headquarters fell asleep in some large and chilly huts near Meaulte.

That day (the 14th) and the next the men worked at their tanks, adjusting the fascines and loading up with ammunition, water, and rations. On the 14th we made another careful survey of our trenches and, through our glasses, of the country behind the German line. On the night of the 15th I walked along the tank route from our next detraining station at Ytres to our final lying-up position in Havrincourt Wood, a matter of seven miles, until I personally knew every inch of the way beyond any shadow of doubt.

At dusk on the 16th I was waiting on the ramp at Ytres for my tanks to arrive, when I heard that there had been an accident to a tank train at a level-crossing a mile down the line. I hurried there. The train had collided with a lorry and pushed it a few hundred yards, when the last truck had been derailed and the tank on it had crushed the lorry against the slight embankment. Under the tank were two men. I was convinced that I had lost two of my men, until I discovered that the tanks belonged to Harris and the two unfortunate men had been on the lorry. The line was soon cleared. The derailed truck was uncoupled, and the tank, none the worse for its adventure, climbed up the embankment and joined its fellows at the ramp.

My tanks detrained at midnight without incident, and we were clear of the railhead in an hour. It was a strange fatiguing tramp in the utter blackness of the night to Havrincourt Wood—past a brick- yard, which later we were to know too well, through the reverberating streets of Neuville Bourjonval, where three tanks temporarily lost touch with the column, and over the chill lonely downs to the outskirts of Metz, where no lights were allowed. We felt our way along a track past gun-pits and lorries and wagons until we came to the outskirts of the great wood. There we fell in with Marris's tanks, which had come by another route.

At last we arrived at our allotted quarter of the wood, three thousand yards from the nearest German. The tanks pushed boldly among the trees, and for the next two hours there was an ordered pandemonium. Each tank had to move an inch at a time for fear it should bring down a valuable tree or run over its commander, who probably had fallen backwards into the undergrowth. One tank would meet another in the darkness, and in swinging to avoid the other, would probably collide with a third. But by dawn—I do not know how it was done—every tank was safely in the wood; the men had fallen asleep anywhere, and the cooks with sly weary jests were trying to make a fire which would not smoke. Three thousand yards is a trifle near . . .

For the next five days we had only one thought—would the

Boche "catch on"? The Ulster Division was still in the line, and, even if the enemy raided and took prisoners, the Ulstermen knew almost nothing. By day the occasional German aeroplane could see little, for there was little to see. Tanks, infantry, and guns were hidden in the woods. New gun-pits were camouflaged. There was no movement on the roads or in the villages. Our guns fired a few customary rounds every day and night, and the enemy replied. There was nothing unusual.

But at night the roads were blocked with transport. Guns and more guns arrived, from field-guns to enormous howitzers, that had rumbled down all the way from the Salient. Streams of lorries were bringing up ammunition, petrol, rations; and whole brigades of infantry, marching across the open country, had disappeared by dawn into the woods. Would the Boche "catch on"? . . .

There was but little reconnaissance for my men to carry out, since the route to No Man's Land from the wood was short and simple. And to see the country behind the enemy trenches it was necessary only to walk a mile to the reserve trench beyond the crest of the hill, where an excellent view could be obtained from an observation post.

By this time we knew the plan of the battle. At "zero" on the given day we would attack on a front of approximately ten thousand yards, with the object of breaking through the Hindenburg System into the open country. It was essential to seize on the first day the bridges over the Canal de l'Escaut and Bourlon Wood. We gathered that, if we were successful, we should endeavour to capture Cambrai and to widen the gap by rolling up the German line to the west.

On the front of our battalion, immediately to the east of Havrincourt itself and opposite Flesquieres, Harris's company and mine were detailed to assist the infantry in capturing the first system of trenches. Ward's company was reserved for the second system and for Flesquieres itself. The surviving tanks of all three companies would collect in Flesquieres for a possible farther advance to the neighbourhood of Cantaing.

On the left was "G" Battalion, with Havrincourt village as its first main objective, and on our right was "E" Battalion, beyond which were the 2nd and 3rd Brigades of the Tank Corps. There was one tank to every thirty yards of front!

Until the 17th the enemy apparently suspected nothing at all; but on the night of the 17th-18th he raided and captured some prisoners, who fortunately knew little. He gathered from them that we were ourselves preparing a substantial raid, and he brought into the line additional companies of machine-gunners and a few extra field-guns.

The 19th came with its almost unbearable suspense. We did not know what the Germans had discovered from their prisoners. We could not believe that the attack could be really a surprise. Perhaps the enemy, unknown to us, had concentrated sufficient guns to blow us to pieces. We looked up for the German aeroplanes, which surely would fly low over the wood and discover its contents. Incredibly, nothing happened. The morning passed and the afternoon—a day was never so long—and at last it was dusk.

At 8.45 p.m. my tanks began to move cautiously out of the wood and formed into column. At 9.30 p.m., with engines barely turning over, they glided imperceptibly and almost without noise towards the trenches. Standing in front of my own tanks, I could not hear them at two hundred yards.

By midnight we had reached our rendezvous behind the reserve trenches and below the crest of the slope. There we waited for an hour. The colonel arrived, and took me with him to pay a final visit to the headquarters of the battalions with which we were operating. The trenches were packed with Highlanders, and it was with difficulty that we made our way through them.

Cooper led the tanks for the last half of the journey. They stopped at the support trenches, for they were early, and the men were given hot breakfast. The enemy began some shelling on the left, but no damage was done. At 6.10 a.m. the tanks were in their allotted positions, clearly marked out by tapes which Jumbo had laid earlier in the night. . . .

I was standing on the *parados* of a trench. The movement at my feet had ceased. The Highlanders were ready with fixed bayonets. Not a gun was firing, but there was a curious murmur in the air. To right of me and to left of me in the dim light were tanks—tanks lined up in front of the wire, tanks swinging into position, and one or two belated tanks climbing over the trenches.

I hurried back to the colonel of the 6th Black Watch, and I was with him in his dugout at 6.20 a.m. when the guns began. I climbed on to the parapet and looked.

In front of the wire tanks in a ragged line were surging forward inexorably over the short down grass. Above and around them hung the blue-grey smoke of their exhausts. Each tank was followed by a bunch of Highlanders, some running forward from cover to cover, but most of them tramping steadily behind their tanks. They disappeared into the valley. To the right the tanks were moving over the crest of the shoulder of the hill. To the left there were no tanks in sight. They were already in among the enemy.

Beyond the enemy trenches the slopes, from which the German gunners might have observed the advancing tanks, were already enveloped in thick white smoke. The smoke-shells burst with a sheet of vivid red flame, pouring out blinding, suffocating clouds. It was as if flaring bonfires were burning behind a bank of white fog. Over all, innumerable aeroplanes were flying steadily to and fro.

The enemy made little reply. A solitary field-gun was endeavouring pathetically to put down a barrage. A shell would burst every few minutes on the same bay of the same trench. There were no other enemy shells that we could see. A machine-gun or two were still trained on our trenches, and an occasional vicious burst would bring the venture-some spectator scrambling down into the trench.

Odd bunches of men were making their way across what had been No Man's Land. A few, ridiculously few, wounded were coming back. Germans in twos and threes, elderly men for the most part, were wandering confusedly towards us without escort, putting up their hands in tragic and amazed resignation, whenever they saw a Highlander.

The news was magnificent. Our confidence had been justified. Everywhere we had overrun the first system and were pressing on.

A column of tanks, equipped with a strange apparatus, passed across our front to clear a lane through the wire for the cavalry.

On our left another column of tanks had already disappeared into the valley on their way to Flesquieres. It was Ward's company, but Ward was not with them. A chance bullet had killed him instantly at the head of his tanks. When we heard of his death later, the joy of victory died away. . . .

At 8 a.m. Cooper, Jumbo, a couple of runners, and myself started after our tanks. We questioned a group of Germans, who confessed that, while they had expected a raid in a day or two, they had known nothing of the tanks. We jumped down into the famous Hindenburg Line. At first we were unhappy: a machine-gun from the right was enfilading the trench and the enemy gunners were still active. We pushed along to the left, and after a slight delay came to a deep sunken road, which cut through the trench system at right angles.

We walked up the road, which in a few yards widened out. On either side were dugouts, stores, and cook-houses. Cauldrons of coffee and soup were still on the fire. This regimental headquarters the enemy had defended desperately. The trench-boards were slippery with blood, and fifteen to twenty corpses, all Germans and all bayoneted, lay strewn about the road like drunken men. '

A Highland sergeant who, with a handful of men, was now in charge of the place, came out to greet us, puffing at a long cigar. All his men were smoking cigars, and it was indeed difficult that morning to find a Highlander without a cigar. He invited us into a large chamber cut out of the rock, from which a wide staircase descended into an enormous dugout. The chamber was panelled deliciously with coloured woods and decorated with choice prints. Our host produced a bottle of good claret, and we drank to the health of the Fifty-first Division.

A few German prisoners, with a large, stiff sergeant-major at the head of them, were halted outside while their escort snatched a hurried breakfast. The sergeant-major was trying earnestly to make himself understood. He seemed to have something important to say. His escort became impatient and irritated, but, before proceeding to more summary punishment, the corporal in charge brought him to me.

The sergeant-major explained to me rapidly that the place would undoubtedly be shelled. He knew that his artillery had already registered upon it. He realised that as a prisoner he must do as he was bid, but he besought me to instruct his escort to breakfast a little farther on. His words were confirmed immediately by a large shell which exploded in the bank above our heads.

I handed over the problem to a Highland officer who had come in for shelter, and we, who had already dallied longer than we had intended, left the corpses, the wine, and the panelled chamber. . . .

In fifty yards or so the cutting came to an end, and we found ourselves in the open with a tank a hundred yards away. We walked to it and discovered my section-commander, Wyatt, with Morris, who had been hit in the shoulder. They told me that we were held up outside Flesquieres, which was being cleverly defended by field-guns. Several tanks had already been knocked out and others had nearly finished their petrol. And there was an unpleasant rumour that Marris was killed.

We took to a narrow half-completed communication trench and pushed on up the hill towards the village, meeting the survivors of two crews of another battalion, whose tanks had been knocked out in endeavouring to enter Flesquieres from the east along the crest of the ridge. The trench was being shelled. From the sound of the guns it appeared that they were only a few hundred yards away. We walked steadily up the trench until we came to the railway embankment, five or six hundred yards from the outskirts of the village, and we could go no farther, for on the other side of the embankment were the enemy and some of my tanks.

Leaving Cooper to keep in touch with the situation, I hurried back two miles to the nearest battalion headquarters with my runner. The infantry colonel would not believe my report. He was assured that everything was going well, and, according to programme, we must be well beyond Flesquieres. So I sent a couple of messages to my own colonel, whose headquarters were at those of the infantry brigade with which we were operating. I pointed out to the infantry colonel that, if we had taken Flesquieres, it was difficult to account for the machine-gun fire which apparently was coming from the neighbourhood of the village, and half-convinced, he sent his scout officer with me to find out what was happening generally, and to endeavour in particular to approach Flesquieres from the west.

We set out at once, taking our direction by a little copse which lies on the hillside a mile or so to the west of Flesquieres itself.

We were tramping across the open down, happily exposed, when the battalion scout officer was convinced by a long burst of machine-gun fire that at least the western end of the village was still held by the enemy. A spent bullet struck the heel of my boot. We hurried on with more haste than dignity, and looking towards the village, I thought I could catch the flash of the gun in the window of a large white house. A particularly unpleasant burst and the scout officer was crawling on his hands and knees towards a convenient trench.

At that moment I knew no one wiser than the scout officer, and I followed his example. For the next five minutes the man in the window of the large white house must have enjoyed himself thoroughly. The air sang with bullets. With tremendous care we continued to crawl, until after a lifetime of suspense we came to within fifty yards of the trench. I jumped up and dashed forward, the scout officer and our two runners following me, and in a moment we were lighting our pipes and feeling acutely that somebody had made a fool of us both. We parted stiffly. The scout officer trotted down the hill to solve the doubts of his battalion commander. I pushed on again towards Flesquieres, keeping to the trench until the curve of the hill interfered with the view of the machine-gunner in the large white house.

Since there was little hope that I should be allowed to approach too closely to the village, I walked to the battalion rallying-place under shelter of the railway embankment, a mile or so to the west of the section where I had been held up a few hours previously. I found a few tanks there and the survivors of some crews.

I gathered that all attacks on the village had been unsuccessful. A few field-guns, cleverly sited in ruins and behind hedges, had knocked out at least a dozen tanks. The infantry, bereft of tanks, had been unable to advance. It had been a stubborn and skilful defence.

Of my eleven tanks four had been knocked out. S., brooding over his misfortune on the Poelcapelle Road, had engaged in a duel with a field-gun; his tank had been hit fair and square by the surviving gunners, and it was thought that he and his crew were either casualties or prisoners. The majority of the remaining three crews had succeeded in getting away. F. and one of his sergeants had shown the utmost gallantry in collecting the wounded under fire and rallying the men.

The other companies of my own battalion, and that company of another battalion which had attacked Flesquieres from the east, had met a similar fate. The village was surrounded with derelict tanks, like a boar at bay with dead hounds. Harris himself, who had gone forward in one of his tanks, was missing, and it was said that he was killed.

Of my remaining seven tanks three had been ditched. Two of these unfortunates in their eagerness to kill had collided and slipped together inextricably into a trench. The remainder had rallied, and were ready, if necessary, to go forward again, but they were alarmingly short of petrol, and the tank with the supply-sledge had broken down. It was impossible, too, at this stage, to secure the necessary co-operation with the infantry, and an attack made by tanks alone would obviously fail.

We were about to start down the hill when I received a message to rally in the Grand Ravine, the title of the insignificant valley behind the front system of the German trenches. I had already sent some of my men to the regimental headquarters in the Sunken Road for food and shelter. I now ordered the remainder of my men to rally there after they had left their tanks under a skeleton guard in the Ravine itself.

An hour later we set out from the Sunken Road on our weary tramp back to the camp in Havrincourt Wood. It was late in the afternoon. We were inexpressibly tired, and of course it began to rain steadily. We plodded along, passing guns, limbers, infantry coming up to make good the victory. The five miles were like fifty, and a year at least went by before we staggered into camp, slipping feebly in the mud. . . .

The adjutant was much distressed, for he had had no news of the colonel, who apparently had left the infantry brigade headquarters early in the day. A pile of messages were waiting for him, including, to my chagrin, those which I had sent him in such haste when I had discovered that the Highlanders were held up at the railway embankment. It was after nine, and I was wondering whether or not to inform the brigade, when the colonel came in with Cooper.

The colonel, who had gone forward early in the battle, had found Cooper in the communication trench by the embankment, where I had left him with Jumbo to keep in touch with the situation. In the afternoon they had collected a few tanks and sent them into Flesquieres. The tanks had paraded through the outskirts of the village, and not a shot was fired at them; but later, when the infantry attacked again, the enemy came up from their hiding-places and let fly with machine-guns. At dusk Flesquieres was still inviolate.

We cared little about anything, except sleep. The colonel told us that we should not be required on the next day. So after a meal and a pipe we turned in for the night.

CHAPTER 11

The Battle of Cambrai—
Bourlon Wood
(November 1st to 23rd, 1917.)

In the morning we were able to look soberly at the situation. We had entered Flesquieres at dawn: the gallant, stubborn major who had defended the village so skilfully with his guns was killed in the final assault. On the left we had swept forward to the outskirts of Bourlon Wood, and tanks of "G" Battalion, including one detached tank of "D" Battalion, had actually reached Bourlon village, but we had not been able to enter the wood, for the few infantry who had reached it were utterly exhausted and the cavalry never appeared to carry on the attack. "G" Battalion had covered themselves with glory.

On the right we were everywhere through the Hindenburg System, although in places there had been bitter fighting. At Marcoing, Hamond had made a gallant but unsuccessful attempt to force a crossing by driving a tank into the canal when the enemy had blown up the bridge,[1] intending to drive a second tank over the first, but the canal was too deep. Of the cavalry which arrived later in the day a few of the Fort Garry Horse alone had been able to cross by the foot-bridges. We had not reached Cambrai—we had not even occupied Bourlon Wood—but it

---

1. It was incorrectly reported later that the tank had fallen through the bridge. I have obtained the facts from Major P. Hamond, D.S.O., M.C., who was in command of the tanks at the bridge.

was reported that there were few troops in front of us and that these were retiring northwards. It was decided, in consequence, to exploit the initial success.

We did not know it at the time, but it was too late. If only the cavalry had pushed forward into Bourlon Wood on the first day, when, according to all reports, it was held only by a bunch of machine-gunners! But it is not for a company commander to criticise, and I do not presume to do so. I am expressing merely a pious aspiration.

We ourselves had lost Ward, Harris, and a third of our men and tanks. It was almost impossible to believe that we should never see again "Roc" Ward, the great athlete, the very embodiment of energy, the skilled leader of men, the best of good fellows—and never hear again his enormous voice rolling out full-blooded instructions. As for Marris, we hoped that he might have been captured, but we feared that he was dead.[2] In my company we had lost S., a stout tank commander,[3] and several of my best drivers.

We were able, however, to form two strong companies, of which I commanded one and Cooper the other, and we set to work in the afternoon of the 21st to put our tanks again in order.

On the morning of the 22nd we received orders to collect every available tank and move to Graincourt-lez-Havrincourt, a large village two miles north of Flesquieres, with a view to attacking Bourlon Wood early on the 23rd.

We first concentrated our tanks in the Grand Ravine, and endeavoured to load up with sufficient stores for the coming battle; but supplies were hard to get, and finally we were told that a large dump would be established at the chapel on the Flesquieres road, half a mile out of Havrincourt. Foolishly credulous, I moved my tanks to the appointed place and waited for the dump to appear.

We had, however, entered the state of open warfare, and we

---

2. He was seriously wounded and captured.
3. Captured.

soon began to realise its disadvantages. My messengers scoured the countryside without success, and at last, when it grew dusk, I despaired and sent on my tanks to Graincourt, intending to arrange that my share of the dump, wherever it might be, should follow them.

I was unable to accompany my tanks, for I had been bidden to attend a Brigade Conference at this most desolate shrine. I had an hour to spare, and I spent it pleasantly enough in a neighbouring comfortable dugout, where a machine-gunner entertained me to a magnificent meal of coffee, hot salmon cakes, and plentiful bread and butter.

When I returned to the shrine, I found the battalion and company commanders of the brigade waiting for the brigade staff. It was chilly with a fluster of rain, my throat was sore, and I longed to return to the warm dugout, but I did not dare. We waited for an hour and a half until our tempers were frayed and we had finished our stock of good stories. At last an officer from the brigade happened to pass by, and, taking pity on us, he informed us casually that the conference was now in full session at Havrincourt Château. He was sorry we had not been told of the change of place. We were all so tired and cold and hungry that for a moment nobody spoke. Finally, the colonel expressed our feelings, and we tramped into Havrincourt.

It was rather a one-sided conference. Generals and people of real importance dashed in and out of rooms. I learned by cross-examination that the dump was somewhere on the road between Havrincourt and Graincourt—he was sorry we had not been told, but of course it was for company commanders to find those things out for themselves—and the colonel discovered that we should attack in the morning with the Fortieth Division.

After this interesting discussion we went out into the night and trudged painfully through Flesquieres, where the battered houses looked a little self-conscious in the dim moonlight, to Graincourt itself. The battalion advance party had discovered excellent cellars, safe though damp. I left the colonel and went in search of my tanks, hoping against hope that by some miracle they had run across the dump which was believed by the brigade staff to be somewhere east of Havrincourt.

I found my tanks where they should be, but, to my utter dismay, the only officers with them had not come with the column, and did not know whether the tanks had been "filled" or not. X., an officer from another company, who was acting temporarily as my second-in-command, was in a dugout nearby, they told me, but nobody knew where the dugout was. I began an endless and intolerable search. Every bank, road, field, or trench in the neighbourhood of Graincourt had its dugouts. There were hundreds of dugouts within quarter of a mile of my tanks.

I might have been a dog looking for its master in London; and it was of the most urgent necessity that I should know for certain what my tanks had on board. I could not even find out for myself—the tanks, quite properly, were locked. I rushed from dugout to dugout, rousing an infinite multitude of sleepy officers and men. I quartered the ground scientifically. I followed every possible clue. How could I possibly go back to the colonel and tell him that I did not know whether my tanks could fight on the morrow or not? The situation would have been ridiculous, if it had not been so serious. I nearly wept with rage.

I had searched for three hours or more and the dawn was near, when, returning in utter despair to battalion headquarters, I was greeted by a familiar voice. It was X.! Thinking that I would surely arrive by the Havrincourt Road, he had taken possession of a dugout on the side of that road, half a mile or more out of the village. My tanks had been lucky. On their way from the shrine they had by chance run right into the middle of the errant dump. Little damage had been done, and though the dump was not as large as it might have been, they had been able to take on board stores sufficient for one day's fighting.

It was no time for speeches. I reported our success to the colonel, who informed me that "zero" would be at 10.30 a.m. My composite company was detailed to co-operate with the infantry, who were attacking up the hill immediately to the west

of the wood itself. Cooper's company was to be on my left. "E"
Battalion was to advance along the ridge from the west with the
Ulster Division, and "G" Battalion was to clear the wood. On
the right, that is to the east of the wood, companies of the 2nd
Tank Brigade were to assist the infantry to capture Fontaine-
Notre-Dame, and to complete an encircling movement round
the north-eastern outskirts of the wood. We should all meet, it
was hoped, in Bourlon village. A rough diagram may make the
plan clear.

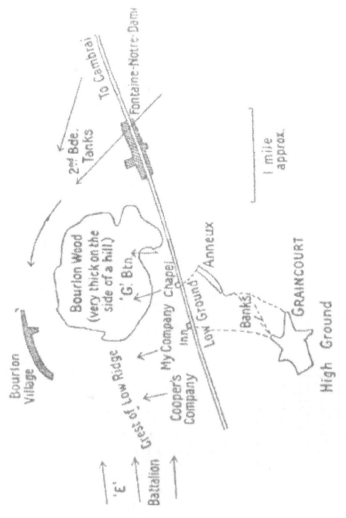

Neither my tank commanders nor I had even seen Bourlon Wood, and we knew our front line only by the map. Further, we had not met the infantry with whom we were to co-operate. These, however, were trifling difficulties. Experts who had seen the wood told me it was plain enough to the eye. I hoped for the best, wrote a few orders, and snatched an hour's sleep. . . .

Our tanks were parked in the western outskirts of Graincourt. An hour after dawn they drew clear of the village, and it may be presumed that the enemy observed them, but he displayed no interest. At dawn he had shelled a little. When dawn had passed and we had made no attack, the shelling ceased. It did not occur to him that we might attack in the middle of the morning, and he settled down to a quiet day.

At 9 a.m. my tanks were just about to move off, when I received a disturbing message from the colonel. "G" would not be able to arrive in time—their supplies had gone astray—one of my two sections was to tackle the wood itself. The situation was a trifle humorous, but I solemnly gave the necessary orders, instructing four of my tanks to assist the 40th Division in the capture of Bourlon Wood.

My tanks started for the battle, and after a little breakfast I walked to the high ground south-west of the village, and watched through my glasses the opening moves of the attack.

Across the foreground of the picture ran the great highroad from Bapaume to Cambrai. It was wide, perfectly straight, and fringed with orderly trees.

Beyond it and to my left was a low hill, which the enemy still held. Our line ran diagonally up the slope of it, and away to the west we were on the ridge. Immediately in front of me on the hillside was the great dark mass of Bourlon Wood, square and impenetrable, covering the highest point of the hill and stretching over the skyline to the farther slope, which we could not see. The wood dominated the whole countryside, and beyond it there was nothing but low open country, extending to the marshes of the Scarpe. We could not live north of Havrincourt while the enemy held the wood, and if we captured the wood there was nothing to prevent us from sweeping northwards to the Scarpe or westwards into Cambrai. At the moment our line ran along the southern outskirts of the wood and to the south of Fontaine, which the enemy held in force.

At 10.30 a.m. the barrage fell and we could see it climb, like a living thing, through the wood and up the hillside, a rough line of smoke and flame. On the hillside to the left of the wood we could mark the course of the battle,—the tanks with tiny flashes darting from their flanks—clumps of infantry following in little rushes—an officer running in front of his men, until suddenly he crumpled up and fell, as though some unseen hammer had struck him on the head—the men wavering in the face of machine-gun fire and then spreading out to surround the gun—the wounded staggering painfully down the hill, and the stretcher-bearers moving backwards and forwards in the wake of the attack—the aeroplanes skimming low along the hillside, and side-slipping to rake the enemy trenches with their guns.

We watched one tank hesitate before it crossed the skyline and our hearts went out to the driver in sympathy. He made his decision, and the tank, brown against the sky, was instantly encircled by little puffs of white smoke, shells from the guns on the reverse slope. The man was brave, for he followed the course of a trench along the crest of the hill. My companion uttered a low exclamation of horror. Flames were coming from the rear of the tank, but its guns continued to fire and the tank continued to move. Suddenly the driver must have realised what was happening. The tank swung towards home. It was too late. Flames burst from the roof and the tank stopped, but the sponson doors never opened and the crew never came out. . . . When I left my post half an hour later the tank was still burning. . . .

At noon I determined to push forward into the wood and discover what had happened to my tanks. We skirted the village, walked along a sunken road lined by dugouts, and started to cross the low ground between us and the road. I at once began to wonder whether it was not perhaps a little early yet to go forward. The path to the highroad was the object of direct or

150

indirect machine-gun fire, and an officer, who was sitting in a trench, told me cheerfully that Cooper and Smith, his second-in-command, had already been hit by chance bullets.

We pushed on, however, to the inn on the highroad, and as the road was being shelled, we took to the ditch until a shell, bursting in the ditch itself, persuaded us to use the road. We did not get very far, and soon we returned to the top of the bank at the side of the sunken road. By this time "G" Battalion were beginning to arrive and their tanks were moving across to Anneux Chapel.

After lunch I went forward again and reached a clearing on the south side of the wood, where the tanks had been ordered to rally. The enemy must have realised our intention, for the clearing was being shelled most systematically. The only tank in the clearing belonged to another battalion. The crew, realising their danger and a little lost, evacuated their tank and joined me in a small quarry where I had temporarily taken cover.

I left the quarry during a lull and walked up a sunken road into the wood, but I soon realised, first, that I should never find my tanks by tramping after them, and second, that I should be infinitely happier in my quarry. So I returned and spent the next hour in watching the rallying-place and in moving at intervals from one side of the quarry to the other. The news was moderately good. The 40th Division, assisted by my few tanks, had driven the astonished Germans to the further fringes of the wood, and were now mopping up a few pockets of the enemy who were still holding out in the vain hope that they would be rescued by counter-attacks. But on the right—so I was told by two immaculate young cavalry subalterns who were reconnoitring forward—Fontaine was defying our sternest efforts.

About three I saw a couple of tanks cross the road at the inn, three-quarters of a mile away. So, as one shell had already burst on the lip of the quarry, I hastened to the cross-roads at Anneux Chapel on my way back to Graincourt. At the cross-roads I met an infantry battalion coming up to complete the clearance of the north-west corner of the wood. The colonel asked me whether my tanks would assist him. I told him that they were already in action. It was indeed a pity that "G" Battalion, which did not arrive until after the main portion of the wood was in our hands, had not been held in reserve for such an emergency.[4]

I reached battalion headquarters about 4 p.m. Both Bourlon village and Fontaine-Notre-Dame were holding out. It was reported, too, that "E" Battalion had suffered very heavily.

I walked along to my dugout, where I discovered that the majority of my tanks had already returned in safety. They had realised the danger of rallying at the clearing and had come back direct to their starting-point, followed all the way by the German gunners.

Two of the tanks, commanded by Lloyd and Hemming, had successfully crossed the ridge and entered Bourlon village, but the infantry were prevented by the intense machine-gun fire from occupying the place. Two more of my tanks had experienced such concentrated machine-gun fire themselves that every man in them was wounded by flying splinters, including Wyatt, who had commanded his section from a tank.

All the tanks had done their work well, having assisted the infantry to the limit of their advance. All of them reported that they had been given excellent targets, while our own casualties were astonishingly light. For us it was a most satisfactory day, spoilt only by the fact that Wyatt and Cooper had been wounded.

My last tank had just come in when the enemy, furious at the loss of the wood, began to shell Graincourt with "heavy stuff." The colonel, realising what must happen, had already departed for the calm of Havrincourt Wood, while we were out of the danger area. To the accompaniment of distant crashes we sat down to our evening meal. . . .

---

4. But it was "G" Battalion that captured the wood a year later.

CHAPTER 12

The Battle of Cambrai—
Gouzeaucourt
(NOVEMBER 24TH TO DECEMBER 1ST, 1917.)

It was pleasant enough to wake up in the musty candle-lit dugout, sniff at the frying bacon, and murmur—

"Yesterday we helped the 40th Division to take Bourlon Wood. Two of my tanks crossed the ridge and entered Bourlon village. All my tanks have returned. A thoroughly sound and altogether satisfactory day's work. . . ."

The morning was fine and fresh, with a nip in the air. We breakfasted cheerily, and then, after a last look at the great wood, unchanged and imperturbable, I started to tramp the six miles back to Havrincourt Wood, leaving the others to follow with those tanks that had not come in until dusk on the preceding day. It was an exhilarating walk through the ruins of Havrincourt, past the enormous crater in the road, over the old trenches, and through Trescault, since transport and troops were pouring forward.

But in the afternoon we were told that the battle of the 23rd had been a most incomplete and melancholy success. "E" Battalion, which had attacked along the ridge from the direction of Mœuvres, had lost the majority of their tanks. Five of their tanks were still missing, and their casualties had been ghastly. On our right the fighting had been heavy indeed. Fontaine had remained in German hands, and the 2nd Tank Brigade had been quite unable, in consequence, to complete their enveloping movement. Finally, at dawn the enemy had counter-attacked and retaken the northern half of the wood itself.

It is not for me to relate the history of the pitiful struggle during the next few days, when the great wood was drenched with gas and half-destroyed by shells. I did not see Bourlon again until exactly a year later, when I passed to the north of it on my way from Arras to Cambrai for a court-martial. If only the cavalry could have taken it on the 20th, according to plan, when it was defended merely by a handful of machine-guns!

We began to make ourselves thoroughly comfortable in Havrincourt Wood, and "temporary structures" arose with astounding rapidity. My own Armstrong Hut, which had followed me for four months like a faithful dog, arrived at last, together with certain kit which had been left at Meaulte, so that we might not be over-burdened in our pursuit of the enemy through the streets of Cambrai.

We felt a trifle guilty in our luxury as we watched the grim infantry going forward to the dark terrors of Bourlon, and my men in their kindness would give them part of their rations, for, during these days, the rations of the infantry were painfully short. But war is war, and, putting Bourlon out of our minds, we made an expedition to Bapaume, had tea at the officers' club, a haircut and a shampoo, bought potatoes and eggs and dined sumptuously.

Only an inspection on the 29th depressed us, for nothing can be more depressing than an inspection. As usual, we had such a lengthy wait before the arrival of the general that, with all due respect, we thought of little except the end of his speech. And, if we had been Romans, we should have cried out in horror, for, during the parade, an enemy aeroplane brought down in flames one of our observation balloons. It was a most inauspicious omen, and that evening I went to bed with an unquiet mind. . . .

We had received orders to entrain within the week at Fins, a railhead about three miles south of Metz-en-Couture, and we had been preparing our tanks for the journey. None of them were now in a proper condition to fight, and most of them needed a thorough overhaul before we could attempt even the short trek to Fins with any feeling of security. Our work had been delayed further by a temporary stoppage in the supply of spare parts. This, however, gave us little cause for anxiety, since there was a whole week in front of us.

Early in the morning of the 30th, Battalion Headquarters, with all our motorcars and lorries, left Havrincourt Wood for Meaulte, our destination and rumoured winter quarters.

If my narrative is to be truthful, I must confess that I was asleep in bed when the colonel departed, and that we did not breakfast until 9.30 a.m. We had barely sat down when we noticed that strange things were happening, and we walked out of the wood into the open to investigate. We could hear distinctly bursts of machine-gun fire, although the line should have been six miles away at least. German field-gun shells—we could not be mistaken—were falling on the crest of a hill not three-quarters of a mile from the camp. On our left, that is to the north, there was heavy gun fire. On our right, in the direction of Gouzeaucourt, shells were falling, and there were continuous bursts of machine-gun fire.

We had not fully realised what was happening, when a number of wounded infantrymen came straggling past. I questioned them. They told me that the enemy was attacking everywhere, that he had broken through near Gouzeaucourt, capturing many guns, and was, to the best of their belief, still advancing.

This was cheerful news and made me think hard. Look at the rough diagram following—Our line on the 29th formed a bulge or salient. I knew the enemy had attacked at A and had broken through. I suspected from the heavy gun fire that he was attacking at B. If these two attacks were successful, our troops inside the bulge would be surrounded and the two attacking forces would meet in the neighbourhood of the + on the diagram.[1]

---

1. It was known later that the two attacking forces were instructed to meet at Metz, a mile or so from my camp.

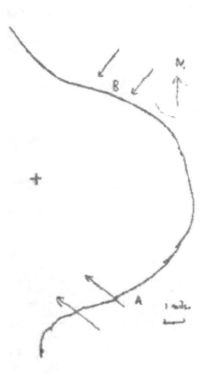

But the **+** also represented my own position on the morning of the 30th, with a batch of tanks in every stage of disrepair and the colonel by now at Meaulte.

I hurried to the camp of "E" Battalion, a hundred yards away, but that battalion was temporarily under the command of a captain, as the colonel and the three company commanders had preceded their tanks in the move to Meaulte. "G" Battalion, the third battalion of the brigade, was encamped on the farther side of the wood, four miles distant, and I had no time to go and see who was in command of it. Besides, the colonel's car had disappeared with the colonel, and I had no transport except three battered motorcycles.

So I assumed command of the two battalions and gave instructions for all tanks that were in any way mobile to be filled and loaded. This took a little time, as the petrol dump was some distance away, and we had no lorries. Then, as it seemed to me that if we were about to fight—and I certainly did not intend to withdraw—we should probably be surrounded, I collected those officers and men who were not actually needed to fight the tanks, and ordered Field, whom I placed in charge, to march them back to Royaulcourt, where I hoped that they would be out of the way.

After I had made these preliminary arrangements I started with Spencer, my servant, in search of the nearest Divisional Headquarters. I had then no idea which or where it was. By this time all the roads into Metz were blocked with transport of every description. The enemy gunners were endeavouring to register on the Trescault road, but they were shooting consistently short or over, and a couple of "shorts" gave Spencer and myself the fright of our lives.

In Metz we discovered the headquarters of the Guards Division. I reported to the Divisional Commander that I was the proud possessor of an odd collection of second-hand tanks. He was not much impressed, but wired the news to his corps and told me to wait for orders.

The cross-roads in Metz about 11 a.m. on the 30th November 1917 would have gratified any German. In spite of the desultory shelling there was, of course, no panic, but the thick confused stream of traffic pouring westwards was unpleasant. It reminded me too vividly of Estrees on the afternoon of Le Cateau, three years before. Mingled with the transport were odd groups of men, the survivors of batteries, stragglers who had lost their units, walking wounded—bitter, because they felt that this sudden counter-attack should have been prevented, and sullen, because although they realised that Metz was no place for men who could fight, they did not know what to do or where to go.

There is nothing so tragical as the bewilderment of a broken army. For every man who retires because he is afraid, there are a thousand who retire because they are not organised to advance.

The A.P.M. proved himself a man indeed. One minute he would be out in the traffic lashing the drivers with a stinging tongue, until, literally frightened, they would perform marvels of driving, and so disentangle a block of traffic. Another minute he would drive a bunch of stragglers into the courtyard, consigning them with deep oaths to the lowest hell. Or he would interrupt passionately with a wealth of curses a gunner subaltern with three men, who, with tears in his voice, was trying to explain that they alone of his battery had survived, and that they had at least saved the breech-blocks and the sights. The A.P.M. was a huge man with mad blue eyes, but, thanks to his intolerant fury, the stream of traffic continued to flow, and no possible fighting man passed beyond Metz. My own servant, who had lost me in the crowd, was arrested as a straggler.

At about 12 noon a message came through from the Corps—

One battalion of tanks will attack Gouzeaucourt from direction of Fins, and one battalion of tanks from direction of Heudecourt.[2]

The general considered that this message was an order for me to attack with my two battalions, but as both Fins and Heudecourt were further from me than Gouzeaucourt, which the enemy had taken, I read the message as a piece of information.

Probably two battalions of the 2nd Brigade were about to advance. The general, however, desired me to attack.[3]

I walked back to the wood, and found that in my absence the tanks had been drawn up in line at intervals of one hundred yards to defend the Trescault-Metz road. This unnecessary deployment caused delay, but by 1 p.m. "E" Battalion had moved off to attack Gouzeaucourt from the west, and the tanks of my own battalion to attack the village by the shortest possible route. I did not know how many of the tanks would reach Gouzeaucourt. They were all quite decrepit.

When I had seen my tanks under way I returned to Metz, reported, and waited for further orders. The situation was dis-

2. I quote from memory, but I am certain of the words "will attack."
3. It was in fact intended to inform the general that two battalions of the 2nd Tank Brigade would attack from the directions indicated.

tinctly obscure. We knew that the enemy had not been able to debouch from Gouzeaucourt, and soon we learnt that the Irish Guards had retaken the village at the point of the bayonet, but the corps told us that enemy cavalry were said to be in Heudecourt, a village south of Fins, and well behind our line. The news from the north was reassuring. Apparently the enemy attack on that flank had been broken.

The tanks of my own battalion had arrived at Gouzeaucourt too late to assist the Irish Guards, but the sight of the tanks on the ridge to the west of the village may have assisted in the discouragement of the enemy, since he made no further effort to advance, although, if he had known it, there was little enough in front of him. Finally, acting under the orders of the infantry commanders on the spot, my tanks withdrew to the neighbourhood of Gouzeaucourt Wood, half-way between Gouzeaucourt and Metz. Of "E" Battalion I had heard nothing as yet.

I went back to camp, where I found that steps were being taken to send rations out to the crews. Just before dusk I received a message from the colonel, instructing me not to become involved and to report to Colonel Hankey commanding "G" Battalion. So Jumbo and I, by now more than weary, tramped round the wood, and after an hour's hard walking came to the "G" Battalion bivouac. I explained the situation to the colonel, who was most kind and understanding, and informed him that I had placed myself under the orders of the Guards Division, and proposed to continue to offer that division any help that was possible. Colonel Hankey agreed.

While I was with Colonel Hankey, our brigade-major arrived and told us that a lot of nice sound tanks were coming up for our use. He was astonished that I had more than twenty mobile tanks under my command. It seemed that in an official return to the brigade we had shown only one tank as "fit for action." However, he appreciated the course we had taken, and confirmed Colonel Hankey's instruction that I should continue to operate with the Guards Division.

I trudged back to camp through the mud, and, after a little

food, finding that no orders had come for me, I walked into Metz, which was by now free of traffic.

The general was arranging a counter-attack at dawn on Gonnelieu and the ridge to the south of it. Gonnelicu was a small village on high ground commanding Gouzeaucourt, and its recapture would be the first step towards regaining the valuable ground that we had lost. To the south of Gouzeaucourt a dismounted cavalry division had managed to form some sort of line, and this division would co-operate with the Guards Division in the counter-attack proposed.

The general and his G. S.O.I, were determining the form which the counter-attack should take. We were in a dim and bare schoolroom. The candles on the general's table threw the rest of the room into deep shadow. Outside there was low eager talking in the courtyard, the tramp of a sentry, the rhythmical rattle of a limbered wagon with horses trotting, a man singing quietly, the sudden impertinent roar of a motorcycle, the shouting of a driver, and then the silly whine and the clear reverberating crash of a shell bursting by night among houses. The general was speaking evenly, without emphasis. . . .

I was called into consultation. Apparently a battalion of tanks from the 2nd Brigade now lay at Gouzeaucourt Wood, ready to assist the Guards. We discussed the counter-attack, and a decision was made. It was becoming dangerously late. The staff-officer hurriedly began to write orders. I left the schoolroom and started to walk up the hill through the frozen night to Gouzeaucourt Wood.

Outside the wood in a rough plantation I discovered the headquarters of a brigade of Guards, and with them the colonel of the tank battalion, with whom I arranged that my tanks should attack Gonnelieu itself, while his tanks should advance with the infantry against the ridge to the south of that village.

A message came through to me from the captain temporarily in command of "E" Battalion that he had lost touch with his tanks, and did not know where they were now. I was in consequence forced to rely upon "D" Battalion alone.

I found my section commanders, and instructed them to move their tanks round Gouzeaucourt Wood, and concentrate to the east of it, so that they could go forward to their final positions prior to the attack without difficulty. I foolishly did not make certain myself that they had sufficient petrol for the fight.

Then I walked over the short grass round the northern outskirts of the wood in search of another brigade headquarters, and ran them to ground in a large tent pitched in the open on the downs. Luckily for me it was a clear night, with a moon and no clouds. The brigade commander had not yet received his orders, and he told me to find the colonel of a certain battalion of Grenadier Guards, warn him that we should make a counterattack on Gonnelieu at dawn, and arrange, as far as was possible, pending orders from the division, the lines on which my tanks would assist.

I tramped on over the cold bare downs—it was now about midnight—until, to my relief, I struck the sunken road coming from Trescault. I followed it, and, just short of the first houses in Gouzeaucourt, I found the headquarters for which I was looking in a dugout at the side of the road.

The colonel had just returned from an inspection of his outposts. The division on the left was working forward from the north towards Gonnelieu, and the colonel had been listening to and watching the enemy machine-guns. The village was thick with them. It was doubtful if the division would be able to advance farther.

I gave him my message, and after a few minutes' discussion he sat down to write his orders. The colonel of the Welsh Guards arrived, and together they analysed the situation. ... I hesitate to write of the Guards, and I dare not describe the scene.

I was about to go back to my tanks when two of my officers suddenly appeared, bringing the worst possible news. The tanks had run short of petrol! Their commanders in the hurry and excitement of the day naturally had not realised how much they had used. And it had not been intended that after they had entered Gouzeaucourt they should withdraw all the way to

Gouzeaucourt Wood. There was no transport. The lorries were with the colonel. In any case it was too late. And the attack would take place in five hours—the Guards were relying on our tanks—Gonnelieu was crammed full of machine-guns. The colonel had just said so.

I felt sick and frightened. My mind flew back to a morning when I was late for school and stood outside the door, desperate and trembling, miserably wondering whether it would be worse to go in and face the smiles of the class and the cutting words of the master, or to stop away for the whole day on the plea that I was really ill. The Guards were relying on our tanks, and Gonnelieu was crammed full of machine-guns!

A moment before I had listened in apprehension to the shells bursting along the sunken road. Now, throwing my officers a few brief instructions, I dashed up the road, and regardless of shells or anything else, I ran at top speed back to the Brigade Headquarters in the large tent, two miles away. It was an eternity before I came choking to the tent and rushed to the telephone. I called up the colonel of the other tank battalion and besought him to send at least a section against Gonnelieu, for I did not know how many of my tanks would have sufficient petrol to enter the battle. He replied that his tanks had already started for their final positions, but he promised that he would do what he could.

I explained the situation shortly to the brigadier and then hurried off to my tanks. I found the crews endeavouring, with little success, to siphon the petrol from one tank to another. At last, when it had become too late to do more, I sent off those tanks which had any petrol at all in them, hoping that by some miracle they would be able to join in the attack. I had done all I could. I slunk back to Brigade Headquarters and waited in anguish for the dawn. The downs were lonely and cruel that night.

There was nothing of a barrage, for our heavy guns were in the hands of the enemy or dismantled in Gouzeaucourt or without ammunition. A slight bombardment and the Guards stormed up the hill. No news came to us at Brigade Headquarters, but we could hear with terrible distinctness the never ending chatter of the enemy machine-guns. We tried to deceive ourselves and to imagine that these machine-guns were our own, but we knew our deceit, and we knew, too, that if we had carried the hill and were fighting on the farther slopes of it, we should hear little of the machine-guns.

About 7.30 a.m.—it was the morning of December 1st—the brigadier and I tramped over the hillside to the sunken road at Gouzeaucourt, passing several machine-gun pits cunningly camouflaged. We crossed the ridge, and as we began to descend I saw for the first time Gouzeaucourt, a cheerful little town in the valley, and Gonnelieu, a jumbled village set on the hillside beyond with the white stones conspicuous in its cemetery, and a church. In a large field below us and on the edge of Gouzeaucourt were hutments, shelled and deserted. They had been left in a hurry, and before one hut was a table laid for breakfast with a real tablecloth. Over Gouzeaucourt and in front of Gonnelieu shrapnel was bursting lazily.

The sunken road was full of wounded. We came to the headquarters which I had visited. They were occupied now by another battalion of Grenadier Guards. For the battalion which I had met in the middle of the night were fighting desperately in the cemetery at Gonnelieu.

The news was disquieting. The Grenadier Guards had not been able to force an entry into the village, while the Welsh Guards on their right had made little progress. Both battalions had lost practically all their officers. They had been withdrawn and replaced by fresh battalions. The dismounted cavalry had managed to establish themselves on the ridge with the help of tanks, but they could make no farther advance until Gonnelieu was cleared. Tanks could be seen on the slopes of the hill. Two, silhouetted against the skyline, were burning fiercely. Of my own tanks nothing could be heard. The colonel was doing valiant things in Gonnelieu.

Then came a grave rumour: "The colonel is badly wounded!" but a moment later he walked into the dugout, his arm in a rough sling and his face drawn with pain. They persuaded him against his will to go to the main dressing station. . . . The wounded were streaming past, walking wounded and stretcher after stretcher.

I left the dugout and went in search of my tanks, but there was no sign of them. They were not to be traced, although I walked down to the Villers-Plouich road, and later, coming back up the hill, climbed a little mound and scanned the opposite slope with my glasses. Certain tanks to the right of Gonnelieu obviously belonged to that other battalion. Perhaps a report had reached our camp at Havrincourt Wood, which was, in fact, nearer to Gouzeaucourt than was Metz-en-Couture.

So at last I turned, and more weary than I can describe— since, like many others, I had been more or less on my feet for twenty-four hours—I trudged up the sunken road and, taking a last look at Gonnelieu and at Gouzeaucourt, struck out across the downs to Havrincourt Wood, a matter of three miles.

At the camp there was still no news. It was now about 11 a.m. I breakfasted and turned in, telling Jumbo to call me if any message came from the tanks.

I awoke at three. The crews had reported. The tanks had not been able to climb out of a sunken road for want of petrol, and had never entered the battle. Of "E" Battalion there was still no news. Tanks from that other battalion had assisted the Guards— that was a little satisfying,—but the Guards had failed to storm Gonnelieu.

I walked out of the wood into the open. A few centuries ago I had stood on the same spot and wondered why there were bursts of machine-gun fire in the direction of Gouzeaucourt.

CHAPTER 13

Havrincourt to Harrow
(DECEMBER 1ST, 1917, TO JANUARY 31ST, 1918.)

We were not yet out of the wood. I was smoking a pipe in contemplative solitude behind my hut after an excellent little dinner, when, without warning, there was a shattering explosion. A shell had burst a few yards away in the bushes, and a moment later a couple fell in the farther end of the camp. Evidently the Germans wished us to remember the 1st December 1917. I shouted to the men to take cover in the tanks, since inside or under a tank is a place of comparative safety. For twenty minutes the shelling continued, and then it stopped as suddenly as it had begun. We investigated the damage. One man had been killed and three wounded.

I ordered the men to sleep under cover that night, so that, although our corner of the wood was shelled four times before dawn, there were no further casualties. I passed the night in a shallow dugout, and I was glad in the morning that I had not returned to my hut, for, when I went to it before breakfast, I found that a scrap of shell had drilled a neat hole through my bed.

Early on the 2nd I received orders from everybody, and if I had obeyed them all "D" Battalion would have remained where it was, entrained at the Fins railhead, and moved to Dessart Wood on the route from Metz to Fins. So I went in a "box-body," which I had commandeered, to seek counsel of Colonel Hankey. I tracked him from the wood to Fins, and found him there at a ruined "cinema" in company with our brigade-major, from whom I learnt that our display of tanks on the hills to the west of Gouzeaucourt had been more valuable than I had realised.

I suggested to the brigade-major that I should withdraw the battalion to Ytres, the railhead at which we had detrained when we had first arrived in this troublesome neighbourhood.[1] We knew the route to Ytres; there were two ramps at the railhead; we should be out of everybody's way; accommodation there should be ample for the battalion. He agreed to my suggestion, and gave me definite orders to move as soon as possible.

With a light heart—for it was a splendid sunny day—I hurried back to discover the battalion plunged into the deepest melancholy. The rations had not arrived! That on one day there should be a shortage of rations might seem to the civilian reader a commonplace of war, and he may marvel when I state with an eye to the whole truth that this was in very fact the first occasion, while I was with my company of tanks, on which rations had definitely not appeared. And the reason for it, as we learnt afterwards, was ample. The enemy had begun to shell the railhead at Bapaume with a long-range gun, and our particular lorries with rations on board had been blown into matchboard and scraps of metal.

We repaired the deficiency by a raid on a dump, which I had noticed, and were packing up when the enemy again began to shell our pet corner of the wood—this time with a high-velocity gun. Thus encouraged, the battalion was ready to move in record time. In the middle of it all our rations arrived: the equipment officer, undeterred by long-range guns, had secured fresh rations and fresh lorries.

I went ahead of the tanks in my "box-body," and that night the men slept peacefully in the brickyard at Ytres, the officers in a large "Adrian" hut at the R.E. dump, and I, who had made friends while searching for billets with an admirable and elderly subaltern in charge of a Labour Detachment, after playing bridge successfully in a hut with a real fireplace, went to bed in

1. See chapter 10

a real bed.

On the 3rd we regained touch once more with the outside world. Four days' mail arrived, sundry foodstuffs, and a new pair of light corduroy breeches; while the colonel motored up from Meaulte to see us, and gave us most gratifying messages from the brigade commander. On the 4th, since I was still without transport, I tramped five miles across the downs in deliciously bright and frosty weather to Fins, and arranged for the entrainment of certain tanks.

That evening after mess I was sitting with the elderly subaltern over a huge fire. We were discussing in extreme comfort painting, the education of artistic daughters, and the merits and demerits of the Slade School. Suddenly we heard a musical and distant wail, something flew past the window, and there was a wee "plonk."

"A dud!" said I wearily.

"They've never shelled the place before," he asserted with confidence.

"It was rather near," I murmured.

We were silent, and then once again we heard the musical wail, which this time was followed by an overwhelming explosion. The hut trembled, and clods of frozen earth rattled sharply on the roof.

He rushed off to his *coolies*, and I came back to the fire after I had given instructions to my officers; but another "dud" fell within a few yards of the hut, so I determined to explore the farther end of the dump, but, of course, when I was walking sedately away, I slipped on the ice and took most of the skin off my thigh.

At last the shelling stopped. We again returned to the fire and drank hot cocoa. I undressed and went to bed, daring the German to do his worst. I was dozing, when a shell burst just outside the hut. The side of the hut appeared to bulge inwards, everything fell off the shelves, and a large piece of frozen earth flew through the window. It was too much, and no man is a hero in silk pyjamas. I wrapped myself in a British warm and ran out into the night—the shell had fallen ten yards from the hut. Another came. I stumbled into a trench, but it was so cold and humiliating there that I returned to my hut, dressed rapidly, and went to spend the night with a friend who lived at the opposite end of the dump. We had just begun to make some tea, when the German gunner lengthened his range. We might have remained where we were, but we were too tired and annoyed. We decided to take a drink off the town major.

In the morning we moved to the brickyard half a mile away. I was making for my new quarters after a little dinner with the town major, and looking forward to a quiet night, when a shell burst in front of me. I ran to the brickyard, but my quarters then were under eighteen feet of solid brick, so, although we were shelled again during the night, we slept most peacefully.

On the 6th I managed to entrain the remainder of my tanks at Fins by anticipating another battalion who were a little late. Then I started off on a motorcycle to warn Battalion Headquarters that the tanks would arrive a day before their scheduled time, but I had magneto trouble at Haplincourt. I completed the journey in accordance with the custom of the country, by securing a lorry lift to Bapaume, a lift in a car from Bapaume to Albert, and then walking to the camp at Meaulte.

Even when the tanks had been detrained at Le Plateau, the most desolate railhead on earth, and driven to the chilliest of tankodromes by the ruins of Bécordel-Bécourt, half an hour's walk from the camp, we were not rid of the war. The line to which we had fallen back was none too stable, and to strengthen it tanks were posted at intervals behind the guns. It was intended that these tanks should break the enemy attack, demoralise their infantry, and act as rallying-points for our own men. This curious method of defence was never tested, perhaps luckily, but we were compelled to take our turn in providing garrisons or crews. Other tanks, manned by my men, were used at night to drag back heavy guns, which had been abandoned in the first flurry of the counter-attack on November 30th, and were now just behind our advanced posts.

During these days I was again in command of the battalion, for the colonel was on leave, and twice it was necessary for me to drive over the Somme battlefield by Peronne to Fins. It was freezing hard, and the wind cut to the bone.

At last we were free even of these duties, and were able to spend our time in repairing a job lot of fifty old tanks, in starting their engines frequently to avoid the effects of frost, and in making ourselves thoroughly comfortable. And we began to look for pigs.

The camp on the hillside above the village of Meaulte at first consisted of large huts, but like good soldiers we added to it as usual a variety of "temporary structures." I could not be parted from my Armstrong Hut; and Forbes, my orderly- room sergeant, would have wept bitter tears if that hut which a party from Behagnies had found "somewhere in France"—it was a dark and shapeless erection—had not provided shelter for himself and his papers.

The camp had its advantages. The canteen at Meaulte was then the finest in France. Albert, within walking distance, had revived, and its inhabitants were fast returning to set up shop and make much money out of the British troops. Amiens and all its luxuries was only an hour away for those who possessed cars. We had something of a football ground.

Then in the colonel's absence I was able to use the colonel's horses, and with the doctor or the adjutant, we would canter over the downs and pay visits to those other battalions who were in huts on the edge of the Happy Valley above Bray.

As Christmas drew near our search for pigs became feverish, but at last we found them, and the beer too arrived; so that we were able to give to each man, in addition to his rations of beef and plum-pudding, one pound of roast pork and one gallon of beer.

Of Christmas Day I have probably a clearer recollection than many. We began badly, for half the battalion paraded in one part of the camp and half in another, and the *padre* was in doubt. Finally we combined and shivered through the service. A little later came the men's dinner. The colonel and his company commanders started to go round, but there had been some slight anticipation. ... .We went away cautiously.

In the evening there was high revelry, speechifying, shouting, bursts of crude song. Some wild spirits endeavoured to abstract the captured field-guns which "G" Battalion displayed temptingly outside its huts, but "G" Battalion was not convivial on this matter and talked sternly of fights. This was sobering, for the last thing we wanted was to fight with our most excellent friends— so, feeling that our joke had been a trifle misunderstood, we drank with them instead. But somebody a night or two later ran the guns down into the village from under the noses of "G" Battalion. It was a pity, because the porridge was cold.

There are other stories about that Christmas which will be told time and again in the mess. You will never hear from me what the old soldier said to the brigade commander in the streets of Meaulte.

We had thought that we should not move again during the winter, and we were just beginning to settle down when a rearrangement of units in the Tank Corps and the arrival of certain new battalions in France unsettled the situation.

You will remember that after the battle of Arras, "D" Battalion, which had now become the 4th Battalion, "E" (5th), and "G" (7th) Battalions, formed the 1st Brigade. To the three brigades in the Tank Corps a Fourth and Fifth were now added. The 4th Brigade was commanded by Brigadier-General E. B. Hankey, D.S.O., and included at first only the 4th and 5th Battalions. This brigade was ordered to billet in the old Blangy area, and one of the brand-new battalions was instructed to take over our huts.

I must state with regret that the advance party of this new battalion was a shade tactless. After all, we were "D" Battalion, formed out of the old "D" Company, the senior Tank company in France. Further, every officer and man of us had volunteered for the job. We were inclined to look for a little respect, perhaps even a little awe, from these newcomers. Now during the fourteen months of the battalion's existence the carpenters had been busy. Forbes, my orderly-room sergeant, had a collapsible desk. There were racks, card-tables, special chairs, fittings of one kind or another which, since we were then allowed generous transport, and the tanks can carry much, we took with us from place to place. These cherished possessions were claimed by the advance party as billet fixtures to be left with the huts, which had been more bare than a dry bone when we had first come to them. Finally, the advance party had the temerity to claim the colonel's own wine-cupboard.

That was enough. We could not suffer this attempted rape of our colonel's cherished possession without some forcible protest. Of what actually occurred I know little, for I was laid low in my hut with a bout of trench fever. My memory cannot be trusted, and the strange things which I heard may be attributed to delirium. I imagined that extra lorries were obtained, and everything possible loaded upon them. I dreamt that during these last days there was no lack of firewood. Half unconscious, I thought of men plying axes.

They put me into an ambulance and sent me to the Casualty Clearing Station at Dernancourt, where my nurse was even more charming than nurses usually are. It was a pleasant ward, and for company there was an ancient A. P.M. with a fund of excellent stories, and a succession of unlucky but cheerful flying men. When we became convalescent the A. P.M. and I would stroll through the snow to the hospital trains that came into the siding, but we decided that we preferred our own nurses.

We could not hope to remain for long in that delicious paradise, and, although we tried hard, the south of France was beyond our reach. The car came for me on a dull liverish morning, and I had to say goodbye. There are lesser tragedies, which leave a wound.

I found my company luxuriating at Auchy-lez-Hesdin, the most desirable village in the Blangy area. It was full of good billets and estaminets, and there was an officers' tea-room where the law of the A. P.M. did not run. Many of us decided that it was indeed time for us to brush up our French. We had neglected it too long.

Soon the company became amazingly smart. This happy state may have been the natural result of careful inspections and concentration upon drill, but I am myself inclined to think that credit should be given to the far-seeing Frenchman who established a cotton-mill in Auchy and employed a number of girls with large admiring eyes.

You will remember that during the last season at Blangy-sur-Ternoise the company had made a name for itself in the football world, and we did not intend to allow this reputation to slip away. No Selection Committee discussed with more care, insight, and real knowledge of the game the merits of each candidate for the company eleven than that over which I had the honour to preside, and as a very natural result we won during the month of January a series of overwhelming victories. But I have not yet decided to my satisfaction whether Spencer was more useful in the centre or on the wing.

And B., a major from the Glasgow Yeomanry, who was attached to the company for instruction, took charge when football was impossible, and led the company with intolerable energy over many weary miles of country.

In the evening he was the life and soul of the mess. We still had that piano which had been taken forward in the first lorry that ever attempted the Puisieux-le-Mont road from Albert to Achiet-le-Grand after the enemy had retired in March. Our guest-nights were unequalled. Who could ever forget our "Beauty Chorus," with B. as "*prima* ballerina," or Happy Fanny singing a song in his more cheerful mood?

There was only one little cloud. The Russian Armies, infected with strange enthusiasms, had left the battlefield. The Italians had their backs to the wall. We heard rumours that the French Armies were sullen and despairing. It was certain that the enemy would make one last enormous effort before the tardy Americans arrived. We were, of course, confident—no man in France even for a moment considered the possibility of ultimate defeat—and we thought that it would not be difficult to break the enemy attack, however determined it might prove to be.

We practised the defence of Auchy, though we thought such precautions to be far-fetched; but it was a more serious matter when we were told that, instead of wintering at Auchy, it would be necessary for the battalion to move up to the neighbourhood of Peronne, where our nights might be interrupted by bombs and shells.

But it was under the command of B. that the company left Auchy for the Fifth Army area. One gloomy day I was ordered home with other company commanders to help form new battalions at the celebrated Bovington Camp. The orders came suddenly, although they had not been unexpected. On the 31st January I handed over the command of the company to B., and the parting was the less bitter because I knew that the company would be safe and happy under him.

I drove away from Auchy on a sunny morning with frost in the air and snow on the ground. I caught the afternoon boat. I could not forget that great farewell dinner, but the sea was kind.

My thoughts ran back a year to Blangy and the dim smoky dining-hall of the hospice, where first I had met my company. Then we had been confident that in the great battle of the year we should utterly defeat the enemy, principally by reason of our tanks,—our imaginations reeled with dreams of what tanks could do. And what a joke those dummy tanks had been! . . .

I recalled our pride when we had been selected to take part in the Arras battle, our annoyance when the enemy retreated and brought our careful plans to nothing, our disappointment that we must fight with old Mark 1 tanks. . . . Then Achiet-le-Grand, the detrainment in the blizzard, the anxious nights at Mory Copse, the sudden conference at Army Head-quarters, the struggle against time, the biting anxiety when no news of my tanks came to me in the Armstrong Hut at the headquarters of the Australian Division, the explanation of the coming battle of my officers in the sheer darkness of the little ruin at Noreuil, the confidence in victory and the despair at failure—could tanks be used again?—tempered by the stubborn thought that we had done our best, and from the hillside the picture of my surviving tank, unfairly crippled by a chance shell.

At Behagnies we had been happy enough. Then after Haigh's show there had been Wailly, with the liquid grass sprouting in the cornices of the church, the delicious summer at Humières, and the dismal foreboding when we heard that we were destined for the Salient. I remembered the everlasting blare of the aeroplanes at La Lovie, the steaming and odorous mud of the tank routes, our noisy adventures at the "Dead End," the long days of weary waiting, the hopeless attempt at St Julien, and the black tragedy of the Poelcapelle Road. Why had tanks ever been sent to destruction at Ypres? There must be whole cemeteries of tanks in that damnable mud. And we had lost Talbot there.

It was more comforting to dwell on that astonishing sight at dawn on November 20—lines of tanks stretching away into the distance as far as we could see,—it was a full day,—the sunken road with its kitchens, the dead and sprawling Germans, the glass of wine in the delicately panelled chamber, the climb up the narrow chalk trench to the railway embankment, and the discovery that we could not enter Flesquieres, the dash back to the unbelieving colonel, the unpleasant quarter of an hour under machine-gun fire, the shock of Ward's death. . . .

And then Bourlon Wood, sitting square and imperturbable on the hillside, with the tank burning piteously on the ridge to the left of it—what a feverish search there had been for X.'s dugout on the night before! How I had thanked the Fates for that convenient quarry until a shell burst on the lip of it!

Finally, Gouzeaucourt, Ytres. Had tanks achieved the successes which we had prophesied? It was a difficult question to answer. Anyway, whatever our successes, whatever our failures, no man had ever commanded a finer company than mine.

The boat slid past the quayside. We crowded at the gangway, and there was the usual rush for the train. I secured a seat as usual by climbing in on the wrong side. We reached London in thick fog. They told me I might just as well take a week's holiday at home before reporting at Regent Street and asking for leave on arrival. It was three hours by District to South Harrow, and at Ealing Common a young officer had walked off the platform and fallen under a train. That made me late.

CHAPTER 14

The Carrier Tanks.
(JANUARY 31ST TO AUGUST 1ST, 1918,)

At my leisure I visited the headquarters of the Tank Corps in Regent Street, and after a somewhat undignified appeal to the good nature of a corporal—the staff-captain was busy, or out at lunch, or dictating—I obtained a fortnight's leave. The fortnight passed expensively, but it was pleasant, if dull, to take the train at the end of it from Waterloo and not from Victoria. In due course I arrived at Wool Station, and with two cheery subalterns, who had experienced enthralling adventures in Bournemouth, I drove in a taxi along narrow winding lanes to the camp on the crest of a hill.

I reported, but the charming officers who received me had not been warned of my arrival and were perplexed. Majors, it appeared, were a drug on the market—unattached majors swarmed in Bovington. Would I go to the depot at Wareham? I refused politely. I knew something of the depot. Two skeleton battalions were just being formed? They might not go out to France this year? I refused again: I did not intend to stop at Bovington any longer than was necessary.

At last it was suggested that I should be posted to the "Carrier Tanks." I had not heard of them, and asked for information. I was told vaguely "that they would carry infantry about," and it was expected that they would embark within the next three months.

So I found my way through the nice, clean, well-ordered

camp to the lines of the Carrier tanks. That night I slept uncomfortably on a borrowed blanket in a bare and chilly hut. It had never struck me that I should require my camp kit at home.

In the morning I was given the command of the 4th Infantry Carrier Company.

The six Carrier Companies were under the command of Lieutenant-Colonel L. A. de B. Doucet, R.E. They were to consist of tanks specially constructed to carry infantry. In the past the infantry had followed the tanks. Now it was intended that they should go forward in the tanks. If, for example, it was necessary to storm a village, the Carrier tanks would fill up with infantry and deposit them in the middle of the village, to the confusion of the enemy. The prospect was certainly exhilarating.

But soon these hopes began slowly to disappear. Perhaps the plan was a little startling. The Carrier Companies would not carry infantry "at first." They must begin their lives by carrying supplies. We were called "Tank Supply Companies," and we began to suspect that we should become finally a branch of that splendid Corps, the Royal Army Service Corps. We struggled vigorously against the depression which the prospect produced—we felt we were not worthy. We refused to believe that we should never carry infantry through a barrage to certain victory.

The Staff, however, were brutally frank. An order was published, informing us that although we were not "fighting troops," we should remember that discipline was useful. This order was none too helpful, especially since it was firmly believed both by officers and men that an officer, alleged to have spent three years of the war in England, was responsible for it. Of course there was no truth in this rumour or the allegation!

From the 12th February to the 12th June I was at Bovington Camp, and never have I liked soldiering less. Bovington Camp must have been designed to encourage men to serve in France. In France there was life, interest, even glamour. At Bovington the bones of soldiering stuck out disgustingly. We saw too clearly the formalities, the severities. But I had not been at the Base. If I had, I should have been more prepared for Bovington.

The raw material of my company was splendid—eighteen out of the twenty officers, and the majority of the men, had served overseas—and, since the company was over strength, I was able to weed out the weaker brethren in the course of training. I found it increasingly difficult to realise that my officers and men were not "fighting troops."

For the first three weeks we concentrated on drill. Then batches of officers and men were sent to be trained by the instructors of the camp. At the beginning of May we drew Mark 4 tanks, and used them by a system of reliefs from dawn to dusk. Towards the end of the month, when we waited breathlessly for every scrap of news from France, we began to train as a Lewis Gun Company, in case it should be necessary for us to be sent overseas at once; but the crisis passed, and we returned to our tanks.

It had been almost unbearable to sit lazily in the hot garden of a Dorchester villa and read of the desperate happenings in France. Why should the newspapers doubt, when we had never doubted, . . . but it was impossible that our line should ever be broken? Those civilians, these young fellows who had never been to France, did not understand what it meant. And my old Company? What had happened to them? They, at least, had had their lesson, and would not be caught unprepared. So day after day passed, and on the worst days I had no heart to train my new company.

At last the clouds began slowly to clear, but I was not satisfied until I had heard that my company was still in being and fighting as a Lewis Gun Company on the Lys Front. Well, it meant beginning all over again, and perhaps the sheer number of the slow Americans would make up for the lack of that skill which hard experience alone can give. . . .

Gradually the company began to find itself, and to feel that the 4th Carrier Company was without doubt the finest company at Bovington. Once again my company's football team was invincible. Our equipment and our transport arrived. Soon we were ready, and eagerly awaited our marching orders.

I have not wearied you with details of training or of life at Bovington, because I have no desire to recall them, but it would not be fair to write only of soldiering. I should be churlish, indeed, if I did not set down how an amateur soldier, stale and tired of war, was refreshed and encouraged. The cold flame of gorse in the clear dusk, the hot lawn of the shabby rectory, the healthy noise and bustle of Dorchester streets, the simple magic of Maidûn, the steady tramp from stuffy Abbotsbury over Black Down with its cleansing winds and through the quietude of Winterborne, the smooth rich downs by Charminster, the little footpath walk at evening by the transparent stream under the dark trees to the orderly cottages of Stinsford, the infinite stretch of half-seen country from the summit of Creech Barrow—these memories bred a stouter soldier than any barrack-square.

At 9 a.m. on June 12th we paraded for the last time at Bovington. The usual farewell speech was made. We marched off in bright sunshine. The band, whose strange noises in the huts behind my orderly-room had so vilely disturbed me, played us down to the station. At Southampton there was the usual delay. In the afternoon we embarked on the *Archimedes* for Havre, and sailed at dusk.

Four years before—in August 1914—I had crossed from Dublin to Havre in the *Archimedes*. Then I was a corporal, slept on a coil of rope, and drew my rations from among the horses. Now I was "O.C. Ship," with an adjutant who saw that my orders were obeyed, slept in the captain's cabin, and dined magnificently. During those four years the *Archimedes* had been employed without a break in carrying troops, and the captain had received a decoration. It was a proud "O.C. Ship" who stood on the bridge as the *Archimedes* made her stately way into the harbour.

We disembarked at the same old quay, though, instead of the Frenchmen, who in 1914 crowded to help us, singing patriotic songs, there was in 1918 a baggage party of Americans with marked acquisitive tendencies. Whether No. 2 Rest Camp was an improvement on the wool warehouses with their fleas is a matter of opinion.[1]

When we were not drawing rations, testing our gas helmets and attending lectures, undergoing medical inspections or feverishly endeavouring to comply with the myriad regulations and formalities of the camp, we would sit in the cosmopolitan mess. Americans in hundreds were passing through, some quietly confident that their army had absorbed the best from all other armies, some humbly hopeful and thirsty for knowledge, and some, as the evening grew late, a little irritating to us who had been in France since '14.

Then there were men on leave from Italy with strange tales of mountain sickness, of No-Man's-Land a few miles wide, and adventurous leaves spent in Rome. Or we would discover in a corner a bunch of sickly, cheerful fellows, who would eagerly persuade you that Salonica was no child's play, tell you how the army was riddled with malaria, and how leave came to them only once in a lifetime. It was not too cheerful a mess. On the whole I preferred the wool warehouse.

We entrained, as the 5th Divisional Signal Company had entrained, at Point Six, Hangar de Laine; but this time, instead of travelling through to Landrecies, with cheers at every level-crossing, we spent the day at Rouen, to the benefit of that sumptuous tavern. Hôtel de la Poste. At dawn on the 15th we found ourselves at Etaples, where we managed to give the men breakfast, and shave and wash, and at 9 a.m. we arrived at Blangy, where the 4th Battalion was once again billeted, and marched wearily to Blingel Camp half-way between Blangy and Auchy-lez-Hesdin.

Blingel Camp had a history. It had been designed many months before as a brigade camp, and beautiful blue prints were in existence, showing positive streets of huts, and a plethora of canteens, recreation rooms, bath-houses, messes, and incinerators. The camp had been commenced. In a few weeks somebody had not been quite certain whether after all the Tank Corps

---

1. See *Adventures of a Despatch Rider,*' p. 15 *et seq.*

would expand, and the work in the camp stopped. The staff in due course relented, and back came the sappers and the China-men—to be taken away in a month or so for more important duties. When we arrived only a small part of the camp had been built. So we helped the three sappers and the five Chinamen,—it was never completed. That was characteristic of the long-suffering Tank Corps, which, in fact, became finally and properly organised ten days after the Armistice.

The command of a brand-new unit, freshly landed in France, possessed its trials, annoyances, and humours. There were so many little tricks of the trade that the Company as a whole had to learn. Veteran officers who had been three months in France came over from other units to smile and advise, and so closely were we all connected that it was hard to explain that some of us had been a little longer than three months in France on a previous occasion. We were regarded, too, with slight disdain, as something newfangled and non-combatant, for by June 1918 the enthusiasts and the experts of the early days were outnum-bered in the Tank Corps by the mass of officers recruited from home and transferred, for example, from the cavalry, who re-garded machinery as a necessary evil, and anything new as an infernal nuisance.

We realised this attitude—the tank battalions had met it from the infantry eighteen months before—and we encouraged our-selves by saying to each other, "We'll show them!" But General Elles can never have realised how he broke our hearts, when he inspected us on our arrival, by telling the three proud com-pany commanders that the men were too good for the Carrier Companies, that probably we should have to send them as drafts to the fighting battalions and receive in their place inefficients, invalids, and crocks. We just pretended that we didn't mind. . . .

We remained at Blingel until July 20th, suffering from that fatal inspection, an epidemic of Spanish influenza, and lack of whisky. We drew twelve tanks (Mk. 4) from old friends at Erin, and trained mightily, carrying out a number of competitions and experiments. Forgetting for the moment that we were not

181

"fighting troops," we discovered and used a revolver-range, and, like proper Tank companies, practised battle-firing at Fleury. We might be Carrier Tanks, whose only duty is to "supply," but you never know.

While I had been snugly at home, my old company had fallen upon hard times. They had moved up in February to the neighbourhood of Peronne, and their tanks had been placed in position immediately in the rear of the trenches. Then came the great German offensive, and they were swept back to Amiens, losing on the way the majority of their tanks, because the bridges over the Somme were destroyed before the tanks could cross, and all their kit and the famous piano, because all the lorries available were required to transport Battalion Head-quarters. In front of Amiens they were used as a reserve Lewis Gun Company. Then they were "lorried" to the Lys front, and for weeks held grimly a section of the line. Now they were back once again in Blangy, refitting and drawing the new Mk. 5 tanks. It was sixteen months since they had left Blangy to detrain in a blizzard at Achiet-le-Grand and fight in the snow at Bullecourt.

There had been a rumour afloat soon after we had arrived in France that in August or September we should turn and rend the enemy. We were inclined to scoff at the thought—the situation was then none too favourable—but staff-officers, though mysterious, were decidedly insistent. We did not expect, in consequence, to be employed until this boasted offensive materialised, but on July 19th we received orders to relieve the 1st Tank Supply Company, who were helping the 2nd Tank Brigade to guard the Arras front. So once again I was driving along that stout ally, the highroad from St Pol to Arras.

The 2nd Tank Brigade at this period consisted of the 10th, 12th, and 14th Battalions. To each of the battalions was allotted an area of manoeuvre, in which it would co-operate with other arms in organised counter-attacks, for the First Army was on the defensive, and Prince Rupprecht was expected to attack. The old method of stationing tanks behind or in the battle zone had been discarded.

The Carrier Company in this scheme of defence was reduced to carrying tank supplies. Each of my sections would attend to the wants of one battalion. In the event of an enemy attack the battalion would dash into the fray, and at the end of the day's work would meet a section of Carrier tanks at a rendezvous and refill without reference to lorries, trains, or other more fallible means of transport.

We moved forward in a multitude of lorries, leaving behind us the tanks which we had begun to "tune" with such ardour. We had been ordered to take over a scratch lot of Mk. 4 tanks from the company which we were relieving, and that company, a maid-of-all-work in the Brigade, had not found time to repair them or to keep them in good order.

My own headquarters were near Caucourt, in a delicious valley sheltered by woods, where happy singing Chinamen were working lazily. Our Nissen huts were gaily painted. Peas and potatoes had been planted, and we had geraniums. In summer the camp was perfection. There was even a demure maiden, who brought us each morning eggs, butter, and milk.

Of my four sections, Ryan's was in Noulette Wood, behind Vimy; Harland's and Westbrook's near the vile and dirty village of Montenescourt, where Brigade Headquarters had been during the Arras battle; and Ritchie's in the famous Winnipeg Camp. We were all contented, and during the daylight safe, but at night we soon learnt that in the past few months the enemy had discovered how to bomb. We were kept awake.

Our one trouble was the Mk. 4 tanks, which for our sins we had inherited. Some of them looked clean: some of them looked dirty. All of them required thorough overhauling and repair, and we worked upon them day and night in case Prince Rupprecht should take it into his head to attack, or we should anticipate his attack by a local offensive.

A visit to the headquarters of the Canadian Corps on our right hurried our preparations. The Canadians, jealous of the reputation which the Australians had won, were longing for a fight. There was talk in the higher and more careful circles of an operation to recapture Monchy-le-Preux.

We soon decided to concentrate the company in the centre of the area, and the staff-captain of the brigade and myself went exploring to find a suitable site for the camp. The Bois de la Haie pleased us. It was bombed, but so were all woods, and this particular wood was not too conspicuous. We called two sappers into consultation and planned a camp complete with all the most modern improvements, down to the very latest thing in grease-traps. We began to say farewell to our gentle damsel. But the camp was never built.

For on the 28th, when I had returned from my daily round rather late—there was much movement of troops on the roads—and was calling for tea, buttered toast, and the cake that had come in the parcel, a code message was handed to me. We did not know the code—Carrier companies were often forgotten—but we interpreted the message that we were now in G.H.Q. Reserve, and should be ready to entrain at twenty-four hours' notice. The order might mean anything or nothing. I suspected a move to the neighbourhood of Amiens, where two success-ful little tank actions had already taken place, and sent McBean, my reconnaissance officer, to make a corner in Amiens maps. We returned to our repairs with desperate vigour and waited in excitement for further orders.

After mess on the 30th I was summoned urgently to Brigade Headquarters and instructed verbally by the general over a glass of excellent port to entrain at Acq early on the 1st. The utmost secrecy was to be observed. The entrainment was to be consid-ered as a practice entrainment. With my doubtful tanks no time was to be lost. Mac plunged into the night with orders for Ryan, who was ten miles from railhead, while my despatch-riders bus-tled off to Ritchie, Harland, and Westbrook. I was more than doubtful whether the tanks under repair would be ready.

Mac reached Ryan in the early hours of the morning, and the section was on the move by 6.45 a.m. Much happened to the tanks on the way, but with the exception of one they made Acq in the course of the afternoon, and the laggard arrived during the night.

Ritchie, who was always thorough, covered his tank with branches, and his moving copse caused much excitement. Westbrook and Harland, who each had a tank in hospital, so inspired their enthusiastic crews that by dawn on the 1st every tank was more or less able to entrain. We were not helped by the fact that we were ordered to entrain "full," that is, with our tanks crammed with petrol, oil, and ammunition. Since before entraining it is necessary to push in the sponsons until they are flush with the sides of the tank, the order involved unloading the sponsons at railhead, pushing them in and then loading the tanks again. We wondered bitterly if there were no supplies at our destination.

We discovered that we were bound for Poulainville, a railhead near Amiens. I looked proudly at our box of maps—the battalions were still asking for them days later. Early on the 1st our convoy of lorries took the road. At 3 p.m. the first train left Acq, and at 5 p.m. the second. All the tanks had managed to scramble on board, although none of my drivers had ever before driven a tank on to a train: that useful accomplishment was not taught us at Bovington. I watched the second train pull out—the men were cheering—and left in my car for the scene of battle. It was quite like old times. What part the Carrier tanks would play in the great offensive I had not the remotest idea: I knew only that I was sorry to leave the milk, the fresh eggs, and the butter.

CHAPTER 15

The Battle of Amiens
(AUGUST 1ST TO AUGUST 27TH, 1918.)

The Officers' Club on the hill above Doullens has a reputation, and we could not pass it without discourtesy. It was a good dinner in its way, and we continued our journey in a cheerful, though not hilarious, mood, through novel country, seamed with brand-new trenches and with all camps and houses heavily sandbagged against bombs.

At last we came at dusk to the railhead at Poulainville, discreetly hidden under the trees at the side of the main road. Tanks were drawn up under any scrap of cover—like frogs sheltering under mushrooms. The staff work was superb. There were so many guides that it was quite two hours before we found our own. Then we waited for the train. It was quite dark, and it began to rain heavily.

The first train drew in at 10 p.m. The tanks displayed a more than mulish obstinacy. Every possible defect developed, and we found it difficult to reach the engines and effect the proper repairs on account of the supplies which we had on board.

My drivers, too, were inexperienced. For two and a half hours[1] we struggled, coaxed, and swore in the utter darkness (no lights were allowed) and the driving rain, before the tanks were clear of the ramp.

We hoped feverishly that we should have better fortune with the second train, which arrived at 3 a.m. . . . Dawn was breaking,

---

1. An average time for detraining twelve Mk. 4 tanks is thirty minutes.

when a wearied R.T.O. told me with icy politeness that if my tank—the last—was not off the train in ten minutes, the train would pull out with the tank on board. The tank heard the remark. She had resisted our advances for many, many hours, but now she "started up" as though in perfect tune, and glided away down the ramp in the best of spirits.

We threw ourselves into the car, limp and soaked. During the night the enemy had been shelling Amiens, four miles from our railhead, with slow deliberation—vast explosions re-echoing among the wretched houses. We drove through the suburbs of the city, silent as a Sunday morning in London. Every third house along our road had been hit by shell or bomb. Then we turned towards Albert, and four miles out came to Querrieu Wood, where we discovered Company Headquarters, unshaven and bedraggled, sleeping in the mud among the baggage. Only our cook, humming a cheerful little tune, was trying nobly to fry some bacon over a fire of damp sticks.

We had become a unit of the 5th Tank Brigade, which consisted of the 2nd, 8th, 15th, and 17th (Armoured Car) Battalions.[2] The Brigade was concentrated behind the Australian Corps, and preparations were already far advanced for a sudden heavy attack. How far the attack would extend north and south of the Somme we did not know, but we had heard that the Canadians were gathering on the right of the Australians, and on our way we had passed their artillery on the road. All the woods were choked with tanks, troops, and guns. The roads at night were blocked with thick traffic. By day the roads were empty, the railheads free—our "back area" as quiet as the front of the 11th Corps in the summer of '16.

We were soon caught up in the complicated machinery of preparation. I attended Brigade conferences without number. Ritchie's section, to my sorrow, was transferred, temporarily, to the 3rd Carrier Company (Roffey's), by way of simplification, and I received in exchange a section of the 5th Carrier Compa-

---

2. The 2nd and 8th Battalions were armed with the Mk. 5 tank, a swifter and handier tank than the Mk. 4, and the 15th Battalion with the lengthy Mk. 5 Star.

ny, equipped with sledges drawn by decrepit tanks, which straggled into the wood on the evening of the 6th. The sledges were so badly designed that the cables by which they were towed were always fraying and breaking. I refused to be responsible for them, and began to collect in their place a job lot of baggage and supply tanks.

My sections had no time to make themselves comfortable in Querrieu Wood. On the 3rd, Ritchie, with his six tanks, left me for Roffey and the Canadians. On the night of the 4th, Ryan crossed the Somme and camouflaged among the ruins of Aubigny, moving to an orchard in Hamelet, not two miles behind the line on the 6th; Harland reached Fouilloy, the next village, on the same night; while Westbrook, on the previous night, had joined the 8th Battalion in a small wood near Daours. The majority of our tanks were still giving trouble, for they were ancient overloaded Mk. 4's.

The attack was to be launched at dawn on the 8th. After mess on the 7th I started from the wood with two old tanks, which had just arrived, in a wild endeavour to rush them forward in time. It was dreary and profitless work. Mac managed to reach the fringe of the battle before the tank, which he was leading, finally broke down, while at three in the morning I lost patience with mine and, leaving it to its commander, returned to camp.

The night was fine, though misty. We waited nervously for some indication that the enemy knew of the numberless tanks moving forward softly, the thousands of guns which had never yet spoken, the Canadian Divisions running[3] to the attack. But the night passed quietly. There was only one brief flurry of gunfire, when the irrepressible Australians raided to discover if the enemy suspected.

At "zero" I was standing outside my tent. There was thick mist in the valley. Through some freak of the atmosphere I could only just hear the uneven rumble of the guns. It was so cold that I went in to breakfast.

Half an hour after "zero" my tank engineer and I set out in

---

3. Certain Canadian battalions only reached the "start-line" in time by doubling.

my car to catch up with the battle, giving a lift on the way to a pleasant young subaltern in the R.H.A. returning from leave, who was desperately eager to find his battery. We left the car stupidly at Fouilloy,—we might have taken it farther forward,—and tramping up the Villers-Brettoneux road, cut across country, among invisible guns, through the mist, which did not clear until we reached what had been the German trenches.

Apparently we had repeated Cambrai. Companies of prisoners, stout-looking fellows, were marching back in fours. Here and there lay German dead on the rough coarse grass, or in the shallow unconnected trenches. A few hundred yards to our right was the Roman road that runs west from Villers-Brettoneux. Light-armoured cars of the 17th Battalion, with the help of tanks, were picking their way through the shell-holes.

Just short of a large ruined village, Warfusée-Abancourt, straggling along the road, and two miles from our old front line, we found a little group of supply tanks with a couple of wagons. One wagon suddenly had exploded on the trek forward. Nobody had heard the noise of an approaching shell, and we suspected a trip-mine, with which the battlefield was sown. We were discussing its fate when a large German aeroplane swooped down and drove us to take cover. A British aeroplane appeared, but the German forced it to land hurriedly. And the enemy began to send over a few small shells.

We moved forward unobtrusively. Read, myself, and Puddy, my orderly, to an inconspicuous knoll. There we lay in comfort, watching the farther advance of the Australians. The country was quite open and bare, though broken with unexpected valleys. A slight breeze had swept away the mist, and the morning was bright and sunny. A few hundred yards in front of us the Australians were walking forward nonchalantly, led by a score of tanks.

Occasionally a shell would fall among them and they would scatter momentarily, but it was rarely that a man was left upon the ground. From the valley beyond, which we could not see, came the rattle of Lewis guns, and once or twice bursts from the enemy machine-guns. To the left and behind us our field-guns, drawn up in the open, were firing for dear life, and away to the right along a slight dip a battery of field-guns was trotting forward. Overhead the sky was loud with the noise of our aeroplanes, some flying low above the battle and others glistening in the sun high among the clouds.

The Australians disappeared with the tanks over the skyline, and the supporting infantry in little scattered bodies passed us, marching forward cheerily over the rough grass. We were already three miles within the enemy defences.

We pressed on northwards to the Cérisy Valley, which we knew had been full of German field-guns. This deep gully, with steep grassy sides, fringed with stunted trees, runs from the tiny village of Cérisy-Gailly, on the south bank of the Somme, to Warfusée. Our gunners had done their work with terrible thoroughness. The bottom of the valley was so broken with shell-holes that it was barely possible to drive a limber between them. Four or five of the enemy guns remained desolate among a wild confusion of shattered wagons and dead horses. A trembling pony, still harnessed to his dead fellow, was the only survivor.

A hundred yards down the valley tanks were climbing the steep bank, and the flag of a tank battalion fluttered bravely on the crest.

We crossed the valley, toiled up the farther slope, and munched some sandwiches on the hill, where sappers were calmly marking out new trenches. At a little distance a shabby Australian field-battery was in action.

In a few minutes we saw something of the display and gallantry of war. A battery of Horse Artillery picked its way across the valley. The men were clean, inconceivably clean, and smart. Their horses' coats gleamed. The harness shone and glittered. The guns were newly painted. Never could a battery more splendidly arrayed have entered the plebeian turmoil of a battle. A series of swift commands and the little guns, with their ridiculous bark, were firing impudently. The Australians were overshadowed—their horses were unkempt and the guns dirty—but they had got there first.[4]

We were reminded by a salvo, which burst nicely just beyond the Australian guns, that, although in this particular battle we had little to do, the enemy could not be expected to realise our position. So we finished our lunch, and walking along the crest for half a mile, dropped down into the valley again, and came upon Ryan's section engaged in refilling the 13th Battalion. Westbrook's tanks were coming in one by one—they had all had their mechanical troubles.

So far as we could learn from our friends in the valley, the huge surprise attack had been a cheap and complete success—south of the Somme. The thick mist at dawn had protected the tanks, while it had not been dense enough seriously to hamper the drivers. The advance had been rapid, and only in one or two villages had the enemy shown any resolute defence.

But north of the Somme it was clear that some- thing was wrong, for the enemy were shelling mercilessly the southern bank of the river. Even the Cérisy Valley was harassed, and we were privileged to watch a brigade of artillery gallop, team by team, over the crest, through the smoke of the shells, down into the comparative safety of the valley. The German gunners must have rejoiced at the target, but they made poor use of their opportunities, for only one horse was hit; the team swerved as the shell burst, and, galloping madly down into the valley, only just missed a tank.

Ten minutes later an enemy aeroplane circled overhead. We held our breath—the valley was packed with artillery and tanks—and listened for the whirr of the bombs or the crackle of the machine-guns; but "Jerry" was for the moment harmless, although in quarter of an hour an H.V. gun made frantic efforts to land her shells in the valley. She could not manage it—her shells burst on the crest or high up on the farther bank.

Westbrook and Ryan were now under the orders of the bat-

---

4. It was, of course, only the luck of the game. This particular battery of Horse Artillery was brigaded with the Australian Artillery and went where it was told. It finished the day in close support of the infantry at Morcourt.

talions which they were refilling, and Harland had completed his job. So Read, Puddy, and I tramped back along the river wearily to Fouilloy, taking tea on the way from a hospitable Australian, whose name I should always have blessed if I had not forgotten it.

Later I heard that Harland had done his work well, following the Mark 5 Star tanks of the 15th Battalion to the Blue Line, the farthest limit of the attack, and forming there a dump of supplies. He led his tanks on a horse, which he had taken very properly from a prisoner. The 15th Battalion carried in their tanks machine-gunners, who were detailed to defend the Blue Line against counter-attack. Luckily, no counter-attack was launched, for the machine-gunners, unused to tanks, fell out of the tanks choking and vomiting and retired by degrees to the nearest dressing station, some, of them on stretchers. The tank crews remained in possession until the infantry came up.

And the light-armoured cars, manned by tank crews, whom we had seen picking their way through the shell-holes—their deeds of daring that day have become historical. It will not easily be forgotten how they dashed through the German lines and planted the Tank Corps flag on the head-quarters of the German corps in Foucaucourt; how they fusilladed the German Staff at breakfast through the windows of their billet; how they captured a train full of reinforcements; how they destroyed a convoy of lorries. We were convinced that light-armoured cars and fast tanks had driven the cavalry into a museum.

I doubt whether in the early days of the Amiens battle my three sections of Carrier tanks were usefully employed. The supplies with which they were overloaded could have been taken forward more rapidly and more economically by lorries or by wagons both on the first day and during the following week, when they dragged across country supplies of petrol, oil, and ammunition to dumps which were served by excellent roads. The true function of the Carrier tank, it appeared to us, was either to follow the infantry closely into the battle area with supplies, or to transport heavy and bulky material. The experiences of Ritchie's section were valuable.

Ritchie and his six tanks had left Querrieu Wood on the night of the 3rd, making for the tank bridge across the Somme by Lamotte-Brebière. In a cutting short of the village the convoy of forty odd tanks—Ritchie was with Roffey's company—met a column of Australian transport. Neither the tanks nor the wagons could turn, and for three hours there was a masterful display of language. At last, after prodigies of driving on both sides, the wagons and the tanks were disentangled, but the night was unpleasantly short, and the tanks were compelled to seek shelter from the day in the village of Glisy.

For once a number of Australians were to know what fear was. Dawn was breaking, and an enemy aeroplane, hoping to catch the belated scurrying for cover, was low overhead. One tank decided to shelter beside a house, but, swinging a little hastily, it carried away the corner of the house, and the bricks and masonry fell with a crash. The Australians, who had heard the noise of the aeroplane, thought at once that a bomb had fallen. They rushed out of the house in their shirts and dashed for cover. Then, as the tank snuggled more closely to the house, they realised what had happened. Luckily the doors of a tank cannot be opened from outside.

On the day of the battle four tanks, loaded with shells, bombs, wire, shovels, and water, started from the ruins of Cachy, immediately behind our trenches, and endeavoured to keep pace with the infantry, but that day the Canadians advanced eight miles. The tanks, accompanied by the D.A.A.G. of the 1st Canadian Division, toiled along after them. It was a hot and weary trek. The D.A.A.G. was saddle-sore, and Jacobs, whose tank he was accompanying, was a little chafed. A halt was made, and a tin of tank grease broached. The remedy was odorous, but effective.

On the heels of the infantry the tanks arrived on the following day at Caix, ten miles from their starting-point, and disgorged. Two of them made a round of the more advanced machine-gun posts, and, despite heated protests from the enemy, supplied much-needed ammunition, returning in triumph.

Some of the men found it difficult to remember that, strictly speaking, Carrier companies were not "fighting troops." Wallace, for instance, a runner, finding the time heavy on his hands, disappeared for a few hours, when he was not required, and joined the Canadians in a successful little bombing raid.

The section returned by night. The enemy aeroplanes, attracted presumably by the glow of their exhaust-pipes, bombed them unmercifully, but without success.

After a series of marches and counter-marches, inspired by false alarms, Ritchie's section returned to Querrieu Wood on the 18th. I had intended to give him a week to rest his men and overhaul his tanks, which had already covered a hundred miles without respite, but I received orders to assist the 47th Division in an attack north of the Somme, and my remaining sections had already been ear-marked for the 1st Australian and 32nd Divisions.

So on the 21st Ritchie's weary old tanks trekked six miles over difficult country to Bonnay, a pleasant little village on the Ancre, a mile above the confluence of the Ancre and the Somme. It was a hurried business: I fetched the necessary maps in my car from brigade headquarters. Two of the tanks loaded up immediately with machine-gun ammunition, and, trekking another four miles, about midnight came to a brickyard just behind our trenches. North of the Somme the enemy was fighting stubbornly, and his guns pounded away day and night. The neighbourhood of the brickyard was shelled and gassed until the crew longed for the battle.

At dawn the two tanks under Jacobs crawled forward into the gas and smoke, and, passing through the enemy barrage, dumped their loads of machine-gun ammunition among the advanced posts and returned with the crews slightly gassed but otherwise unharmed.

Two of the remaining tanks went forward with infantry supplies late in the morning when the struggle was swaying to and fro over the Happy Valley, a couple of miles south of our old camp at Meaulte. There was never a more deadly struggle, and the issue was always in doubt.

The first tank was led by Sergeant Bell. He came to the place where he should have unloaded his stores. The Germans were pressing fiercely, and the tank was in the forefront of the battle. Under bitter shell-fire and machine-gun fire Bell endeavoured to unload at least his precious ammunition, but two of his crew were killed and one man was seriously wounded immediately after they had left the shelter of the tank. Bell collected another party of infantrymen, but by this time the Germans were close to the tank, and our infantry, who had lost heavily, were withdrawing.

Bell could do nothing, for a Carrier tank possesses only one Hotchkiss gun to fire ahead, and, as his tank had turned to provide cover for the unloading party, that gun would not bear. He was unable to move the tank, because by this time every man of his crew had been killed or wounded. He waited helplessly until the Germans had almost surrounded the tank, and then, firing one last burst from a Lewis gun which he had secured, he ran across to a trench in which our infantry had rallied. The tank stayed in No-Man's-Land. Twice during the day Bell, with two of my men, tried to crawl out to it and drive it in, but the German machine-guns were too vicious.[5]

The second tank was led by Holt. He had just climbed inside for a moment, when a shell pierced the sponson and burst, killing instantly Holt and one of his men and wounding the remainder.[6] We could recover nothing at the time, although Wallace made a brave attempt; the Germans had regained too much ground, and to approach the tank was certain death.

It was a disastrous day. The attack had failed and the failure had been costly. The Happy Valley was strewn with derelict tanks, and the cemetery on the Meaulte road is very full.

On the 23rd Jacobs, with his two tanks, carried ammunition forward to isolated machine gun posts, although his men were

5. Sergeant Bell was awarded the D.C.M. He was killed in action on September 28.
6. Lieutenant F. M. Holt was one of my most promising and gallant subalterns, who, if he had lived, would certainly have received early promotion. He was a charming companion in the mess. We could ill afford to lose him.

still shaken and suffering from gas and returned without casualties. I then ordered Ritchie, who had himself been in the thick of the fight, to withdraw his battered section by easy stages to Querrieu Wood.

Since the 8th we had indulged in a series of expensive nibbles south of the Somme. Although on the day of the great surprise we had penetrated south of the Somme to a depth of ten thousand yards, disorganised the enemy's communications by concentrated bombing and the raids of armoured motorcars, and captured innumerable prisoners and an enormous quantity of material, the Germans with astounding skill filled the gap with fresh troops, who defended their positions with the utmost resolution.

In these minor operations the tanks suffered heavily. We could not understand why they had not been withdrawn. Obviously the enemy were aware that there were tanks on their front, and they made every possible preparation to receive them. And the Mk. 5 was not so handy and so fast a tank that it could afford to despise field-guns whose one object was to hit tanks.

If the tanks had been withdrawn after the big surprise attack, the striking power of the British Armies in the next "full-dress" offensive would have been increased by one strong, fresh tank brigade. . . .

From the 14th, Ryan's, Harland's, and Westbrook's sections had not been used. The men were given a few days' rest—I brought them back to Fouilloy or to Querrieu Wood—and I arranged for the majority of the officers to go in turn by car or lorry to Doullens for a breath of civilisation. Then we set to work on the tanks, and by the end of the week the tanks of the two sections were once again fit for action. We waited for orders.

It was decided to attack on the 23rd at Herleville and Proyart, two stubborn villages a few miles south of the Somme. My company had been placed directly under the orders of the Australian Corps; and, after I had completed the preliminary arrangements at an interview with the Brigadier-General, General

Staff, of the Corps at Glisy, I instructed Harland and Westbrook to work out the details with the staffs of the divisions involved, the 1st Australian and the 32nd.

On the 21st Harland's tanks in the Cérisy Valley, near War-fusée, were loaded with a splendid assortment of barbed wire, water, detonated bombs, grenades, rations, picks, shovels, and other necessaries. During the night of the 22nd they moved forward, and by 2 a.m. they were in position behind the line, severely shelled and bombed.

At dawn they followed the attack closely, and, when after stiff fighting the Australians had reached their final objective, the infantry were supplied instantly with food and water, with barbed wire to defend them against counter-attacks, and with all the ammunition they could need.

The tanks made two journeys, the second in the broad light of day, within full view of the enemy gunners, who naturally did their utmost to prevent this impudent unloading of stores under their very noses. One tank was hit on the track, but succeeded in crawling away. All the tanks were shelled briskly enough, but good fortune attended them, though by the rules of the game they should never have escaped. One of my men was killed and five were wounded. The Australians, who assisted in the unloading, were less lucky.

At Herleville, Westbrook with three tanks had been equally successful. Two tanks had followed the infantry through the ruins of Herleville, and seen to their wants at the moment of victory. After the third tank (Rankin's) had unloaded, a nest of machine-guns was discovered behind our support lines. The "fighting" tanks had already withdrawn. The Carrier tank with "soft" sponsons,[7] and its solitary Hotchkiss gun, decided to attack, and the colonel of a battalion of Highlanders climbed on board to act as guide, but before the tank could reach the nest an interfering officer with a battery of Stokes guns had forced the surviving Germans to surrender.

---

7. At that period the sponsons of Carrier tanks were made of boiler-plate, which was not proof against bullets.

Company headquarters had not been entirely inactive. Mac, of all reconnaissance officers the most conscientious, who on one famous occasion had described so clearly to a section the routes they should not take, that the section nearly forgot which route they should take, had spent the night of the 20th with Dron his orderly in finding a way for Ritchie's tanks through the difficult country to Bonnay. In the course of their wanderings they came upon a mysterious camp, deserted and full of stores. There were even several cases of whisky in a tent. I can conceive no greater tribute to the discipline of the Tank Corps than the fact that this reconnaissance officer, after making a note of this important discovery, did not dally in the tent for a moment, but went out into the night.

On the 22nd he reconnoitred a route for Westbrook's section from Bayonvillers, where the tanks were camouflaged, to the forward posts. There was no time to lay tape: white stakes were placed at intervals across difficult stretches. It was not too easy to discover a convenient "lying-up place," because the "fighting" tanks had already secured the desirable "banks," and we had been instructed not to go too near them for fear of confusion on the morning of the battle.

My tank engineer and his men had been indefatigable. Our tanks were obsolete, and usually they were overloaded. The crews were inexperienced.

Tank after tank would break down, and a stream of demands for spare parts flowed into headquarters. On more than one occasion it became necessary to lift out the whole engine complete and give the tank a new or more often an overhauled engine from the field stores. At Querrieu Wood we were short of men—the establishment of a Carrier Company is not generous—so that when heavy spares arrived, everyone, from the mess-cook to the adjutant, would lend a hand. Before the battle the tank engineer would rush on his motorcycle from one invalid tank to another. At Proyart, for example, a few minutes before "zero," he was repairing under continuous shell-fire a spare tank which had broken down tactlessly at a cross-roads immediately behind the line.

With his sections operating independently on a wide front the company commander could only tour the battlefield, for once the plans were laid he could exercise little influence upon the result. So you may imagine him visiting Ritchie and his tanks north of the Somme, paying a brief unhappy visit to Pro-yart, and then with Westbrook pushing forward to a gully beyond Rainecourt to look for Rankin and his tank. The enemy were unkind that day.

In these later actions the Carrier tanks had proved their worth incontestably. South of the Somme forty-six tons of stores and ammunition had been carried by nine ancient, unsuitable tanks, manned by eight officers and fifty men[8] to nine different points, each within 400 yards of the enemy, and each inaccessible by day to wheeled transport. If the old bad system of carrying parties had been employed, 2500[9] men would have been needed instead of 58. Further, these loads were carried forward eight to nine miles in all, and at least sixteen lorries were therefore set free. Lastly, the Carrier tanks followed so closely the advancing infantry that in the majority of cases the stores and ammunition were handed over as soon as they could be received.

The success and importance of the Carrier tanks were pleasantly recognised. One general wrote a special letter of thanks and congratulations about us to the 5th Tank Brigade, stating that the Carrier tanks were "a great feature of the day's operations." An Australian General recommended one of my section commanders for a decoration, and at the first opportunity sent by his car a present to the section of two jars of rum and a few cases of chocolate.

It had become increasingly difficult for us to convince ourselves that we were not "fighting troops." We had followed the infantry "over the top"; we had dumped supplies in full view of the enemy; one of my tanks had received a direct hit, and had been set on fire; another tank had been abandoned practically

---

8. The numbers include orderlies, cooks, batmen, &c.
9. For the actual carrying—cooks, &c., excluded.

in No-Man's-Land because every man in the crew except the tank commander had become a casualty; a third tank, with a Highland colonel on board, had started to mop up a machine-gun nest. We began to wonder whether, after all, we were a fit receptacle for "crocks." And we did not forget that Carrier Tanks were manned only by skeleton crews, and that, in consequence, every member of the crew was driven to work day and night.

We set ourselves at once to make ready our fourteen surviving tanks, in case we should be required again, and I issued orders for the reconnaissance of the forward area south of the Somme; but on the 21st August the battle of Bapaume had commenced, and on our front the enemy began to withdraw to the Canal de la Somme, with the Australians in pursuit. Our brigade were placed in G.H.Q. Reserve, and I was ordered to concentrate my company at Villers-Brettoneux. On the 26th we received instructions to entrain.

CHAPTER 16

The Hindenburg Line
(AUGUST 27TH TO OCTOBER 8TH, 1918.)

We had become masters of our tanks. Faults had been traced
and eliminated; defective parts had been replaced—three tanks
had received complete new engines—and invaluable experience had been acquired not only in the upkeep and repair of
tanks, but in the art of extorting "spares" from Field Stores, in
preserving the necessary "stock" in the technical quartermaster-
sergeant's stores, and in arranging for the correct "part," even if
it were an engine complete, to be rushed forward by lorry to the
invalid tank. I knew now that, if I ordered a tank or a section of
tanks to trek any reasonable distance within a reasonable time,
there was no need for me to wonder how many of my tanks
would reach their destination. This may seem a small thing, but
you must remember that five months before not half a dozen of
my men had had the slightest idea of a petrol-engine's insides.

So it mattered little that, when I received instructions to
entrain at Villers-Brettoneux, my tanks were scattered over the
countryside—Ryan's at Hamelet, Harland's and Westbrook's in
the Cérisy Valley, and Ritchie's survivors at Querrieu Wood. On
the 26th, the tanks trekked without incident to an orchard half a
mile from the ramp, camouflaged and, pushing in their sponsons,
made ready to entrain, while Mac, with an advance party, dashed
away to Boisleux-au-Mont, our destination.

On the 30th, after I had seen Harland and Westbrook entrained in great style from a travelling ramp, I drove north to

Boisleux, which lies just half-way between our old friends, Wailly and Behagnies. There I discovered Mac weary and wrathful after a tussle with a battalion commander over some choice dugouts which we coveted. We consoled ourselves with a clean stretch of turf at the back of some old trenches, against the *parados* of which we afterwards constructed shacks and stores, and fortunately well away from the village.

At 1 a.m. on the 31st Westbrook's train pulled in to the ramp at Boisleux. Read, Mac, and I had been waiting for it since 9 p.m. After we had spent an hour or so in listening to German aeroplanes, admiring the ineffective patterns which the searchlights made, and wondering whether the ramp might not be bombed, we procured some chairs and dozed.

We were suddenly awakened by a hideous crash, the grinding of enormous timbers and frightened shouts. We listened for the noise of the engine and the hiss of the next bomb—until in the blackness of the night we realised that it was only a tank train which a foolish engine-driver had driven into the ramp. . . .

At Boisleux we rested pleasantly after we had thoroughly overhauled our tanks, fitted grids inside the sponsons to prevent the loads from falling into the engines or the crew, and drilled a little. There were, of course, minor diversions. On two or three nights the village was bombed, but we, who were in the open, escaped. We did not escape so easily from a storm which blew down the majority of our numerous tents. There was much shouting for batmen that night.

I took the opportunity of indulging in a little Paris leave. On the second night Paris was bombed. I was awakened by a discreet tap at the door of my room. Sleepily I heard the calm voice of the unruffled Swede who owned my favourite hotel in Montparnasse—

"It is an air-raid, and my clients gather below; but *M. le Commandant*, who is accustomed to war's alarms, will doubtless prefer to continue his sleep."

It was too absurd to be bombed when stretched comfortably in the softest of beds with a private bathroom next door. . . . I thought that I must be dreaming. Anyway, nothing on earth or above it could have induced me to leave that bed.

My car met me at Amiens on September 25th. The driver told me that my Company had moved forward to Manancourt, a village a few miles south of Ytres, and was expecting shortly to take part in an attack. So with the famous air from that sophisticated operetta, "*La Petite Femme de Loth*," running in my head, I drove through Villers-Bretonneux and Warfusée to Proyart, where I dropped an austere American Staff Officer, who had come with me in the train from Paris, and thence over the Somme through the outskirts of Peronne, to a tidy little camp on clean grass by a small coppice half-way between Manancourt and Nurlu. I found the Company making ready for action.

At Boisleux we had come under the orders of the 4th Tank Brigade, which had suffered such heavy losses during the battle of Amiens, both in a series of actions with the Canadians and later in the Happy Valley, that it had been placed in reserve. The stern defence of Bullecourt by the enemy, who held it as desperately in 1918 as they had in 1917, nearly drew the brigade from its rest; but at last even Bullecourt fell, and the British Armies swept on to the suburbs of Cambrai and the Hindenburg Line.

It was with the Hindenburg Line that the 4th Tank Brigade was concerned.

On the front of the 4th Army, with which our brigade was now operating, the Hindenburg Line, a series of defences 7,000 to 10,000 yards in depth, was itself defended by the St Quentin Canal. For three and a half miles, between Vendhuille and Bellicourt, the canal passes through a tunnel, and this stretch it was determined to attack. But before the main operation could take place, it was urgently necessary to capture certain outlying points of vantage known as The Knoll and Quennemont and Guillemont Farms. Already we had attempted unsuccessfully on three occasions to carry them by storm.

A final attempt was to be made by the 108th American Infantry Regiment on September 27th, and one section of Carrier tanks was ordered to assist. Ryan, who had been in command of the company during my absence, had detailed his own section for the job.

On the afternoon of the 25th, Ryan and I reported at the Headquarters of the American Division concerned, the 27th. The American Staff was a little flustered and confused, . . . but we found to our gratification that Australian Staff Officers were "nursing" the Americans—there were a number of Australians with each American unit—and we soon obtained the orders and the information which we required. The Australians knew us and we knew the Australians: nothing could have been more satisfactory. The Americans, on the other hand, had never heard of Carrier tanks, although they appreciated in theory their use at once.

Ryan's tanks moved by easy stages to a copse three-quarters of a mile from Villers-Faucon, where they were loaded on the 26th with ammunition, wire, water, and sandbags. They were joined by unloading parties of American infantry, eight men to each tank, bright young fellows who had not previously been in action. I doubted whether they would be of use: to follow a slow Carrier tank into action and to unload it in sight of the enemy under heavy fire needs the coolness and skill of veterans.

It was a little characteristic that, while the quartermaster who brought the supplies to Ryan's tanks was more than eager to help and almost embarrassed me with his explanations and suggestions, the unloading parties gave us a sad fright by arriving at the last moment. They had received no written orders, and, after wandering aimlessly round the country "for some other tanks," came in at dusk dead-tired.

On the night before the battle the tanks moved up to points in the rear of our posts, and thirty minutes after "zero" they followed the fighting tanks and the infantry. The shelling was severe.

The first tank under Sergeant Broughton reached its objective, but, as the unloading party had lost touch with it on the trek forward, the crew were compelled themselves to unload the tank. Apparently the attack had been checked, for Sergeant

Broughton found that he was so close to the enemy that he could see them firing. He completed the dump, swinging the tank to give the men as much cover as possible from machine-gun bullets, though without help it was painfully slow work, and half his men were wounded. On the way back the tank struck a land-mine, and it was set on fire. The survivors crawled back into camp late in the afternoon.

The second tank, under Thomas,[1] became "ditched" in a huge crater a few hundred yards from its objective. It was so heavy loaded that the unditching beam could not be used, and such intense machine-gun fire was directed at the tank that Thomas quite properly did not ask his men to attempt to unload the roof. It would, in any case, have been a laborious job, since the unloading party had missed the way. Three attempts were made to extricate the tank from the crater into which it had slipped, but each attempt failed. The German gunners were more successful, for by dusk they had blown the tank into a fantastic tangle of twisted wreckage.

The third tank struck a landmine on the way forward. Two of the crew were killed instantly, and a third man was severely wounded. Ryan, who was walking beside the tank, was badly injured—his ankle was shattered by the force of the explosion.

Read and I had tramped up to Ronssoy, a large industrial village in which were the headquarters of the 108th Regiment. It was a damp steamy day. The Americans were puzzled and disconsolate. Their infantry, led gallantly by tanks of the 4th Battalion, had undoubtedly advanced, but the reports were so conflicting that no one could say definitely how the line ran. It appeared that the Americans had not "mopped up" with any success, since there were parties of the enemy between the Americans who had attacked and the posts which they had left at "zero."

In places the Germans seemed to be farther forward than they had been before the attack commenced. Of the fighting tanks the majority had received direct hits,[2] and the crews,

---

1. Lieutenant (later Captain) S. A. Thomas, M.C.
2. It was in these local attacks that tanks suffered most severely.

mostly wounded, were staggering back by twos and threes into Ronssoy. It was no wonder that Sergeant Broughton had found himself under the very noses of the enemy. With the main attack still to come, the situation could not have been more unsatisfactory.

Even the headquarters of the 108th Regiment were to suffer. We had noticed a little nervously that although a German observation balloon was looking into Ronssoy, a crowd of orderlies and officers were collected in the road outside the head-quarters. The lesson was sharp. Twenty minutes after we had left the village in an ammunition lorry a salvo of 5.9's, entirely without warning, burst among the crowd.

Of the land-mines which had proved fatal to two of my tanks and to several tanks of the 4th Battalion we had received information, but the information was found to be inaccurate. Warning had reached us of a British anti-tank minefield laid in March, and we had marked the mines on our maps. The minefield, however, was in fact five hundred yards from its supposed position, and its full extent was not discovered until on the 29th ten American tanks endeavoured to pass across it and were destroyed.

On the 28th it was clear enough that, although parties of American infantry were out in front of their original line, The Knoll, together with Quennemont and Guillemont Farms, remained in German hands. The attack of the 108th Regiment was more than unsuccessful.

If it had never been launched the attack on the 29th might have taken place at least under cover of a barrage; but now that scattered bodies of Americans, surrounded by the enemy, were ahead, no barrage could be employed.

While the survivors of Ryan's section, under the command of Thomas, were salving what remained of their tank equipment, the three remaining sections moved forward from Manancourt with the battalions to which they had been allotted. Fortunately, my officers reconnoitred their own routes, for two of the convoys with which they were trekking temporarily lost their way.[3] My tanks were detailed once again to carry supplies for the fighting tanks, a dull and thankless task.

Two hours after "zero," on the 29th, my car felt its way through thick mist into Hargicourt, a dilapidated village a mile or so from the "infantry start line." The Brigade had ordered that the Refilling Point for tanks should be an open stretch of rough pasture on the farther side of the village. The map reference of the point was L5b4.1. It was intended that on the afternoon of the battle lorries should bring supplies to the Refilling Point, that the loads should there be transferred to my tanks, and that my tanks with a day's supplies on board should follow the fighting tanks across the broken desolate country of the Hindenburg system of trenches. I had decided in consequence to make L5b4.1 my headquarters.

The enemy did not approve of this decision. As soon as the mist began to clear Hargicourt itself was shelled methodically, while the proposed Refilling Point, which was surrounded by a number of half-concealed batteries, was the object of a bitter hate. A wireless tank, destined for the same unhappy spot, had retired into the garden of a cottage, and I accompanied the wireless tank. It belonged to my old battalion. We heard all the news, and the driver knew how to make tea.

Soon it became clear that for once the battle was not proceeding in accordance with plan. Obviously the enemy was still clinging to the Quennemont Ridge, and the left flank of the attacking infantry was uncovered. The direction from which the bulk of the shelling came could not be mistaken. Hargicourt itself was being shelled with light stuff, while, if we had reached our objectives to time, the village would by now have been out of range.

The news was melancholy. The wounded, streaming back through the village, told us that the enemy machine-guns were murderous; reports from tank officers showed that an appalling number of tanks had received "direct hits"; of the Americans nothing had been heard. From our right, however, came the

---

3. In any case it was bad policy for Mk. 4 's and Mk. 5's to move in the same convoy.

astounding rumour that the 46th Division had achieved the impossible by forcing the passage of the canal and capturing Bellenglise.

A gunner officer was being carried down the street of the village on a stretcher. He was so badly wounded that his nerve was gone, and he asked me piteously as he passed me whether he was now quite safe. I had left him and was fifty yards or so away when a field-gun shell burst close to the stretcher. For a moment the smoke enveloped the little group. Then it blew away—the stretcher-bearers were standing quite still. I hurried to them. Not one of them had been touched. Mercifully the officer had lost consciousness. The stretcher-bearers just grinned, gave their straps a hitch, and strode off down the street again.

Soon Ritchie, Harland, and Parslow reported to me that they had dumped their loads and, seeing that the proposed refilling point was being heavily shelled, had come to me for orders.

I instructed my sections-commanders to concentrate at certain points in the rear of the village, and pushed forward along the Quennemont road myself. In a few minutes I met Major Hotblack, the intelligence officer at Tank Corps Head-quarters. He had been wounded in the head. Later I learned that he with two tanks had just captured Quennemont Ridge, which for so long had defied us. And the tank crews had held the ridge until they were relieved.

I obtained as much information as I could from the many walking wounded—our attack on the left had been checked—and returning to my head- quarters, which were rapidly becoming distasteful to me, despatched a report by wireless.

There was an element of humour in this delay to our advance. It was so unexpected that many headquarters found themselves farther forward than they had intended. Puzzled mess-sergeants, pushing on blindly to villages which were still in the enemy's hands, were hurt and indignant when they were warned to return. The neighbourhood of Hargicourt was crowded with pathetic little camps, disconsolate staff-captains and suspended headquarters. Personally I had no wish to remain even in Hargicourt. The enemy had begun to use gas shells, and one heavy howitzer at least made Hargicourt its target for a time. The Refilling Point could not come into operation; the surviving tanks would find plentiful supplies at the dumps which my section had already made.

On the other hand, two miles back, there were some excellent quarries at Templeux-le-Guérard, where we could rest in safety and comfort until we were wanted. You will remember that, as we were not "fighting troops," but merely a humble collection of "supply tanks," we could retire from the fray without hurt to our self-respect.

I was fortunate enough to meet the General's car between Templeux and Roisel. He approved of my suggestion. I returned rapidly to Hargicourt, and withdrew my miserable headquarters to a grassy depression near the quarries, where Harland's section had rallied. Mac went in search of suitable dugouts, while I listened to Harland's report.

Harland, like a good section commander, had given his men an excellent breakfast before the day's work—fried bacon, hot toast, and tea, followed by rum.[4] Each tank had been loaded at Manancourt Copse with 240 gallons of petrol, 40 gallons of oil, 80 gallons of water, 40 lb. of grease, 20,000 rounds of Hotchkiss ammunition, and 400 rounds of 6-pdr. ammunition. Thus heavily laden, they crawled on for three hours, until they reached the appointed spot for unloading, immediately behind our original line. They were noticed by an enemy aeroplane flying low, and shelled heavily in consequence. Small dumps were formed in shell-holes—the operation was completed with astonishing celerity—and the tanks, running light, raced away. One man had been gassed and one wounded.

Within the next two hours the German gunners destroyed half the supplies which had been dumped, but they were not required, since the majority of the American tanks, for whose

4. We could always obtain rum: every tank carried a supply to revive its exhausted crew. At Cambrai each of my tanks carried a bottle of whisky in place of rum, but this innovation tended to bunch the infantry—Argylls—dangerously near to the tanks, and in subsequent actions we reverted to rum.

benefit the dumps had been formed, lay derelict on the mine-field, which had blown up two of my tanks on the 27th.

Ritchie's section had experienced no adventures. They had dumped their supplies punctually, and rallied without hindrance from the enemy.

We retired at dusk to our dugouts in the quarries above the village of Templeux-le-Guérard.[5] These quarries penetrated confusedly into a steep and isolated hill, upon which a stout castle might have been built. The workings were approached by slippery paths. The hill was a very maze of tunnels, ravines, pits, shelters, which provided impenetrable cover for numerous guns and a brigade or more of infantry. The enemy appreciated its qualities, and refused to waste shells upon it. Their gunners confined themselves to the lower slopes and to the level-crossing in Templeux itself.

The quarries were tenanted with wrathful Australians. It had been planned that the Americans should storm the first trench-system of the Hindenburg Line, and that the Australians, passing through the Americans, should continue the attack by storming the second trench-system. But when the Australians went forward an hour or so after "zero," they discovered to their cost that in many places the enemy infantry were sitting happily in the trenches which the Americans had captured. Large numbers of Americans had disappeared.

Not even our aeroplanes could tell us what points they had reached, or how many had survived. The result was that the Australians, with an unknown quantity of Americans "out in front," did not dare to use their artillery. They resigned themselves to the inevitable, and attacked the Hindenburg Line grimly with bomb and bayonet. They hammered in little wedges of men, and foot by foot, with savage cunning and merciless determination, fought their way through the gigantic system of intricate defences, often coming suddenly upon detached bodies of Americans, helplessly surrounded, but still holding out.

---

5. I hope I shall be forgiven if I mention the fact that this village; was commonly known as "Teddie Gerard."

It was indeed true that on our right the 46th Division, "equipped with lifebelts, and carrying mats and rafts," by a gallant feat of arms had crossed the St Quentin Canal and established themselves on the eastern bank,—the right flank of the Australians was thus secured; but to my mind even the feat of the 46th Division did not surpass the astonishing exploits of the Australians, who took disaster by the throat and choked victory out of it. For various reasons this phase of the battle has been somewhat obscured. . . . By October 5th the Australians had broken through the Hindenburg Line, and with the help of tanks stormed Montbrehain. They had fought continuously since September 29th.

In these intermediate actions we took no part. After two nights in the quarries I moved my company to Haute Wood, a stunted copse sheltering a quiet grassy slope, a couple of miles out of Templeux, on the Roisel road. There we remained placidly until October 7th in the multitudinous tents which we had by this time collected, overhauling our tanks, playing a little football, and visiting as frequently as our duties permitted the strictly rationed canteen at Peronne. We were disturbed only by an occasional shell from a long-range gun.

Once Montbrehain was stormed the enemy could cling only to the farther fringes of the Hindenburg Line, and on October 8th we drove them out of organised trenches altogether into the clean open country. My tanks were again employed to follow the fighting tanks with supplies, but on this occasion my sections were not allocated to battalions, but remained under my own command, so that we were able to choose our own times and places, and by "pooling" supplies to effect very necessary economies.

On the 5th I had reconnoitred with Mac and my section commander a route forward from Haute Wood to the vicinity of Bellicourt. It was a dismal tramp over ground shelled to utter destruction—a maze of crumbling trenches and forgotten posts, strewn with derelict equipment, deserted dumps of ammunition, dead stinking horses, and too often the corpses of unburied Germans. Here and there ran light railways, which we did not desire to damage in case they should be needed; and near Bellicourt was a wilderness of sidings and stores and huts and roadways.

From the high ground above Bellicourt we looked across the log-road to Quennemont Ridge—outwardly a peaceful dark-green down, but in fact a loathsome graveyard on which the corpses lay scattered in handfuls, and blackened metal tombs that had been tanks. The distant gunners were still tormenting this hill, which was already dead, and shells, lazily exploding, stirred again the loose mud, rotting bodies, and rusted rifles.

The log-road over the trenches, narrow and insecure, was crammed with thick traffic moving at less than walking pace, for it was the only road from Hargicourt to Bellicourt. It might have been a bridge over a river impassable to all transport except tanks.

To the south were low dark ridges stretching to St Quentin. They were fringed with bursting shells. And in front of us was Bellicourt, tattered, but with red-brick cheerful in a gleam of sun—not utterly submerged by war, and with but a faint spirit of the place hovering above the levelled ruins, as were those ravished places which had known war for year after year. Bellicourt, shattered but undismayed, still lived to point gallantly to the tracks of the retiring enemy and the goal for which we had always fought—open country.

On the 6th my tanks moved into the trenches, spending the night near Hargicourt, and on the night of the 7th trekked down a valley, less destroyed than others, to Bellicourt, and over the tunnel canal and the main St Quentin road. The sections pitched their tents by some trenches. I had advanced my head-quarters meanwhile to a clean stretch of turf by the St Quentin road, just outside Bellicourt, leaving at Haute Wood my stores and heavy baggage, which I had been able only within the last few days to bring forward from the copse at Manancourt. Lor-ries were none too plentiful, and I had collected a great quan-tity of stores in case I should find myself out of touch with the sources of supply.

The night was noisy, but no damage was done, and the morning was splendidly fine. My sections had moved soon after dawn. I followed later in my car.

We drove along the canal to Bellenglise, then, bearing to the left, took to the old Roman Road, along which the 5th and 3rd Divisions, defeated, broken, and more weary than I could describe, poured confusedly through the rain on the night of August 26th, 1914. We passed by the strange cottage, still unharmed, where we despatch-riders had given stew and hot coffee to the bedraggled Staff and had slept amongst the straw, and came to Harland's tanks a mile or so short of Estrees, waiting dully to supply the tanks of the 301st American Battalion.

So we arrived at the dismal dilapidated village itself, momentarily empty except for innumerable notices in German and a derelict whippet tank standing in the little square in which our Signal Company had rallied four years since. We slipped into a by-road, left the car, and walked across country to a half- grown copse under the shadow of Beaurevoir. There we found Ritchie's four tanks with that excellent Mac of the 1st Battalion, who had helped us to detrain at Achiet-le-Grand. While we were consuming tea and sandwiches with them, it was reported that certain tanks had run short of petrol near Serain, the first of the redeemed villages. I sent two of Ritchie's tanks forward to help. . . . Ritchie's tanks duly arrived at Serain, where they were overwhelmed by the embraces of the pale hysterical villagers. Both Ritchie's and Harland's tanks trekked back that afternoon to Bellicourt.

Two of Harland's tanks passed through a valley crammed with a brigade of cavalry, who at the eleventh hour of the war were hoping for an old-fashioned, sabre-waving pursuit. It was a little ludicrous to think that my old supply-tanks could have put to flight the brigade in the valley. As it was, they merely gave the horses a severe fright. We completed our round, gathering the news and calling at various necessary headquarters. Finally we returned in gentlemanly fashion for lunch. . . .

That night we began to realise the unbelievable—there was not a trench between us and Germany. And yet this thing, for which we had been yearning four long years, had come about in the ordinary course of the day's work. That gay, splendid break-through of our imaginations was in fact but the successful completion of a day's fighting disappointingly like any other day's fighting. We could just repeat the words again and again, doubting their truth, yet rejoicing soberly in their significance—

We are through to the open country!

CHAPTER 17

The Second Battle of Le Cateau
(OCTOBER 9TH TO OCTOBER 30TH, 1918.)

On October 9th the enemy broke off the engagement, retiring six miles to the neighbourhood of Le Cateau, in order
that they might re-form and again present some sort of front
to our advance. Clouds of fast tanks should have pursued them
closely and prevented them ever from rallying. In the absence
of tanks the cavalry pressed forward on either side of the Roman Road, gallantly charged machine-guns, and returned more
than a little shaken with news which the aeroplanes had already reported. We wondered what would have happened if the
enemy rearguards had possessed a few "whippets" in addition
to stoutly-fought machine-guns. It is a desperate business—to
charge machine-guns, and it is pure suicide for cavalry to await
the attack of tanks.

My old Carrier tanks were not to be left behind. On the
11th I moved my headquarters to a deserted inn on the Roman
Road in the neighbourhood of Beaurevoir. The sections were
encamped close by. This inn, which, together with a few houses
and a beetroot factory, was known as Genève, had its advantages.
The rooms were large and comparatively undamaged; within a
few yards was a German R.E. dump: it was conveniently on the
main road and the direct tank route forward.

It had, however, been the centre of a stiff little fight. Within
a radius of a hundred yards were thirty to forty corpses, mostly
Americans. We commenced reverently to bury them, but one

morning a somewhat severe American *padre* came in and bade us exhume his compatriots, and carry them to a little cemetery half a mile away, of which we had known nothing. We were only too glad to help him, and I lent him some men and a limbered wagon.

The mile along the old enemy defences to the village of Beaurevoir was a dolorous walk. The defences were only holes, scratched on the reverse side of banks by entrenching tools, and shallow machine-gun posts. The dead had not all been buried, and sometimes the searcher would discover a man who must have been long in dying—open warfare is not pleasant for those who fall wounded in hidden places.

Beaurevoir itself, set on a hill, was not yet empty of the dead. The ruined cottages had been evacuated hurriedly, but in each cottage the handloom had been smashed, and not by shells. The statue of Jeanne d'Arc had been taken from its pedestal, and had not been found.

The only live civilian near Beaurevoir was a cow, which kept Thomas's section supplied with milk until the Chinese came to clear the battlefield.

We were given but a few days to explore the country at our leisure. The enemy apparently had determined to make their first stand on the line of the Selle River, a very definite obstacle. Le Cateau itself was doubtful territory.

A series of conferences was held at brigade head-quarters, which had suddenly jumped forward to Serain. It was determined to attack on the 17th. Now that we had reached good roads and open country my tanks were not required to carry supplies for the fighting tanks, but, as a measure of precaution, I was instructed to send a section forward to Maurois, a ten mile trek from Genève. Parslow's tanks completed the trek without incident on the 15th.

I motored up to see him, and every yard of the road was for me a solemn triumph. We were avenging the confused retreat of the British Army on the afternoon and night of the first battle of Le Cateau; we were driving through really clean unshelled country, which might never have been touched by the finger of war if it had not been for the craters blown at the cross-roads and the occasional corpse by the roadside; and never in my life have I seen happier people, men and women more flustered and confused with happiness, than the thin underfed villagers who stood gazing in the crowded main street of Maretz.

Short of Maurois village the Germans had blown into the cutting the road-bridge over the railway from Cambrai to St Quentin. The traffic was being diverted, when we arrived on the scene, over heavy fields to a level crossing, and the engineers were working against time to construct a new bridge capable of bearing the heaviest transport. It had been raining, and the men were finding it difficult indeed to haul the great girders into position. A couple of hundred yards away were Parslow's tanks. The remedy was obvious. A tank was brought round on to the rails and spent a profitable hour in doing a job which would have taken fifty men a full day. The bridge was completed rapidly, and the traffic once more flowed steadily over the bridge instead of floundering over the fields.

On the 17th and 18th Parslow's tanks were not required. On the 19th they trekked back to Genève. The 4th Tank Brigade was being relieved by the 2nd Tank Brigade. We expected orders to move to Hargicourt for entrainment, and we made an expedition over the log-road to discover the whereabouts of the ramp. But a railway accident outside Cambrai delayed the arrival of the 2nd Carrier Company,—to our disgust we were ordered to remain temporarily with the 2nd Tank Brigade.

We became involved at once in our last battle of the war. From the 17th to the 20th we had straightened our line in a series of fierce and costly little attacks. The enemy had been driven definitely from Le Cateau and now lay just beyond the outskirts of the town. To the west of the town we had crossed the Selle. The army commander decided to throw the enemy back to the Mormal Forest by a grand attack on a fifteen-mile front. I received orders from the 2nd Tank Brigade to assist the 13th Corps by carrying supplies.

I instructed Parslow's section, which had just Completed a ten-mile trek, to return with Thomas's section to the camp by Maurois Station, and when they were on their way I reported at Corps Head-quarters. I arranged with the Corps Staff that Thomas's section should operate with the 33rd, 34th, and 35th Infantry Brigades of the 11th Division, while Parslow should help the 25th Division. The corps further requested urgently that any spare tanks which I might have should be detailed to carry ammunition for the 104th Army Brigade R.F.A., the guns of which could not be reached by horse transport without difficulty on account of the nature of the ground. I brought up Harland from Genève, gave him two tanks, and ordered him to carry on.

On the afternoon of the 20th I established my advanced headquarters in an orchard, quarter of a mile from the bridge which we had helped to construct. After mess we all attended a first-rate "show" given by the Divisional *Troupe* of the 25th Division, and returned to our camp greatly encouraged, but a trifle unhappy that we had not billeted ourselves in one of the many excellent houses in Maurois.

That night one officer at least was disturbed in his slumbers. The enemy shelled Maurois persistently, sending over a few shells to the neighbourhood of the bridge. Finally a large aeroplane bombed along the main road, dropping one group just short of the camp, and another group, intended presumably for the bridge, between the bridge and the camp. The aeroplane was flying so recklessly low—it was a clear night with a moon— that for once our machine-gunners brought her down in a field about a mile beyond the bridge.

Much damage had been done in Maurois. We were thankful that we were in tents outside the village and had not been tempted by the houses. One shell had exploded just behind the hall in which the concert had been held. For such shelling and bombing the casualties were heavy.

On the 21st I was quite busy. After a visit to my rear headquarters at Genève to arrange for the supply of spare parts by lorry, I reported again to the corps for final orders. Then with

Parslow I visited the 25th Division and went with the divisional commander to see the commander of the brigade to which Parslow's tanks would be attached. We settled every detail to our satisfaction.

In the afternoon I ran over with Thomas to Reumont, where we hoped to find the nth Division, but a relief had not yet been completed and its staff had not arrived. We spent our spare time in walking out to the cottage, which had been the head-quarters of the 5th Division on August 26, 1914, but time had swept away every trace of that first battle. The pits which had been dug on either side of the road to shelter the signallers had been filled in. The tiles of the cottage, loosened by the scaling-ladders of our intelligence officer, had been replaced.

The little trenches had disappeared. But there was the hedge from the cover of which our one heavy battery, the 108th, had fired—it ran short of fuses in the old-fashioned way, and Grimers was sent hastily down the road on his motorcycle for more. In that barn to the left we had slept hoggishly among the straw on the night before the battle, the first night's sleep since we had detrained at Landrecies and the last until we reached the Aisne. To my amazement the church behind the barn was still standing, intact except for a couple of shell-holes. I could have sworn that four years ago, as I was riding out of the village, I saw flames bursting from the roof. The Germans certainly entered the village not long after I had left it. Perhaps they may have extinguished the flames and repaired the damage.

I had no time to question the good people of Reumont or to discover whether those exiguous, badly-sited trenches on the Le Cateau road were still to be distinguished. The 11th Division had at last taken over, and the G.S.O.(i) of the relieved division was describing his experiences among the outposts to his successor. I reported, and was referred to the "Q" branch of the division, located doubtfully in Maurois.

We searched Maurois without success. We were somewhat delayed by a stream of ambulances bearing through the rain and the darkness the gassed civilians of Le Cateau. These civilians—

men, women, and children—had refused to leave their homes. Even the French mission could not move them. They protested airily that in a day or two Le Cateau would be safe. Now through Le Cateau passed the stores and ammunition of a corps: the cellars contained infantry; the houses sheltered guns.

The enemy accordingly shelled it heartily with gas and H.E., and the gas was fatal to the civilians. We sent forward as many gas-helmets as we could, but even if they had been sufficient it would have been beyond man's wit to distribute them among the inhabitants, who had gone to ground in cellars. I found it difficult to blame the enemy. Who, then, was to blame for these tortured children with their ghastly green faces, and the still bodies covered with carefully-mended sheets?

At last we met an intelligent staff captain, who directed us to Maretz. There we discovered an appreciative colonel with whom we commenced to make necessary arrangements. The final details the section commanders worked out for themselves with the staffs concerned. We arrived back at our camp a little weary and bedraggled, hoping for a quiet night. Our hopes were fulfilled.

The morning of the 22nd was spent in reconnaissance. At dusk Thomas's and Parslow's sections, accompanied by unloading parties of infantry, moved forward from Maurois: Harland had already commenced to supply his guns with shells.

As soon as it was light on the 23rd, Mac and I drove to the railway embankment, from which Parslow's tanks had started on their trek into the battle. We walked over a few fields until, at a road which at "zero" had been our front line, we overtook a Carrier tank which had been much delayed by mechanical trouble. We followed the route of the attacking infantry through orchards and rich enclosed fields—here and there were dead, the prey of machine-guns—until we came to a mill stream, overhung by thick undergrowth, which had so troubled our intelligence officers that elaborate preparations for building field-bridges had been made. We crossed it by the shallowest of fords.

To our astonishment shells began to fall behind us; later we knew that on our right the enemy were not dislodged from the edge of the Pommereuil Wood until the following day. We pushed on over more delicious fields, friendly gardens, and fine pasture, leaving the village of Pommereuil on our right, until, having followed the unmistakable tracks of our tanks,[1] we ran Parslow's section to ground in an enclosure. His tanks had not yet been unloaded. The situation in front was obscure, and it was doubtful whether they could usefully carry their supplies farther forward.

Parslow told me that the experiment of attacking at 1.30 a.m. instead of at dawn had not been quite successful. The fighting tanks had been handicapped by the darkness, thick mist, and gas. The infantry, running blindly upon machine-gun posts which the tanks could not see, had suffered heavily. It was not until dawn that any appreciable progress was made. Parslow, immediately behind the battle, was compelled continually to stop, but fortunately his tanks escaped shells and his crews gas.

His miserable section passed the night in the enclosure where we had found them. On the 24th another attack was launched to clear the right flank, but it met with little success. The dense undergrowth in the woods and hollows in the ground screened the enemy machine-gunners. At last on the 25th the wood finally was cleared and the Carrier tanks were able to move forward and dump their loads, returning to Maurois on the 26th. It will be clear that the best use was not made of this section. Lorries and limbered wagons can carry up supplies after the battle. To use tanks for such a purpose is pure extravagance.

We left Parslow to his chilly nights and began our five-mile tramp back to Le Cateau along the Landrecies road, keeping a good look-out to the north for Thomas's tanks, but seeing only transport moving on the skyline along the Bavai road, which had known the 5th Division in advance and in retreat. We wondered what the 5th Division would have thought of the thirty or forty aeroplanes fighting mazily overhead in the cloudless sky,

1. These were easily distinguished, as my tanks were the only Mk. 4's in the neighbourhood. Mk. 5's and "whippets" leave a different track.

or what effect these aeroplanes would have had upon the battle. In those days you were not believed if you told your fellows that there had been three aeroplanes in the sky at once.

So in company with an anecdotal *padre* we came at dusk to the town of Le Cateau, which had been so furiously shelled that, as we discovered later, the German artillery officer responsible received a decoration. Torn, shattered Le Cateau remained an ancient and dignified town, an aristocrat who had suffered cheerfully the blows and buffets of a desperate fight. Old women in their best black-silk dresses stood chatting at the entrances to their cellars. A few children were playing soberly in the quiet streets.

Groups of happy soldiers billeted in the place were strolling up and down with their usual air of consummate self-possession. Here and there angry old Frenchmen were searching for valuables among the rubbish and rubble that had been their homes. Along the traffic routes the noisy transport in endless columns shouted and clattered. But the old houses remained undisturbed, proud and a little aloof; you could hear one say to another—

> Of course, my dear, last night was dreadful, but I remember my mother told me that in the year 1554 the French before they set fire to the place. . . . Of course these plebeian factories and gaudy young villas! How can they know that Cateau Cambrésis was stormed at least ten times during the fifteenth century? After all, we have only been French for a trifle over two hundred years. The old bishop was so charming and such a gentleman. . . .

We left the old houses to their talk, and passing through the seediest suburbs, great yards, solitary warehouses, sidings and stations, we came to our car, and drove back to Maurois at walking-pace—the roads were terribly congested. Thomas reported in the evening.

Thomas and his section had moved forward to the neighbourhood of Montay, a little village immediately to the west of Le Cateau, at dusk on the night of the 22nd-23rd, arriving about

8 p.m. The crews had no sleep, for the enemy shelled and gassed Montay unmercifully, the bombardment becoming a barrage in the early hours of the morning. Thomas and Connor pressed forward to make a final reconnaissance of the route. It was necessary for the tanks to cross the Selle by a specially-constructed bridge. The ground on either side of the route was marshy.

One tank under Sergeant Fenwick had been equipped with a special apparatus for laying cable. The tank, accompanied by a signal officer, passed over the bridge at dawn, and following closely behind the infantry laid cable throughout the day to the enormous content of Divisional Headquarters. No sooner was an objective reached than Fenwick arrived with his cable. On one occasion he was a little premature, overrunning the advance, and as his tank drew shell-fire, he was ordered back angrily by a disturbed colonel.

The remaining tanks, heavily loaded with stores, rations, and ammunition, crossed Montay Bridge in column. The first tank caught the door of its sponson in the rails of the bridge, and Thomas, coming back wrathfully to investigate the cause of delay, found the tank commander and one of his men up to their waists in the cold and muddy water fishing for the door, which had been lifted off its hinges. They found it, hauled it up and replaced it; but even Thomas was astounded by the extent of the tank commander's vocabulary, and, his rebuke dying on his lips, he hurried away to the calmer atmosphere of the battle.

The division with which Thomas was operating advanced in three bounds—on a brigade front, the second brigade "leapfrogging" the first, and the third the first and second. Thomas's section was divided into three sub-sections, each of which attended to the wants of one brigade. Thus, when the first brigade, after stiff fighting, had reached its objective, the first sub-section of Carrier tanks which had followed the attack arrived with rations, water, bombs, ammunition, wire, spades, picks, &c., reported to the staff captain of the brigade, and unloaded at sequestered points. The second and third sub-sections followed the example of the first.

In each case the scheme worked with mechanical perfection. The infantry were never disappointed. Without employing much-needed fighting men as carrying parties—without frenzied efforts to push forward tired horse transport over shelled roads, often impassable, a staff captain could be assured that his brigade would receive the necessities of existence as soon as they could be used. And, however far forward the infantry might be, however dangerous the approach to them, the problem was the same for the Carrier tanks.

The tanks serving the first two brigades returned to Maurois when their day's work had been completed, arriving in camp at dusk. The third sub-section came back on the following day. Fenwick and his cable-laying tank was so useful that it was as much as I could do to extract it from the division on the third, with its crew cheery but thoroughly exhausted.

We received letter of congratulation both from Thomas's Division and from the corps; we had, to my mind, given conclusive proof of the utility of Carrier tanks, properly employed, even in semi-open warfare. Before the battle we had helped to build a bridge. During the battle we had kept the divisional commander in communication by laying cable forward as the advance progressed; we had carried stores for three brigades, supplying them on the spot with the necessaries of warfare; we had transported an enormous quantity of shells from the roadside over country impassable to horse transport.

And this we had accomplished with obsolete tanks, entirely unsuitable for carrying bulky loads. On no single occasion did we fail "to deliver the goods." Again we were independent of roads when good roads were so scarce that a corps was fortunate if it possessed one road to itself. We could avoid shelled areas, and we could afford to neglect shell-fire or machine-gun fire. At a pinch we could fight. To my mind our experiences in the later stages of the battle of Amiens and in the second battle of Le Cateau show clearly the remarkable future which must lie in front of Carrier tanks.

Coxhead's Company continued the good work, until the 4th

Army had passed beyond the Mormal Forest. Near Landrecies a section of his tanks captured an important bridge-head in curious circumstances.

The tanks were laden with bridge-building material, heavy girders, timbers, hawsers, and so on. According to programme the bridge-head should have fallen to the infantry, the tanks arriving with material for the reconstruction of the bridge, which it was anticipated that the enemy would have destroyed. There was unfortunately a little hitch. When the tanks came on the scene, the enemy were still defending the bridge-head with the utmost vigour. The section commander did not hesitate. His tanks continued to move forward as though they had been fighting tanks. The infantry, who had trained with tanks, advanced in the proper formation. The enemy broke and fled. It was a bloodless victory gained, curiously enough, by officers and men who were not rated as "fighting troops."

We had been relieved formally on the 25th. Thomas's and Harland's tanks trekked back to Genève on the 26th, Parslow arriving on the night of the 27th. There was no rest for the crews. We had received orders to entrain on the 30th at Roisel, and Roisel was thirteen to fourteen miles by tank route from Genève, which in its turn was more than twenty-five miles from the farthest point which my tanks had reached on the 23rd.

But the men were cheerful, and the tanks were carrying only light tables, wire beds, cupboards, deckchairs, felt and planks from the German R.E. store, jam and *goulash* from a German ration dump near Le Gateau, fresh vegetables from Maurois, tents from three Armies,—they meant nothing to tanks accustomed to carrying ten tons without flinching, and we knew that whatever our destination we should find there nakedness. The weather was fine, the route was familiar, the going was good; in spite of multifarious mechanical troubles we made Roisel on the 29th and entrained on the 30th for the railhead at Beaumetz, a few miles from our old quarters at Wailly.

CHAPTER 18

The End of the War

(OCTOBER 31ST, 1918, TO JANUARY 12TH, 1919.)

We returned from the bustle of active warfare, the sharp interest of solving immediate problems, the pleasantness and at times the comfort of clean country, to a squalid village on the edge of old, rotting trench systems. It was as if the offensive had failed miserably, and we had been thrust back to '16. At first we were exhilarated by the prospect of billets and faint incredible rumours that the end of the war was near. . . .

On the 31st I established my headquarters in a farm at Bailleulmont, the squalid village. The tanks crawled in on the morning of the 1st. The men were distributed among ramshackle barns and leaky huts. We set ourselves at once to make the place tolerable, and were, perhaps, a little successful. Other tank units were not so fortunate. No villages could be found for them in northern France, and they were compelled to spend weeks in erecting laboriously new huts.[1]

On November 10th there was some excitement at Brigade Headquarters—it was possible that an Armistice might be arranged, but "we had heard that tale before." On the 11th a telegram was brought to me before breakfast, while I was in bed, that hostilities would cease at "11 hours."

The news was so overwhelming that I could not absorb it,

---

1. One battalion, or at least one company of it, spent the first Christmas after the Armistice in building a camp for itself, although there were several pleasant villages in the neighbourhood.

and I am inclined to think now that, because there had been no anticipation, we lost at first the fine savour of it. I could not understand—until two of my officers started to ring the bell of the village church. The day became a smiling dream. I found myself walking up and down the village street, stopping everybody I met and saying—

"Do you realise that in one hour the war will be over?"

At 11 a.m. I stood opposite the church and exclaimed in a loud voice to nobody in particular—

"Gentlemen, the war is now over—absolutely!"

The company, naturally enough, had begun already to celebrate the occasion with appropriate rites, and its steadiness on parade, when before lunch the general came round to make a little speech, was truly remarkable. Only one officer in the rear was humming a little ditty to himself, and only one man interrupted the speech by a faint "hear! hear!" Salutes at the conclusion of the parade were superb. . . .

We had a cold lunch, but one faithful mess waiter served us nobly with a set face. The two cooks with arms around each other's waists were strolling up and down outside the window. I think they must have been singing.

In the afternoon we went for a long walk—the news had come too early in the day. We returned a little refreshed. At night there was a bonfire; but I cannot do better than quote from the vivid narrative of one of my most trusted officers:—

November 11th was a great day—and a greater night. The dreariness and loneliness of the place vanished suddenly on the receipt of the news of the enemy's capitulation. Would we not soon all be back in Blighty? The thought came like champagne to our thirsting souls. Imagination responded promptly. The bareness of officers billets vanished before visions of cosy sofas and armchairs, carpeted floors and clean-sheeted beds. Better still, faces of those we longed to see, especially of those we longed to kiss, came to us. Their owners moved amidst the pictured cosiness, sat in those armchairs, shared their sofas. . . . What a picture after the gritty holes and cramping caves of earth-covered ammunition boxes in the Cérisy Valley, or the stuffy, fly-ridden dilapidation of billets in Fouilloy! And it was the same with the men. No doubt their visions were as fair. The delight of these things shone in every one's faces. Unwonted cheerfulness was general. Everyone smiled.

And at night every one cheered. A way must be found to give free and full expression to bounding spirits. A huge bonfire was decided upon. . . . At twenty hours the massed logs that had been heaped on the top of the fallen masonry were saturated with petrol, a match was thrown, and a sheet of flame shot up. A war of cheering followed. Songs burst forth. Everyone sung who could or thought he could. The rest shouted.

It didn't matter—noise was the thing. Half an hour later the officers joined the shouting throng. The din grew louder. Someone shouted Speech! . . . Next the adjutant, and in turn every other officer was called. Reversing the order, the officers then called upon the sergeant-major and senior N.C.O.'s. Finally, the 'other ranks' vociferously sang of the officers, 'For they are jolly good fellows,' and the officers in similar fashion paid compliments to the men. By this time the flames had died down. Flickering light and shadow replaced the ruddy glow, and slowly the crowd broke up. But for hours yet a small group of enthusiastic maffickers sat around the dying embers. . . .

I should like to leave you with that picture—I feel that after "dying embers" the word "*Finis*" might suitably be written—but, if this halting chronicle is to present an honest picture, it must stumble on for a few more paragraphs just as my company dragged out a wearisome existence for a few more months.

There were compensations. Christmas brought its festivities; we played football desperately, and all but won the Brigade Cup; we were second in the Brigade Cross Country Run; a Concert Party visited us; a lecturer was heckled by our pet Socialist. It was, however, an almost impossible task to find the men something to do. We heard vaguely of an Army Education Scheme, or, more correctly, we read much about it in the newspapers, and we endeavoured to organise classes to shorten the long evenings, but we had no lamps or candles, no paper, no pencils, and no books.

We could think only of demobilisation, and soon my order-ly-room staff was allowed to think of little else. We were over-whelmed with complicated regulations. We struggled through them, and discovered that Private X., who, entering the army notoriously under pressure, had arrived in France quite recently, was due to go at once, while Sergeant T., an old and trusted N.C.O., was to remain in France indefinitely. The system of de-mobilising men by classes could not possibly have been meant to apply to a company billeted in a filthy village on the edge of an old trench system.

Such a system disregarded entirely the natural feelings of the men—"First out, first back,"—and it was very necessary to con-sider such feelings after the Armistice. The men were no longer soldiers; they were civilians impatient of control and eager to get home. Only an army, which was undoubtedly the best dis-ciplined army in France, could have suffered such a system of demobilisation with so little disturbance. It was astonishing to us that the *émeutes*, the existence of which is now common knowl-edge, were not more numerous. The system, admittedly perfect in theory from the standpoint of industrial reconstruction, could not be administered strictly without disregarding entirely the ordinary soldier's sense of justice.

Well, after four years of war we amateur soldiers were not dismayed by regulations. We made no fuss. We would receive an instruction to despatch a certain number of men to be demobi-lised at certain specified centres, and the men were despatched to time and in good order. By some mischance Sergeant T. went into the first batch and the demobilisation of Private X. was un-accountably delayed. It was unfortunate, but I was not sorry. The Company remained happy and contented. Further, we found to our amazement and delight that the vast majority of officers and men belonged to certain favoured classes, with the result that the demobilisation of the company proceeded with remarkable rapidity. . . .

The days were long and indescribably monotonous, until on January 11th I received the bunch of papers for which every officer and man in France was yearning, and on the 12th I slipped away from my already depleted company.

I was desperately sorry to leave my men and my tanks. It must break the heart of a man to retire from a famous regiment in which he has spent his life, but the regiment continues to live. A Carrier Company was a humble, temporary unit in a vast organisation, a momentary improvisation. Like every other company, it had found itself and created its own personality. It had fought for its existence against the ignorance and laughter of the more conservative elements in the Tank Corps. I knew that soon the remnants of the company would return home and the company finally be dissolved. Yet there it was—something which I had "formed" though not created. From an odd crowd of men with a few obsolete tanks and some cases of equipment it had become a "Company" of whose honour we were jealous, whose achievements we extolled, whom all of us could leave only with lasting regret. . . .

I was motored into Arras, and travelled down to the coast in a cattle-truck with thirty-one soldiers and civilians of all ranks and classes and four nationalities. The train was bound for Calais, but the driver in answer to my appeal said that he might be able to pass through Boulogne. I do not know whether he had any choice in the matter—strange things happened on the railways in France—but at 10 a.m. on the morning of the 13th the train did stop outside Boulogne, and the stoker ran hastily down the line and helped me to throw my luggage off the truck.

A train-load of prisoners from Germany had just arrived— childishly feeble, still shamefaced, and so emaciated that when I saw a man stripped to the waist washing, I could have cried for the pity of it. Outside the station three of these men, excited by their release, were jeering at two shabby cowed German boys pushing a barrow. . . .

I crossed that afternoon a little sadly, and as usual obtained a seat in the Pullman by climbing in on the wrong side,—I shall never be able to afford a Pullman again. At 10.25 a.m. on the 16th I was demobilised at the Crystal Palace. I felt that I should have been demobilised twice as I enlisted twice. . . .

Now I travel daily to St James's Park station by the 9.31, and when a "file" returns to me after many days, I sometimes wonder how I ever managed, without writing a single "minute," to command a Company of Tanks.

LEONAUR

ALSO FROM LEONAUR
AVAILABLE IN SOFTCOVER OR HARDCOVER WITH DUST JACKET

DOING OUR 'BIT' *by Ian Hay*—Two Classic Accounts of the Men of Kitchener's 'New Army' During the Great War including *The First 100,000* & *All In It*.

AN EYE IN THE STORM by *Arthur Ruhl*—An American War Correspondent's Experiences of the First World War from the Western Front to Gallipoli and Beyond.

STAND & FALL by *Joe Cassells*—A Soldier's Recollections of the 'Contemptible Little Army' and the Retreat from Mons to the Marne, 1914.

RIFLEMAN MACGILL'S WAR by *Patrick MacGill*—A Soldier of the London Irish During the Great War in Europe including *The Amateur Army*, *The Red Horizon* & *The Great Push*.

WITH THE GUNS *by C. A. Rose & Hugh Dalton*—Two First Hand Accounts of British Gunners at War in Europe During World War 1- Three Years in France with the Guns and With the British Guns in Italy.

EAGLES OVER THE TRENCHES *by James R. McConnell & William B. Perry*—Two First Hand Accounts of the American Escadrille at War in the Air During World War 1-Flying For France: With the American Escadrille at Verdun and Our Pilots in the Air.

THE BUSH WAR DOCTOR by *Robert V. Dolbey*—The Experiences of a British Army Doctor During the East African Campaign of the First World War.

THE 9TH—THE KING'S (LIVERPOOL REGIMENT) IN THE GREAT WAR 1914 - 1918 by *Enos H. G. Roberts*—Like many large cities, Liverpool raised a number of battalions in the Great War. Notable among them were the Pals, the Liverpool Irish and Scottish, but this book concerns the wartime history of the 9th Battalion – The Kings.

THE GAMBARDIER by *Mark Severn*—The experiences of a battery of Heavy artillery on the Western Front during the First World War.

FROM MESSINES TO THIRD YPRES by *Thomas Floyd*—A personal account of the First World War on the Western front by a 2/5th Lancashire Fusilier.

THE IRISH GUARDS IN THE GREAT WAR - VOLUME 1 by *Rudyard Kipling*—Edited and Compiled from Their Diaries and Papers Volume 1 The First Battalion.

THE IRISH GUARDS IN THE GREAT WAR - VOLUME 2 by *Rudyard Kipling*—Edited and Compiled from Their Diaries and Papers Volume 2 The Second Battalion.

LEONAUR

ALSO FROM LEONAUR
AVAILABLE IN SOFTCOVER OR HARDCOVER WITH DUST JACKET

ARMOURED CARS IN EDEN by *K. Roosevelt*—An American President's son serving in Rolls Royce armoured cars with the British in Mesopatamia & with the American Artillery in France during the First World War.

CHASSEUR OF 1914 by *Marcel Dupont*—Experiences of the twilight of the French Light Cavalry by a young officer during the early battles of the great war in Europe.

TROOP HORSE & TRENCH by *R.A. Lloyd*—The experiences of a British Life-guardsman of the household cavalry fighting on the western front during the First World War 1914-18.

THE LONG PATROL by *George Berrie*—A Novel of Light Horsemen from Gallipoli to the Palestine campaign of the First World War.

THE EAST AFRICAN MOUNTED RIFLES by *C.J. Wilson*—Experiences of the campaign in the East African bush during the First World War

THE FIGHTING CAMELIERS by *Frank Reid*—The exploits of the Imperial Camel Corps in the desert and Palestine campaigns of the First World War.

WITH THE IMPERIAL CAMEL CORPS IN THE GREAT WAR by *Geoffrey Inchbald*—The story of a serving officer with the British 2nd battalion against the Senussi and during the Palestine campaign.

STEEL CHARIOTS IN THE DESERT by *S.C.Rolls*—The first world war experiences of a Rolls Royce armoured car driver with the Duke of Westminster in Libya and in Arabia with T.E. Lawrence.

INFANTRY BRIGADE: 1914 by *Edward Gleichen*—The Diary of a Commander of the 15th Infantry Brigade, 5th Division, British Army, During the Retreat from Mons

HEARTS & DRAGONS by *Charles R. M. F. Crutwell*—The 4th Royal Berkshire Regiment in France and Italy During the Great War, 1914-1918.

TIGERS ALONG THE TIGRIS by *E. J. Thompson*—The Leicestershire Regiment in Mesopotamia During the First World War.

DESPATCH RIDER by *W. H. L. Watson*—The Experiences of a British Army Motorcycle Despatch Rider During the Opening Battles of the Great War in Europe.

LEONAUR

ALSO FROM LEONAUR

AVAILABLE IN SOFTCOVER OR HARDCOVER WITH DUST JACKET

CAPTAIN OF THE 95th (Rifles) *by Jonathan Leach*—An officer of Wellington's Sharpshooters during the Peninsular, South of France and Waterloo Campaigns of the Napoleonic Wars.

BUGLER AND OFFICER OF THE RIFLES *by William Green & Harry Smith* With the 95th (Rifles) during the Peninsular & Waterloo Campaigns of the Napoleonic Wars

BAYONETS, BUGLES AND BONNETS *by James 'Thomas' Todd*—Experiences of hard soldiering with the 71st Foot - the Highland Light Infantry - through many battles of the Napoleonic wars including the Peninsular & Waterloo Campaigns

THE ADVENTURES OF A LIGHT DRAGOON *by George Farmer & G.R. Gleig*—A cavalryman during the Peninsular & Waterloo Campaigns, in captivity & at the siege of Bhurtpore, India

THE COMPLEAT RIFLEMAN HARRIS *by Benjamin Harris as told to & transcribed by Captain Henry Curling*—The adventures of a soldier of the 95th (Rifles) during the Peninsular Campaign of the Napoleonic Wars

WITH WELLINGTON'S LIGHT CAVALRY *by William Tomkinson*—The Experiences of an officer of the 16th Light Dragoons in the Peninsular and Waterloo campaigns of the Napoleonic Wars.

SURTEES OF THE RIFLES *by William Surtees*—A Soldier of the 95th (Rifles) in the Peninsular campaign of the Napoleonic Wars.

ENSIGN BELL IN THE PENINSULAR WAR *by George Bell*—The Experiences of a young British Soldier of the 34th Regiment 'The Cumberland Gentlemen' in the Napoleonic wars.

WITH THE LIGHT DIVISION *by John H. Cooke*—The Experiences of an Officer of the 43rd Light Infantry in the Peninsula and South of France During the Napoleonic Wars

NAPOLEON'S IMPERIAL GUARD: FROM MARENGO TO WATERLOO *by J. T. Headley*—This is the story of Napoleon's Imperial Guard from the bearskin caps of the grenadiers to the flamboyance of their mounted chasseurs, their principal characters and the men who commanded them.

BATTLES & SIEGES OF THE PENINSULAR WAR *by W. H. Fitchett*—Corunna, Busaco, Albuera, Ciudad Rodrigo, Badajos, Salamanca, San Sebastian & Others

Lightning Source UK Ltd.
Milton Keynes UK
UKHW011923151118
332420UK00001B/87/P